Shift Happens

a memoir

Margot Jarvis Genger

Time moves in one direction, memory in another.

William Gibson

Shift Happens shares my memories of growing up. One gift of writing this memoir has been to learn how much my brothers' memories differed from my own. I claim no larger truth to what I've written. I do know I made a life path based on what I believed to be true.

I wrote extensively during my psychotic breakdown. I used those notes to write that portion of *Shift Happens*.

I kept a journal throughout my trucking experience, and used those notes to write the greater part of this memoir. The trucking incidents are accurate.

I did not record the location of the Motel 6 in Los Angeles. I made that up as well as the location of the AA meetings. I used stories from current meetings in place of stories I heard in Los Angeles.

With the exception of my husband, I've changed the names of people I've written about in order to protect their privacy.

Please consider writing a review on your booksellers site. Thank you so much for reading my story. It's been a long time coming...

You can reach me on my 'about' page at <www.mjgenger.com> I would love to hear your comments, and will answer questions if I can.

ISBN: 978-0-9996325

Cover design by Mariah Sinclair

Bumpfoot
Media
Eureka, Ca

www.mjgenger.com

To Alcoholics Anonymous

Cabover Truck Schematic

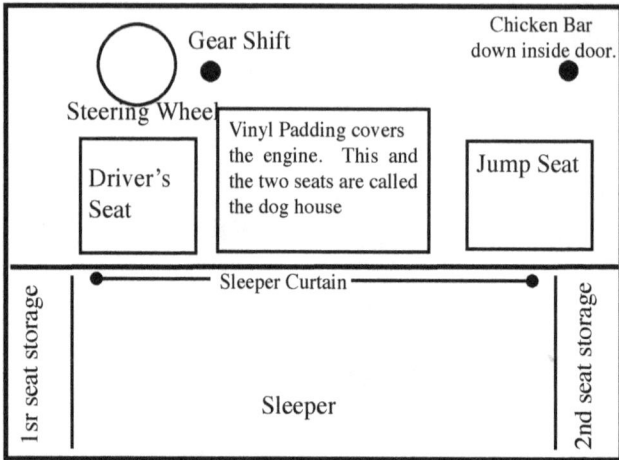

Gear Shift

Chicken Bar
down inside door.

Steering Wheel

Driver's
Seat

Vinyl Padding covers
the engine. This and
the two seats are called
the dog house

Jump Seat

1sr seat storage

Sleeper Curtain

2nd seat storage

Sleeper

Inside Cab - View From Top

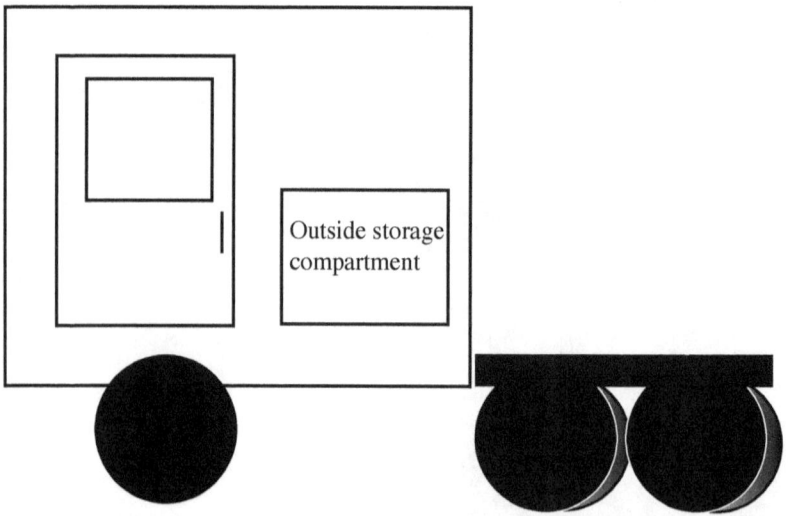

Outside storage
compartment

Steering Tire

Tandem Axels
Two sets of Duals on each side.
8 wheels altogether.

Driver's Side View

Contents

Foreword

Shift Happens is a hero's journey told from the perspective of a woman. While most hero's journeys tell the story of men's exploits and bravery, overcoming obstacles, like sirens who try to steer them off course and monsters out to kill them, a woman's hero's journey is the story of losing everything in order to find oneself. Think of Celie or Sofia or Mary Agnes in *The Color Purple.* Think of Janie in *Their Eyes Were Watching God.* Think of *Dana* in *Kindred.* Think of Eliza Doolittle in *Pygmalion.* Think of Margot Jarvis Genger in *Shift Happens.*

Margot and I came of age together in Eureka, California. Our lives appeared very different — she grew up rich, her father was a doctor, her family had a maid, their house had the only swimming pool, besides the high school, in town, a helicopter ferried her from her wedding at the country club, for god's sake — a wedding I wasn't invited to. My father owned a bar, the Vista Del Mar, that Margot came to frequent during her lost years. My family was asked to leave the First Presbyterian Church because my father's bar "promoted" devilish acts like drinking. Margot's friends had contests, like who can go the longest without wearing the same clothes twice, and my friends and I worked after school, on weekends, and throughout the summer to buy the few clothes we owned.

And yet, because we grew up during the 1960s, we were more alike than all those material assets and class differences portray. We graduated high school in 1969, during the height of the Vietnam War, the sexual revolution, the women's movement. Very little of which penetrated rural Humboldt County where we grew up. Our lives were still pressed flat by the hallowed myths of virginity and the accompanying guilt, the vision of whoever gets the best husband wins, and the idea that lots of money means happiness. And neither of our lives turned out the way we imagined.

During one meandering, delightful conversation about *Shift Happens*, Margot said, "I always wondered why you left Eureka. I heard that something shameful happened, but I never knew what it was."

Yes, something shameful happened. My former husband beat me in front of the Catholic church in downtown Eureka. He tore hunks of hair from my scalp, broke my nose, and battered my body. It wasn't the first time during the nine months of our marriage. When he fell into a drunken sleep, I found the keys he used to keep me locked inside and I fled, wearing a bikini and a bloodied white fisherman's sweater. For nine months I lived in fear of his hands, of drives into the country where he might kill me and bury my body. I lived in fear that if I fled, he might harm my mother or my sister.

But I'd also heard rumors about Margot that she carried with her: Her husband, the great quarterback, divorced her. She got on stage at a local bar and danced topless. She was crazy.

Part of Margot's memoir tells these stories—sometimes directly, sometimes through flashbacks, sometimes through conversations. But what is clear is that her story of overcoming addictions, of learning to cope with mental illness, of grounding herself through an 18-month journey as a truck driver will serve as a blue-print for others who need a road map for their lives.

Margot's memoir told through her road trip — more Thelma and Louise than Jack Kerouac — demonstrates how the journey cracked her sheltered, privileged childhood to learn about the lives of working class men and women, opens her up to a humanity that escaped her as a child where she met few people of color, or people who lived in poverty or people, other than their live-in help, who were blue-collar workers.

What I expected when I read Margot's book was the sexism she encountered while riding with truck drivers. What I didn't expect, but loved, was how those truck drivers imparted lessons about life while they taught her how to drive.

Often blue-collar work is seen as lacking intelligence, yet throughout the book, Margot shows the ingenuity and skills of the truck drivers. Mike Rose, professor at UCLA Graduate School of Education and Information Studies, wrote a wonderful book *The Mind at Work: Valuing the Intelligence of the American Worker.* He discusses what Margot showed about truck drivers throughout her memoir:

> *As someone who comes from a blue-collar background*
> *and who now, as a professor of education, studies issues*

like learning and intelligence, I am troubled by the way we as a society readily acknowledge the intelligence required for white-collar and professional occupations, but rarely honor the thinking involved in physical work. Listen to the language we use. The work of the "new economy" is "neck-up" while old-style industrial and service work is "neck-down". In the body only. Mindless.

But what I saw growing up was anything but mindless. My uncles — who were machinists, welders, and factory workers — would show me how to do things with tools or explain how something worked. And my mother was so competent in the restaurant, so in command of what seemed to me to be chaos. All this has affected how I understand intelligence, learning outside of school, and the immense knowledge and skill of the everyday work that makes life possible.

I was especially moved by the trucker who stopped in a rainstorm when Margot and her partner Kent lost their brakes. The trucker, Big Red, showed Margot how to temporarily fix the brakes with two pennies and a dime:

Got a dime?" Red sat on the pavement and water bubbled up on him like he was a rock in a rapid. The water reached above the soles of my waterproof boots, but my butt was still above the river. Big Red looked like a drowned rat.

"What are you doing?" I handed him a dime.

"If I plug this line, the air can't get to this pot and leak out." He pushed the coins around with his little finger trying to lodge them in the service line just right. "I've gone five hundred miles like this. You'll make it to Nashville if I can get this dime in right."...

Showered, in dry clothes again, I climbed in the sleeper, chastising myself that I didn't invite Big Red to a truck stop for a meal. Never in my life had I met someone so generous. My mind wandered as I vibrated and flopped around in my sleeping bag while Kent drove. I couldn't imagine my Dad sitting in the rain fixing some stranger's truck. The truck and the sleeper and all the noise falling away, I wondered if Dad had ever operated on anyone for free. Dozing off, I couldn't think of a single time I'd ever helped another human being. I'd never even shared my candy. And then sleep actually came to me in a moving truck.

Throughout the memoir, Margot shares moments of coming into awareness of her privilege, but as a reader, I also felt her heart opening, her growing appreciation for humanity.

In every encounter we had, Margot demonstrated this same openness to learn. After I read the book, I called her and shared a few concerns I had about her portrayals of poor sections of town and fat people. I worried about this phone conversation, expecting her to be defensive. The book was "done" — why would she want to go back and rewrite sections? Instead Margot thanked me for my honesty, and we had long talks about poverty, addiction, obesity, womanhood.

As I close the final chapter, I celebrate the woman Margot has grown to be, and I mourn that 50 years of lost opportunities to help each other navigate becoming women during troubled times. This book will be a mentor text for those young women, coming of age in these #MeToo times, to understand how becoming your true self becomes a bedrock for your life.

Linda Christensen (lmc@lclark.edu) is Director of the Oregon Writing Project at Lewis & Clark College in Portland, Oregon, and a Rethinking Schools editor. She is author, most recently, of Reading, Writing, and Rising Up: Teaching About Social Justice and the Power of the Written Word (2nd edition.)

Shift Happens

Is This The Beginning?

I will tell you the story about myself that I can't yet hear.

June, 1977
Eureka, California

The night before our wedding, on the way home from his bachelor party, my fiancé stepped out of a moving pickup and fractured his skull. An unbelievable stroke of luck. I didn't have to marry the lying, argumentative cokehead after all. I actually looked up and thanked God that night.

From the hospital, the poor bastard came straight to my house, not because he lived with me, but because his room had already been rented. I fed him, changed his sheets, washed his clothes, and found my backbone.

"We're not getting married, Jeff."

"What do you mean?"

"I don't want to get married anymore."

Two weeks passed. He'd eaten a month's worth of pain meds. I hadn't seen him get out of bed. He hadn't looked at me, or spoken to me. Day fifteen, I'd had it.

"I need you to move out."

"Where am I gonna go?"

"Call a friend."

"Like who?"

Not a single person had called or come by to visit. "How about calling that guy who was supposed to work on our car."

Another ten days dragged by. Jeff made no attempt to get out of bed or communicate. The doctor would not refill his pain medication, said Jeff should be getting exercise, walking would help him feel better.

Two days before the July 4th weekend, after Jeff had lain there for a month, I said, "I'm leaving for the weekend. When I come back, be out of this house. If you're here when I get back, I'll put your stuff in the street." I walked out and, despite its loose steering and bald tires, I drove the 1940s black Volvo, up past Salyer and spent the next three days on the Trinity River with my dog. Sonny, a big, protective, loving, concerned, German shepherd, never left my side.

Eureka, on the coast, rarely got above seventy degrees, but inland the dry heat could reach triple digits. That weekend, the temperature climbed upwards of 85, but a warm wind, that felt like cotton, blew downstream and kept me content to sit there.

I stared at the river. Sat there in my lawn chair. Didn't even bother with lotion.

How did I get into this mess?

I had sold my Rambler and was now stuck with this piece of junk I'd bought to advertise Jeff's future catering business in Wisconsin, where he was raised. Where his parents still lived. When I was head over heels I'd thought it was a good idea. Good advertising. Using a cool car as we drove around delivering food for our catering business. I'd prep for him till he got established. Then maybe I'd go back to teaching.

I'd wanted to get out of town, but Wisconsin? I didn't even know exactly where Wisconsin was, except somewhere near the great lakes. Fourteen weeks ago, head up my ass, Wisconsin only meant four seasons, a white Christmas. Giant mosquitoes didn't even occur to me, much less the heat and humidity.

I'd lived in Eureka — population 30,000 — all my life. Plenty of rain and fog, not too hot, green all year round. In the heart of the towering redwood forests, Humboldt County had pristine beaches, clean rivers, and wildlife. If I hadn't been so focused on turning my life around, maybe I would have noticed how much home meant to me.

Jeff asked me to marry him three weeks after I'd met him. He had a plan for his life, and so I attached myself. An adventure and an answer. Just what I'd been looking for. Marrying Jeff was my ticket to see a wild birth of new green in the spring, a stark dying back of foliage in the fall, and snow. Way back in March, when we were all hot with his plan, I bought this Volvo on Jeff's recommendation.

"I've got a friend that will fix the steering." But two months had passed and I still hadn't met the friend.

I'd quit waiting tables because we were moving. My morning job at Eureka City Schools paid three times what I made waitressing, but I'd quit that job a few weeks earlier, having slammed the receiver in my boss's ear after yelling a few obscenities. My first unemployment check hadn't arrived yet.

A thousand bucks up Jeff's nose every month. My thousand. We'd hardly saved enough for the new tires we needed to start our big trip.

I poured Purina into Sonny's bowl. Brought water up from the river. Cracked open *Watership Down*, by Richard Adams, but kept reading the same paragraph and not remembering what I'd read. So I rolled a joint.

I'd met Jeff in February, the first night on my job. He'd flirt with me as I walked by his ovens to dump my dirty dishes at the washing station. Short, maybe 5'8, but handsome. Maybe Italian. Dark wavy hair, blue eyes, tan skin. We hung out together after hours, and three weeks after I'd met him, he proposed. I hadn't even slept with him, but I said yes. How stupid was that?

Jeff was adamant. "I mean now. Let's get married now."

I hadn't divorced Aaron yet, although we'd been separated for over two years. Nevada didn't require a waiting period like California, so I called an acquaintance who lived in Reno, stayed with her, and went through the whole process in three days. Jeff and I set our wedding date for the last weekend in May, three whole months from the day we met. We bought the car, but Jeff wouldn't move in with me.

"Jeff, we'll save rent money."

"I want to wait till we're married."

No amount of protest on my part budged him an inch. I did get him to sleep with me. He claimed he'd had too much coke, he was nervous.

"Okay. I understand."

A month before the wedding, my stomach hurt so bad I could barely eat. Why didn't I call it off then?

Jeff insisted our wedding invitations include a little phrase at the bottom. *We'd prefer money instead of presents.* He'd quit his job at the restaurant, to remodel his friend's kitchen, although he had not one iota of experience with a hammer.

A week before the wedding, he bullied my brothers, acted like know-it-all and ordered the most expensive meal on my Dad's dime.

"I'd like my salad AFTER the meal." Jeff pontificated, waving his arms. "And bring me another whiskey, with a water back. Red wine with dinner. And I'd like to see the bottle before you open it." When he started explaining to my father his expertise with wine, I excused myself to the bathroom.

I sat on the toilet, elbows on my knees, head in my hands. *Why didn't I call it off then?*

A few days before the wedding, I watched Jeff pound raw 2x4's in the lawn and then nail boards on top that were torn from abandoned pallets he'd found. "What are you doing?" I asked.

"Benches. For the wedding." His "bench" tilted off to the left. He straightened it and pounded some more on the seat-board.

"They could get splinters, Jeff. Look." I pointed at his seat-board. "That could poke someone."

"We'll put dish towels over them. Do you have any nice towels?"

No one would sit on those benches. They weren't big enough for two people. I knew if a two-hundred pounder sat on one, Jeff's bench would split. Actually, if anyone rocked back, say, because they were laughing, the bench would have toppled.

That same day, I lost the star sapphire out of the ring my mother had given me ten years previous. I dug around in my yard for an hour and finally accepted the loss as a horrible omen. But by this time, it was too late to call off the wedding.

Nobody had thrown me a wedding shower or given me a bachelorette party.

Jeff went to his party. Later, they told me they were bringing him home because he had gotten so wasted they wanted to get him to bed. But he came-to in the pickup, protested, and stepped out while it was moving because the driver wouldn't stop.

Jeff went to the hospital. The wedding was off. And a month later I sat on the Trinity River, smoking a joint because I couldn't concentrate enough to read.

I smoked, cried, pet Sonny, drank beer, and watched the river. Sonny lay by my side. I didn't hike, didn't even walk far from the tent. I just sat there in my little lawn chair, reefer in hand, cooler by my side. I thought about throwing a stick for my dog, but didn't.

Sleep was a pipe dream. I couldn't get all the rocks out from under the tent. With Sonny snuggled up next to me, I just spun my life out forwards and back and couldn't make sense of it.

I sat there for three days and all I came up with was "Why Me?"

Eating made me sick to my stomach.

Back home, Jeff was gone. He'd left a note on the table insisted that we talk soon, that we work this out. The car guy had let him put up a tent on the back of his property out in Elk River Valley.

Jeff came to visit every day. He stuck letters in behind the doorknob when I wasn't home, long letters about our beautiful future together and how we were made for each other. If I answered the door, I'd have to stand there, blocking his entrance, accepting the letter while his arguments escalated from pleading to anger.

I took a job as a bar maid at the Vance on weekends, a popular hang-out with live music, a crowded dance floor, and lots of drinking. My brother's band, the Heart Beats, played there often. The most popular band in the county, they'd pack the room shoulder to shoulder.

I'd lost twelve pounds and, enjoying my thin self, I continued to eat as little as possible.

I dropped acid, smoked pot, drank, and partied at the Vance.

A month passed. In mid-August, Mom invited me to have lunch at her work. Coincidentally, she introduced me to Lewis, a therapist who was joining us for lunch. "I can't afford a therapist," I said, aware of the set up.

"Maybe you can't afford not to see a therapist," the counselor countered. "Group Therapy. Once a week. You won't find anything cheaper. If you don't like it, you can quit."

Something Big's Coming Down

And I'm in on it.

August 1977

Eureka, California

I started counseling that Thursday and immediately, Lewis cut off my complaints about Jeff. "When he comes to the door, you walk to the telephone. You say, 'Leave, or I'm calling the police'."

"Okay."

"Tell him you'll get a restraining order put on him if he comes again."

"Okay."

"Have the number ready, and if he doesn't leave, you start dialing."

"Okay."

"Can you do this?"

"Yes."

I did, and Jeff quit coming around.

Next week Lewis forged ahead. "So you trip 'em and beat 'em to the floor."

"What do you mean?"

"You pick up men, fuck 'em and leave 'em."

"It's not like that."

"Oh yeah?" He makes like he's holding a glass and glugging down the liquor. "You do this a lot?"

I glared at him.

"Ya know, Margot, if you were to line up next to ten women, and you all put bags over your heads, a guy wouldn't know the difference."

I considered walking out right then, but I was too chicken-shit.

I went for a motorcycle ride up the coast with a guy in my therapy group but didn't sleep with him.

In September, Lewis held an all-day session, "Goal Setting." We made charts. 'ME' went in the center. Long-range goals went on the edges of the paper and we flow-charted the steps to reach our goals. I decided to take the steps I'd charted to produce a readers' theatre of my own poetry.

I contracted with the Ferndale Theatre, reserving January 13, 1978 for my performance. I contacted Terry, my brother, to ask if his band would play their music around my poems. I called my Readers' Theatre professor at Humboldt State University, to inquire about getting a few students to read for me.

As soon as the Heart Beats agreed to play their music, I knew I'd have a full house. Now, I could not only afford the venue, but I could afford to pay a lighting tech and someone to build a simple set. I set up a meeting with my HSU professor, for a critique of my poems, which, up until that point, I'd never shared with another soul. At our meeting, he told me the department had given approval for their students to earn a unit for working my show.

He pushed pretty hard, and even though I didn't want to, I slept with him, even though he was married. The experience brings to mind a hammer, or a pickaxe, nothing so kind as a drill. Now I realize we were having a power play, but at the time, I thought I was irresistible.

"This is just temporary. You understand, right? We're clear on that, right?" My HSU professor was absolutely clear.

"Of course. No big deal." But what wasn't clear, I wrote in a poem and threw into my bottom drawer.

I focused on advertising. Called "I'd Be Proud To Be Your Movie Star," the debut of my poetry was going to push me into another world. Everyone would know I wrote poetry. I might become famous before Terry's band hit the charts. I started designing a poster. I decided to add "...because I've been a damn good audience all my life" to the title. I was feeling pretty good.

Much better than being a Business Education Coordinator (my title at that Eureka City Schools job). Much better than waiting tables. So much better than being the sugar mama for a cokehead.

22

Seven women readers volunteered, and the rehearsal schedule soon became a nightmare. Just when I'd get a time schedule nailed down, one or another of the girls would cancel and I'd have to re-schedule. No one had a message phone. I made a million phone calls.

I remember looking out the window at my lawn. A rich green because I loved watering it. The grass was above my ankles, but instead of mowing it I spent my time listening to telephones that no one answered and driving to HSU to pick up messages that weren't there.

I stopped sleeping.

"So don't sleep," I'd say to myself, rationalizing that just resting was enough.

I thought about how my relationships would form with these seven women. I would be an authority, a teacher. What a wonderful position. Maybe if this works out I'll put an ad in the paper, 'poetry lessons'. I could teach.

I worked out the logistics of class size and how much I'd charge. And no tight-shoed grunting administrator to deal with. The more easy, natural, on purpose, flowing, and right-on this seemed, I thought 'What if teachers actually had the freedom to teach? What if we abolished administrators altogether?'

That thought became "Someone needs to step up!" Why would I think all this up in the first place if I wasn't supposed to do it?' In the coming weeks, what began as a poetry reading, grew to a full-blown revolution.

Adrenalin rushed through me. I would be famous. I watered my budding plan with enthusiasm.

With no more administrators, there would be money to fund a kind of clearing house for students not interested in going to class. Don't want to be in class? Fine. Hang out at the municipal auditorium. See a counselor.

But how would new teachers break in to the system, contract for classrooms or equipment or textbooks? Who would get to use the P.E. facilities?

I tried to tell my brother about it. I tried to tell my ex-husband. I expounded on my idea to group therapy on Thursday evening. They didn't get it.

I needed to write it all down. Clarify. Take it to the Secretary of Education. I'd leak it to the news, call a press conference, go on a speaking tour.

I wrote bullet points on a legal note pad. Page after page. When I hit a wall, like with insurance issues, or background checks, or hard-core juvenile delinquents or Special Ed kids, I'd recite my poetry as I wanted my readers to perform it. My clarity of purpose ballooned. Exhilarated, I drank Tab. Ate candy. And hardly slept.

Plenty of days got used up. I lost track, except that I noticed the weeds taking over my lawn. I just didn't have time to haul out the mower.

After work one night, I slept with this guy, started my period, and bled heavily all over his bed. The next night I started sobbing out of control at a party and didn't know why. I went back to the poor man's house again, and while he slept on the couch, I wet the bed.

I walked over to visit my motorcycle friend from group therapy but couldn't find his house, even though I'd been there before, and I knew my small home town like the back of my hand. I sat down in the gutter and cried.

From there I walked all over town until I recognized Lewis' office, and walked in. He was with a client and had me wait in a small room off the kitchen. I calmed down and left before his appointment ended.

I picked up some guy in the bar, brought him home, and abruptly made him leave. I went out again the next night, picked up Ed, someone I never even liked in high school, and brought him home.

In the morning I noticed a penny stuck to his leg. A bug! I knew it! I was being bugged! I started watching his every move, but then he left abruptly. Suddenly, I realized Ed had been planned for me. My psychologist had set up this meeting. It made perfect sense.

Just go see Lewis. He evaluates you, what you're like as a person, then this other guy, in my case Ed, lays you and reports back as to how good you measured up.

Except in my case, Ed blew it by giving the code word away. At that point, I knew I was being picked for something important. I couldn't wait to find out what. And since I was being bugged, I had to be careful about what I said.

I realized what was wrong with everybody else's relationships. I needed to get to David and Tina's house, to help them break up. I wet my hair down, greased it back and put rubber bands in it. I put rubber bands around the rotary dial on my phone so it would stay on '7'. I walked to David and Tina's, jumped right in with convincing arguments, implored them to separate.

Out of the blue, my mother was on the phone. At David and Tina's house! I hung up on her. Then my therapist called, which excited me because I knew he was the next step for whatever big was coming down. Mafia, I thought, or National Geographic, or the Secret Service. His call reassured me. I knew I'd made the finals. I could win.

My mother called back. "Stay there bunny, I'm coming to get you."

I thought she'd figured out what I needed, created this ruse on the phone, and would help me break up this couple when she got here, but instead, Mom wanted to take back to her house in Trinidad, a half-hour drive up the coast, give me a nice hot meal, help me get some sleep.

"No!" I shouted. I'd never shouted at my mother before.

She took me to my house, where I physically prevented her from coming inside. I looked away from the tears on her face, and noticed the lawn. Up to my shins. Full of weeds. Sonny had trampled it. Poops everywhere. They'd get stuck in the lawn mower, I thought. I turned back to my mother, whom I'd never, ever made cry, and conceded to play one song on the piano for her if she would leave, but then she cried harder and I hadn't practiced so I gave in and let her bring me back to her house, a half-hour drive, to eat and get some sleep.

I didn't feel like eating. I couldn't sleep, though the sun had set long before we got to Trinidad. Suddenly, I couldn't stand to be there and lashed out, swearing, shouting again at my mother and stepfather for their control issues. I slammed their front door, intent to walk to the Vista, a local fisherman's bar in Eureka, a twenty-five-mile hike.

My stepfather found me walking up the on-ramp to the freeway. Standing on the shoulder of highway 101, we argued about where I needed to be and decided we'd let the psychologist decide for us. I got in Ben's car, we took the next exit and found a phone booth. Took turns talking to Lewis. Forty-five minutes later, Ben drove me to the hospital. 25

Calibrating Reality

Yeah, I slept around a lot. So what? It's the truth that counts.

October 1977
Eureka, California

I passed the entrance exams, signed in for seventy-two hours and waited in my room. Because I was at General Hospital, where my Dad practiced medicine, I flashed that I'd be asked to testify against my Dad for hypnotizing all of us kids when we were three-year-olds and programming our brains. They had my Dad up on charges and needed my testimony. I didn't know what I was going to do.

A nurse stood in the doorway. "No smoking in this room."

"Well, I'll just go out and sit in the goddamn hall and have my cigarette."

This thing I was being picked for had something to do with who I was. My Dad was a doctor. I was in General Hospital. I'm the fourth child and only daughter and obviously my parents had made some sort of agreement way back when, that someday, coming up real soon apparently, I would be in control of something big. I mean really big.

I hated having to sit on the floor in the hall to smoke my cigarettes, waiting for them to get their act together and tell me what I was supposed to do. Three times I asked for the doctor. Each time, they denied my request.

I yelled out, "You tell Dr. Suchandfuckingso that if he doesn't get over here in fifteen minutes he can kiss my ass."

No one answered, so I marched up and down the hall like I was in front of two thousand people, cheerleading, taunting the huge nurse like in *One Flew Over the Cuckoo's Nest*. I'd come up behind her and whisper in her ear, or I'd bump her with my hip as I walked by.

"You've got a good seventy more hours to go, my dear." She cajoled me down the stairs and through a door. "You behave like that and you'll spend the whole time in here." The door closed and I heard the lock click.

Maybe eight feet by ten, a perfectly white room with yellowed linoleum. A single mattress. No blankets. A small window, higher than my head. Daytime. A high overcast sky. The door had a window. No glass in it, just wire.

I couldn't keep track of time or make any sense of it.

I went through birth. Could have gone on for hours or taken five minutes. The womb was all watery and warm. Squeezing through the birth canal, I struggled, waves of convulsions pushing against my skin. Me pushing back. Finally, I opened up my arms, wiggled my legs and slowly, opened my eyes to the blue-striped ticking crushed against my cheek. I shivered and tucked myself into a ball to keep warm. A night sky out the window, lit by a street lamp. Where the hell am I?

"Margot, you can come upstairs now." A nurse opened my cell door.

Daytime.

I'm damn mad. "If that man can talk me into a box then he can damn well talk me out of a box," I yelled at her.

"What man?

"I'm not coming out of here till he tells you what's going on and if you don't know who I'm talking about then you'll just have to find out." Told her off good.

"Will you have some breakfast?" Sweet as candy.

"No, I don't want anything to eat. Leave me alone." Fuck you and the horse you rode in on.

I couldn't let anyone dominate me. Minutes or hours passed. I agreed to go upstairs to help them find out who *he* was. I knew they were testing me, to see if I could stand the pressure. To see if I measured up.

The day room was full of women. Student nurses having a meeting, they said, but I knew they were women from all over the world. They were here for their countries just as I was here for my country. They were holding me for some deadline. Oh my God. December 7th. It was going to be December 7th.

I heard voices in the other room, Mom and Ben's, and started heading that way.

"You can't go in there." Two nurses shouldered up to me.

"But I just want to see who's there." I've heard damn good voice impressionists before. The two nurses flew off me and bounced against the wall when all I did was shrug a little bit.

I'm in a straitjacket. The two women are dragging me into the cell. I knew I wasn't supposed to beat them up because I was a girl, so I cried.

Back in the little room with one window over my head. Daytime. High overcast. Books Margot. Think. Why did you read all those books? Then I saw the *Catch 22* sign taped above my door. The escape signs with arrows. I took the hint.

Being a patient here meant everyone was free to not substantiate me. Night-time.

When the nurses weren't looking, I snuck down the hallway and pushed the button by the door. They buzzed me! I opened the door and took off. Down the steep drive on H street in slippers, hospital pajamas and bathrobe. Turned left on Harris. Ran. Where?

Down the middle of the street. Someone would see, call someone. I'd be saved from this hostage situation, this prison. I saw the bars on the cells, just above the grass here on the outside of the hospital. Inside, the window was above my head. Outside, a cemetery! A prison cemetery! I'd made it out just in time.

I noticed three men watching me. They'd call. I'd be saved. Darrel and Katie's bus was parked there, but what if it was a trick? I couldn't trust it. I had to keep running. No traffic. Night. Down the white line.

The ward clerk caught me as I passed the liquor store on the corner of Harris and K. "You can really run." He was panting.

"Yeah." I panted back. I should have ducked through back yards. Too late now.

"You can go home in the morning, Margot. That's not much longer. Come back to the hospital."

Out of breath and too tired to wrestle, I knew my house would be cold and dark and I didn't have the key to get in. I let him hold my shoulders, guide me back to the hospital.

Ten men and I had a party all night in the day room. I did a gymnastic tumbling routine down the linoleum hallway. The nurse made me stop even though I felt no pain.

I'm home. Did I walk? Where's Sonny? Colder inside the house than outside. Lawn like wet green hay.

In bed in the afternoon. Gary, the opium dealer from Hawaii, had bugged my house. He hid in my attic with all his electronic equipment. Messages came to me through the TV. Through the radio. In the Halloween commercials. I needed to listen carefully. Sometimes the TV and radio collaborated on a message for me to interpret. Then, I saw a woman burning up in the old fall-out shelter under my kitchen. No smoke, no smell or heat, but she glowed. I took off walking to report the murder. At Zane junior high, I pulled the fire alarm and waited.

The fire engine showed, but I couldn't get the words out. All I could say was E=MC squared.

The police arrived. I threw my glasses to the ground and stomped on them.

In General Hospital again, I talked to the president of Mexico who pretended to be the janitor. He explained the law. Suddenly, finally, I knew the why and what and wherefore of it all!

Those women from all the countries, the ones they said were student nurses... Bullshit! Year after year, they had prevented WWIII! Each year, one country offered up a woman in October. If she had sex, then we would have WWIII. If she didn't have sex, we got another year without a world war. My mother couldn't do it. She started WWII. Those women had been keeping us out of war for thirty-five years. And now, this year, the United States' year, I had been offered up! I FINALLY KNOW WHAT I AM SUPPOSED TO DO: No Sex till December 7th. I could do this! I've got to get out of here. Prove myself. I've got to prevent WWIII.

I got stuck half way out the iron bars on a window in the lunchroom. Hips wouldn't budge. They removed a bar to get me unstuck. Another very kind ward clerk said someone on the outside saw me stuck half way out the window and called in.

Home again. Cold, cold house. Kennedy was not dead. WWII was still going on. Listening to the radio and the TV for any messages, they mentioned Thanksgiving turkeys. What happened to Halloween? I wasn't prepared. I spotted something shiny in the back of my closet. I reached, and pulled out a perfectly round blue marble, a purie! The sign I needed! I'm doing the right thing. I've got to be brave. Show that I'm not having sex. Prove it. I walked to the Red Lion. Entered the bar. The band was taking a break. Background music played softly through the speakers. I went up on stage, unsnapped my shirt (my favorite thrift-store red plaid shirt that tied at the waist if I wanted). No bra. I didn't have the nerve to slip the shirt over my shoulders. Maybe I wouldn't have to. I danced. I let my shirt hang loose. I'd say 'no' to any guy that approached me.

The police escorted me out.

There was a little man in the piano at General Hospital. I took the piano apart looking for him.

"Stop worrying." I snarled at the nurse. "I do this all the time with my own piano."

The little man moved to the top of the water tower. I couldn't understand what he said to me.

Me and some guy, a loony-tunes, are in the back seat of a white government car going south on highway 101. I never did get that piano put back together.

Napa State Mental Hospital
Medicated

November 1977
Napa, California

I woke up strapped to a single bed with my feet next to a pink wall. My head in the middle of the room. About four feet above my toes I could see sky through a two-foot square window secured with an iron grate. Daytime. Twigs were touching the iron grate. A big tree out there threw shadows across the wall to my right. Without my glasses, I couldn't tell if the sky was cloudy or a high overcast. Other than the door, and my bed, that was it.

The strap was leather, very much like a belt, with knots and loops to hold the leather against itself. Maybe more like an old harness of some kind. I felt the bed's cold steel bar above my head. I pulled out the hard pillow, tried to fluff it, shoved it back under my neck. I drew my knees to my chest, and the sheet came along. I rubbed my feet.

"Hey. Is anybody out there?" I called.

No answer.

The leather ran twice across my stomach, down around a rung of steel attached to the bed, back up through loops and buckles, across my spine, more loops and buckles, down around the steel rung attached to the opposite side of the bed and back up across my stomach, two-fold again. This long hundred-year-old piece of leather around my waist was all that held me in bed.

I wanted to turn around and face the door but just sitting up tightened the leather enough to pinch my waist. I stuffed the sheet between me and the strap and waited for the leather to adjust. Sitting Indian style, stomach sucked in to the max, I managed the 180-degree turn, only to stare at the door and wonder what to do next.

I didn't know where I was or why. The fuzz in my head buzzed like little mosquitoes. I wanted a drink of water. "This is definitely me and I'm definitely not dreaming," I said out loud, testing my voice. I was me. I started crying and wiped my nose on the sheet.

"I have to use the bathroom," I called.

Nobody came.

I began analyzing the strap. By pushing and pulling just right a knot loosened a bit, like macramé. I slid that bit of the leather down, and the strap pinched my back, so I stuffed some sheet in back there. But I could see a marked increase in the slack below the knot so I started pushing that piece of leather through its course, sort of like threading elastic through a waistband with a safety pin. Working the strap around the steel rung of the bed, reward! A blue plastic bedpan sat on the linoleum. I thought my hips might cramp from stretching to reach it, but what a relief to pee and not have to sit in a wet bed.

Renewed, with a clear head and purpose, maybe forty-five minutes later, I managed to slither out.

Now what?

Immediately, two women met me at the door when I opened it. Their hands cupped my shoulders. I did nothing to resist them, said nothing. They deferred to a third nurse standing down the hall, and after a minute, they eased off me, and walked away.

I stood in the long wide hallway, with open doors all down one side, and closed doors the length of the other side, my side. No one talked to me or told me what to do. A woman brought sheets and a blanket, led me through an open door down the hall to my left, gave me the bedding and pointed to the bed closest to the door.

"That's your bed. No smoking in the room."

The bed next to mine was occupied by a lump. All I could see was greasy strands of gray hair. I thought she was dead. The two other beds were empty.

In the day room, zombies sat on plastic chairs watching a TV affixed up in the corner to the ceiling. Cigarette butts decorated the floor. The overflowing stand-up ashtrays looked like little parking meters between the chairs.

We all wore scuffs. (Flat terrycloth slippers. Jam your toe in the front, leave your heel hanging out the back.) A cigarette butt got stuck to my scuff. I tried using a chair leg, and then the base of an ashtray to get it off, but I needed something pointed and the butt was probably covered with spit. I didn't want to touch it.

Some of us had grayed-out, blue scuffs and I got an old pink pair. Everyone wore the same frayed terrycloth bathrobes, pajamas and these awful scuffs that required us to shuffle so they wouldn't come off.

One big woman had a dull red bathrobe. She had wild black hair like straw that had fallen out in clumps. Her hair got on my scuffs too. She had her neck crooked back so she could watch the television while she smoked. Fresh ashes lay on the floor to her right, because she didn't bother using the ash tray. She looked frozen. She never moved except when her hand came to her mouth. She inhaled the smoke, and blew it out straight at the TV.

Ashes, ground in from all the shuffling, coated the floor. I could tell the ashtrays had been moved recently because circles of white linoleum, like little dinner plates, dotted the floor. A small woman, in a blue bathrobe, picked up a standing ashtray, spilled cigarette butts and ashes all the way back to her chair, and set the ash tray on her right as if to say, "I'm parked here now."

Maybe seven or eight zombies roamed the room. One zombie followed the wall around, a monotone sound coming out of her. A big woman. Maybe 5'10". A sure win in a fight.

At the nurse's window, I showed her my cigarette, expecting a light. She pointed to a small hole in the far wall. "Over there."

Above my eye level, a car lighter broke the blank stuccoed wall like a blackhead. But the big woman rounded the corner en route to the lighter. I waited till she passed. Quickly, on tip toes, I stuck the cigarette in my mouth, shoved my face up to the wall, hit the target with my cigarette, and sucked.

I ashed on the floor.

Twenty steps to the wall opposite the blackhead, a short plastic shower curtain served as the door to the bathroom. Privacy only to the knees, we knew who sat in there, broadcasting their noises.

No way to change channels. How can they watch TV with their necks crooked back like that? How can they hear with the shuffling going on behind them, the constant mumbling?

I paced and smoked.

At night I was scared the lump had a butcher knife.

Daytime. I ran out of my room to see the commotion. A zombie had thrown a chair, grabbed a stand-up ashtray, threatened another zombie or maybe the TV. She got hauled off. The day room twittered. The mumbling grew louder. I paced the hall.

"When do we eat?" I said to no one in particular.

No one answered. I ambled up to the office window and asked again.

"You just ate." She didn't look up.

I waited.

Finally, she said, "Dinner is at 5:30" which didn't help because I couldn't see any clock and I didn't have a watch.

I found a library of about twenty beat-up books, tried hard to read, but the words flashed and my thinking was all cut up. After a few pages, I tucked a book away in my suitcase, for when I could read again. *Gift from the Sea,* by Anne Morrow Lindberg.

Bobby, my brother, and his friend came to visit me.

"What do you get to eat?" Bobby asked.

"It's all white." I said, and they laughed, knowing how much I hated white food. I fake laughed.

"Texture?"

"Mushy." More laughter.

"Do they make you eat tomatoes?" Both Bobby and I hated tomatoes.

"What's it like in here? I mean, what do they let you do?" The friend asked.

"If I behave, I'll get a pass to leave the room, but if I don't behave, I get taken someplace else. That's all I know. There's a TV but it's on the ceiling."

Dad came and checked me out for the day. He could do that because he was a doctor. We drove forever around Napa Valley in his Volkswagen bug, and I sat there, miserably uncomfortable, on the sticky plastic seat, unable to move, feeling sick with all the visuals whizzing by. Telephone poles hit my eyes, bushes blurred like tripping on acid. I stuck my hands under my legs to hold myself against the rocking, to keep from getting carsick. Dad and I didn't talk. He didn't try to teach me anything. I didn't ask any questions. We ate lunch and drove all that way back to the hospital.

They gave me a grounds pass, which allowed me out of the ward for a couple of hours each day. I walked to the hospital store, where I could buy cigarettes with no money. The oldest mental hospital in the state, four-story buildings fenced off a large square of green lawn, some trees, and a few benches. Roads and sidewalks bordered the square. I met a fellow. Another Bobby, just like my brother, and we palled around together until he wanted to have sex in the stairwell. I wouldn't do it. Not because I didn't want to, but because I was afraid we'd get caught.

But Bobby had a radio and we'd sing along when the Bee Gees came on. We littered because littering gave more people jobs. We walked. We went to the store. We smoked cigarettes.

"Another Elvis Presley song. Jeez. What's the deal," I said, as Elvis crooned 'Don't you step on my blue suede shoes...' on Bobby's radio.

"Just respecting the dead, is all."

"Elvis is dead?" I asked.

"You don't know Elvis died? How can you not know that? Where you been?"

"Well, in here. When did he die?"

"Way back. Like in August."

I didn't even know Elvis Presley had died.

"So do you know who the president is?" Bobby asks.

"Jimmy Carter is the president. Duh."

"What a wuss, that Carter is." Bobby blamed Carter for the economy.

"He ought to go back to his peanuts."

"I think he's nice." I hadn't kept up with any news, much less news about the economy.

We bought cigarettes. Walked back to the square. Nobody sat on benches. We all walked. Round and round.

"When you're from the South, you can't be trusted." Bobby said.

"Why's that?"

"Well, for one thing, he's white."

"Who?"

"President Carter." Bobby looked at me. His eyebrows traveled around his forehead. "No black person's gonna trust a white guy with his money. So of course the economy was doomed at the start."

"Well that's fucked."

"Don't swear, Margot. It's not good."

"Oh." Pause. "So when do you get out of here?"

"They don't tell you that stuff. You know when you're getting out?"

"No."

"That way, they can keep you here as long as they want. You got to play their game."

"They took this lady away the other day." I told him. "She was screaming and held one of the ashtrays like a baseball bat. She wanted to hit someone."

"She won't be getting out. You gotta be careful. This is a hospital for violent people."

Back from my off-grounds, lunch was white again. More meds.

The lump was gone. A different person napped in my room. A long, thin one. Her covers smoothed over her, she looked like a long pencil stuck in the bed. She had some cap on her head, like a swim cap but flesh colored, like the eraser. I liked her being a pencil. I took a nap.

More days and nights. More meds. And then I got out. Rode back to Eureka behind the driver in another white government car, directly to Beverly Manor, where they checked me in before they told me I couldn't go home.

Beverly Manor

If you go there, don't inhale.

November/December, 1977
Eureka, California

The crazies lived in Beverly Manor. Forever. The place smelled awful, like pee and vomit that had never been aired out. Like cat shit. Like smelly, old people. Like the same air has been inside the smoke-stained walls since they built the place. I checked in to the last room on the left. Nobody slept in the other bed.

Bobby came to visit. We sat in the lobby, because visitors weren't allowed access to any other part of the building.

What's happening with my house?" I asked.

"It's still there. Don't worry."

Silence. "What are you doing for Thanksgiving?" I asked.

"Same old, same old," which meant he and Terry would eat at Mom's house. Ben would roast a turkey in the barbeque. Liquor for the parents. Beer for the kids. Wine with turkey. Home by 10:00. Probably lots of laughing.

I felt ashamed to miss Thanksgiving, but truthfully, I didn't want to see them. I had nothing to say and nothing to laugh about.

The only wall cigarette lighter, just outside my door, drew crowds. They mumbled and complained while waiting in line to light up. Across the hall from my room, the door to the smoking room banged every minute. Clouds of smoke wafted into my room. The windows didn't open. No windows opened.

So much smoke, my eyes stung but wouldn't water.

There was nothing to do.

December. I spent my 26th birthday in Beverly Manor. Thorazine kept me stiff as a board. I couldn't get away from the smell. The small

37

courtyard on the north side generated a kind of claustrophobia with its overgrown wet, moldy, dead sword ferns that hadn't been cut back since Lincoln was assassinated. There was no dry place to sit out there, no sun, and even if I could sit, my bones ached with the cold.

My court-appointed social worker came to visit.

"I need a lawyer. I have to get out of here."

"How about a month, Margot."

"A month?" I shook my head. "Oh, God no. I need a lawyer."

"Margot, a lawyer would take longer than a month to get you out of here. How about just after the new year? January sixth. I can't get you released until then."

"Okay." My social worker didn't treat me like I was crazy, even though I was wearing a bathrobe.

"But you have to take your medicine. I can't get you out if you quit your meds."

"Okay."

I paced the hallway, which simulated a two-lane highway with smoking zombies dodging in and out of the double yellow lines. I'd weave through the traffic jam at the cigarette lighter to get to my room.

The activities director posted a sign-up sheet to go on a walk. I wrote my name down. I'd seen these groups for years. I'd be driving to visit my mother, who worked just around the corner from Beverly Manor, and they would be clumped on the sidewalk, or walking, or waiting to cross at the stoplight. They had stiff arms, and shuffled along watching their feet, following the leader. They all stopped when he stopped. I'd thought they didn't even know why they stopped, and if not for the activities director, they'd walk right into the street, like so many lemmings walking off a cliff.

We walked by my mother's office, me in the pack of zombies. I was too gone on Thorazine to feel the shame, and with stiff arms I too, watched my feet, not because I had a dead brain, but because the light hurt my eyes. If I looked up, the flashing started, like little lightning interruptions in my vision.

A couple days before Christmas, 1977, a huge earthquake hit during a storm. A big tree fell in the moldy north courtyard. The power went out. Beverly Manor was all a titter. The next day, Bobby came for a visit.

"Margot, we made national news!" I tried to love Bobby's enthusiasm.

You should see the Eel River. It's right up by the highway! All the Arcata bottoms are flooded. Old Arcata Road is out. Ferndale is practically under water."

"Wow." I felt so left out.

Silence. Bobby switched gears. "So, how about we celebrate Christmas after you get out?"

"Okay." Bobby left.

The putrid smell overwhelmed any fragrance the Christmas tree in the lobby might have shared.

I tried to watch the news, but with the TV at a normal height, crazies stood in front of the television. One guy changed the channels without any thought of who might be watching, and then left. No smoking allowed, but no quiet required. The door banged. Three of them argued and stormed around. It was insane. I was in an insane asylum.

Years later, locals still remember the *Storm of '77*. When the subject comes up, I am carried back to the terrible smell, the Christmas tree decorated with maybe ten unbreakable balls and a few bows, the unbearable sadness, insurmountable loneliness, and how much I hated the Thorazine.

Christmas passed and somebody cut up the tree and hauled it away. The hallway traffic continued. The jam of people remained constant outside my room. I acclimated somewhat to the smell, the smoke, and the noise. I took my medicine.

I didn't join the New Years Eve festivities in front of the TV.

I waited for January 6th.

I understood why Mom didn't visit, why Bobby didn't stay longer than ten minutes. There was nothing to say.

Choose

Crazy but medicated or sane and humiliated

January, 1978
Eureka, California

After my release, Bobby moved in with me because I couldn't take care of myself. Then Terry, who'd been taking care of Sonny for the last two months, kept my dog permanently, because I couldn't take care of an exuberant German shepherd.

I couldn't even smoke a cigarette gracefully. Like wearing a back brace with boards strapped to my appendages, an invisible torture chamber, Thorazine ran stiffness up my spine into my crown, down beyond my tailbone clear into the balls of my feet. Just let me lie down, the only position remotely comfortable.

If I absolutely had to go out, I pretended nobody saw me. Didn't look at other drivers, other cars. Hunched over, staring at the pavement, I'd make my way into Longs Drugs to buy groceries. I avoided Safeway. Aisles and aisles of choices. Food I wouldn't cook. Worse, people I'd know from as far back as grammar school. Instead, I bought food in cans. Tuna, soup, peanut butter. Crackers, chips, candy, coke. Didn't look at the store clerk. Just paid and left.

Fast food worked the best. Hot and tasty. I could stay in my car.

Thorazine stopped the racing thoughts. Those pills cut my thoughts into little pieces. Like in Napa, I tried reading, but the sentences didn't even fit right and whole paragraphs skewed themselves into puzzles. When I tried to think, words wouldn't come through the fog, like I had blank pages up there. No sense bothering to blink while staring at my lap. Looking up or out for a visual to think about brought on little seizures. I lay down with my blank page and stiff back for much of the next year.

The psychiatrist, whom I had agreed to see as a requirement of my release, said I'd have to swallow that shit for the rest of my life if I wanted to be sane.

"If I could trade, I'd cut off my little finger. I swear, I'd easily give up my little finger if I didn't have to be like this." I told Bobby, talking about my psychotic break, as we now called it.

"Margot, right now you remember it all big, all the time." Bobby said, "Eventually, you'll only remember it for a part of every day. Then that will pass and you won't have thought about it for a week. One day, you will remember all this only a little, like you can't even remember it very good any more."

"Yeah. I guess." I held on to the tiny thread of hope he'd given me.

I walked to the day activities center for mentally ill outpatients. Stiff as a post and just as dumb, I fumbled around, felt awkward, and walked home.

The social worker visited.

"All I want is a man to take care of me."

"Beverly Manor can do that," he said. "You don't need a man to take care of you."

He told me about a fellow that moved here from Florida. Got into some trouble and had to register as a sex offender. "An amazing artist. He's recovering from a break too." He handed me information about where to see this guy's art.

Not interested. The guy was a pervert, for God sake.

The social worker set me up with a male patient. To help me get out of the house. Start talking to people. I walked to the patient's house. We sat on his porch and didn't talk. I was too stiff and he was too short. I didn't want to go bowling.

"We think you should quit taking that medicine, Margot." Mom was sitting in a chair I'd cleared off for her in the kitchen. Bobby sat at his workbench, in his 300 square feet of my house, which opened into the kitchen. Technically, he lived in the dining room and slept in the living room. I kept the kitchen, bedroom and bathroom clean, so I considered those rooms as my 300 square feet.

"That medicine isn't helping you, Margot." Bobby lit a cigarette, inhaled, and emptied his tuna can full of butts into the garbage sack under his bench.

"The psychiatrist says I have to take it or I'll go crazy." I sat down across from Mom at the table.

"I think I'd rather have you be a crazy than a zombie."

"Bobby!" My Mom interrupted.

"It's true, Mom. Bobby's heartfelt voice practically echoed off the linoleum and smoke-stained walls.

"Honey," Mom spoke softly. "What do you think about quitting that medicine?"

"I hate the shit, Mom, but I don't want to go crazy again."

"You're not going to go crazy again, Margot." Bobby's cigarette dangled. His pencil moved across white paper. Two hamburger cartons interrupted my view of what he was drawing.

"Bobby could watch you. If you started to..." Mom couldn't say it. "have an episode, you could get right back on that stuff. Okay?"

At my next appointment, I told the doctor about our plan.

"If you quit taking the medicine, I won't see you." Point blank.

In spite of my fear, in April, I quit my meds.The psychiatrist quit me. Mostly I stayed in bed and waited.

A month passed. I was still sane.

For years, when the storm of '77 came up in conversation, I'd talk about the tree falling at Beverly Manor. Questions would direct the conversation and I'd offer that I believed people stay crazy because sane, the humiliation was too overwhelming. People choose to stay crazy. Now, I'd say people live with an untreated chemical imbalance.

I no longer see zombies when the stiff-bodied people shuffle across the street. I imagine a former teacher, or maybe a wife with children. My heart still hurts when I remember.

Mom got me a job at the answering service her office used. A minimum wage job as an answering service operator. I expected to be fired, that I wouldn't be able to figure out how to plug in all the cords. Just two years prior, in another lifetime, I'd held a high school English teaching position. That baffled me completely. How in the world did I get from there to here?

But the answering service job fit me. I could talk to people without them seeing me. Nobody knew me as a mental patient, that I'd gone crazy, tried to take my clothes off at the Red Lion.

By June I had a new workday routine. I watched the game shows in bed, got dressed by 2:30 and to work by 3:00. Home at 11:15. A little wine in bed with Johnny Carson. Lights out.

Days off were long. I watched TV. Even golf.

Meanwhile, Bobby, always busy, cluttered up every available space in his 300 square feet with projects: cartooning, sand blasting, sculptures, graphic design. Bobby's life never had a dull moment to spare, so his clutter included fast food wrappers, pizza boxes, rotting food, and plenty of empty beer cans.

I watched TV, sat at the answering service, ate out of cans, paid the bills and emptied the garbage. In eight months, I gained forty pounds.

A week or so before Christmas, having had enough, I made my plan. A wonderful release followed. Unexpected, I felt almost light-hearted for the next several weeks.

Topping off at 165 pounds, I had a will drawn up, and in mid-January, I left it on my pillow, headed to a motel, and got in the bed with a delicious mint grasshopper. I downed a whole bottle of Thorazine and turned out the light.

What I learned about Thorazine from the library gave me confidence that it would do the job. Too much of the stuff, and my stomach would paralyze. The crap wouldn't get in my system. Not enough, and I'd be one miserable stiff cookie. I'd measured just right. I'd be a goner for sure in the morning.

I sipped my grasshopper in the dark, the TV flashing some commercial for clean floors. I hated cleaning floors.

I'd used the motel so my house wouldn't be tainted. If committing suicide meant I'd stay in purgatory forever, I didn't want to haunt my own house. And if I didn't know I was dead, well at least I'd get to float around and watch everyone. But I didn't believe any of that. I believed dead was dead. All she wrote. The will tied up the loose ends. Mom and Bobby could have everything.

I couldn't go on hiding. I could find no reason to continue.

The TV buzzed away and I got dizzy. I put my drink down before

I spilled it. With my head in the pillow, I had a small thought of wanting some way out of this, but that thought got cut up, and there was nothing.

Knocking. Talking. I remembered the TV. Haven't died yet. The TV was arguing, having gunshots. A commercial. More knocking. Why doesn't someone answer the door? Noisy fucking neighbors. Then I heard loud talking. Banging. Maybe my TV was bothering them. Maybe they were knocking on *my* door.

I opened my eyes and saw daylight seeping through the crack in the curtains. I tried to call out to whoever was knocking, but I couldn't talk right. Chain-locked from the inside, they wanted me to unlock the door.

Somehow, I dialed my mother and got some words out. Too hard to lift my head. Blanked out.

A ton of noise. Pounding. Hammering. The door came off. A whoosh of cold air filled the room. People. Loud. My Mom rushed in and sat next to me.

"Margot!" She patted my face, rotated my neck. "You told me the wrong motel!"

Men took me out of the room on a stretcher. I could feel the jiggling and bumping. Lots of official talking and directions and quickness. I couldn't do a thing about it. I didn't care.

They didn't have to pump my stomach. Mom sat with me in the emergency room all afternoon while the nurses observed me. Finally, she took me home to her house and put me to bed, up in Ben's office, the loft.

Failed at suicide. For days, my family tip-toed around while my head cleared.

I came home and sat in the kitchen for another couple of days.

And then it happened.

As simple as buying apples, or opening a door, or turning on a light, the weight lifted. I said, out loud, "If I can't even die, I might as well live."

The black cloud dissipated. The sun came out. Later, I thought, "and since I've lost all face, I don't have to worry about my face anymore!"

My cheeks puffed into a grin. My step got a spring in it. Energy to spare, I turned off the TV and made the bed. During that two-week period in late January when the sun shines every day before the rain settles in again, I walked all over town.

It flat isn't in the cards for me to have a man, I thought, *so I might as well do something fun if I'm going to be alone in this life.* While drinking a chocolate milkshake in Denny's, I stared out the window at 5th street, U.S. Highway 101's route through town. I watched a great big truck drive by. Then two more. The idea burst forth like I'd known it all my life. *I'll go truck driving and write a book about it! I'll call it* "Gidget Goes Long Hauling".

"What?" Mom's eyes looked like marbles with eyebrows on top when I told her.

"Why not? I'll keep a journal. It'll be fun."

"But..."

"Mom, I've never done anything on my own."

"You went to Hawaii."

"That was different."

"How?"

"That was just me getting out of town. This is like, going somewhere."

"Hawaii is somewhere."

"I've never seen any part of the country, except from Dad's airplane. I've never seen the Rockies, or the salt flats or the amber waves of grain," I started singing. "Oh beautiful for spacious skies..."

"I hear you, sweetie." I stopped singing. I'd embarrassed her.

"Mom, what would it feel like to be completely surrounded by black people? I mean, we might see one black person here, totally surrounded by white people. What do you think that person feels like?"

"You want to visit black people?"

"Mom," I groaned. "It sounds fun to me to put myself in places that I can't possibly imagine what to expect. You can see that can't you?"

She hugged me then. That warm squishy hug, smelling of Benson & Hedges, the scent of dry cleaning chemicals on her black cashmere.

45

Good as perfume, my mother's hug.

A nutritional counselor helped me with my diet, and I started taking the pounds off. Anything I wanted, as long as it was fresh. Nothing processed. I ate a lot of peanut butter and apples. I walked the two-plus miles to work and got a ride home with a co-worker. I enrolled in the truck driving class, worked, and exercised. I looked strangers in the eye.

Still, when a former co-worker got out of her car in the Safeway parking lot, just three cars down, she practically craned her neck backwards to avoid eye contact. She'd been invited to the wedding and had also witnessed first-hand parts of my psychotic break. The avoidance thing happened again, in Longs Drugs, with a high school friend, and then again with a friend of my ex-husband's. Go crazy in a small hometown, suffer the consequences. I don't remember a single "Hi Margot! How ya doin?" I kept score. The people I could call by name who looked the other way, led by about a hundred percent.

I quit smoking on November 1st.

The nutritional counselor recommended I read *The Eden Express*, by Mark Vonnegut. Published five years earlier, Vonnegut recounted his bout with a psychotic break. Vonnegut's book stunned me, as he described thoughts identical to mine. I had no idea what I was crying about.[1] It makes perfect sense![2] He described his obsession with the meaning of all the books he had read.[3] Just like me, he had inappropriate sexual experiences, had to save the world, and continually tried to appear normal while attending to the grandiose demands being put on him.

But he'd had friends. They'd hung in there for him.

I started going back to The Vista. I could smile, laugh, play pool. I had Bobby's wrecked cars towed away and asked him to move out, which strained our friendship for months. I cleaned my house and mowed the lawn. The answering service made me a supervisor and gave me a raise. The Truck Driving class sparked my enthusiasm and gave me plenty to talk about. The weight of having failed as a person became "who gives a fuck?"

I was going to write a book about long-haul truck driving, eighteen wheels, loaded and rollin'.

Truck Driving Class

"Clutch! Less throttle! Punch it! Clutch!"

Fall 1979 To Spring 1980
Eureka, California

Two semesters of truck driving at College of the Redwoods, along with the right to take my driving test cost a hundred bucks. Sixty students enrolled in the first semester competed for the thirty spots available in the second semester. I had plenty of strong will but marginal driving skills. For all his yelling, the instructor, Dick Dart, was actually quite supportive.

Dart wore blue mechanic's overalls. The material pulled at his snap fasteners and pinched his armpits. A rotund man, maybe he'd gained weight and hadn't upgraded his work clothes. His clean overalls had plenty of grease stains. Mr. Dart had a large square-ish head, a booming voice, clean-cut black hair, and the beginnings of a set of jowls. His pant-legs stopped inches above his ankles, which were inside buffed-clean black boots.

He sat in the passenger seat. A student sat at the wheel, and four more students rode in a converted sleeper, sitting on a long bench waiting for their turn to drive. Between Mr. Dart and the driver, two three-foot tall stick shifts loomed up from the floor.

I bubbled straight to the top as the worst driver in our group.

Before getting behind the wheel, we were required to thump the tires, listen for air leaks, adjust the trailer brakes, check the oil and lights, look for anything askew, and double check that the king-pin, which connects the tractor to the trailer, was actually hitched. "Any flat tires?" Mr. Dart would ask.

"Is this one flat?" I'd take him to check out a tire that sounded dead.

"No. The sound is lower. Your thumper won't bounce if it's flat."

Dart had us watch him, and in turn, he watched each of us adjust the trailer brakes. "Screw it up tight, back it off a quarter turn. You never know who had your trailer before you got it. Save your life. Check your brakes."

We hauled slabs of cement along all the narrow roads of Humboldt County. Called a conventional, the truck's engine stuck out in front, and I couldn't see over the top of it. "Place yourself in the middle of the lane, not over there by the center line." I'd learned to gauge my position and flat roads were fine. Even curvy roads were okay.

Dick mandated that we drive over the Ferndale Bridge. A narrow, two-lane bridge, built in 1911. Mere inches were between our truck and the bridge's cement siding. Cars going the opposite direction hugged the double yellow line just like we did. Paralyzed at the wheel, Dick Dart powered us over the bridge with his booming voice. "Get over more. More!" This two-lane bridge survived the '64 floods, the only bridge in the county that could claim this fact. (Years later, a student would hit the bridge railing. No injuries, either to on-coming cars or the bridge, just a dented fender on our truck.)

The school's truck, a Kenworth tractor, had twenty gears. Called a five-by-four, the stick-shift closest to the driver shifted the five "big" gears and the stick closest to Mr. Dart shifted the four gears in-between the big gears. The speed of the engine had to match the road speed to make a successful shift. Any miss-matched shift sounded like a chainsaw cutting on metal.

With a failed shift attempt, while listening to the chainsaw, the engine speed slowed, the truck slowed and the driver needed to quickly find a different gear to match the ever-slowing road speed. Rev the engine *and* get it in gear. In the wrong gear though, the engine wouldn't pull the load. Fail continually to find a gear and the truck comes to a complete stop, always with a line of cars trailing.

"When slowing down, always make your up-shift first." Dart lectured us in class on Tuesday nights. Easy to understand in the classroom. The little gear got shifted three times, all the way down to 1st, and in a

48

two-stick shift, the little gear went back up to 4th, before the big gear could drop into a lower gear. I practiced the shifting pattern at home constantly.

"Up-shift first! Make your up-shift!" Dart would yell. "You've got to drive by the seat of your pants."

If I was riding dressage, I could feel my pants, no problem. But I had no sense of what was going on underneath me in that truck. I wanted to watch the tachometer and make my shifts by the numbers. But any change in the road grade changed the rate of my engine speed and I would sweat profusely after I missed my shift, and once again come to a complete stop, literally trembling.

"Down a gear! Down another gear! Faster! You're too slow!" Dick would yell. I lost it completely every time we came to the incline on US 101 at the Hookton Road exit.

Starting up again, on an incline, created the absolute worst driving nightmare. Hit the throttle, clutch and shift a ton of times, the truck went forward. Miss the shift, the truck bounced like a huge earthquake before it stalled. The earthquake/stall thing happened to me twice before Dick put his hand on mine to help me feel the rhythm of his shifts and yelled "Clutch! Less throttle! Now punch it! Clutch!"

I got a 76 on my driver's test. They didn't require me to drive up the Hookton Road incline.

Mr. Dart made connections with one of his former students, Bob, and got me a long-haul job. Sam Tanksley Trucking. Cabovers. 10-speeds. "Margot, this is an entry level job."

"Like the greasy spoon of restaurants?"

"I'm serious. You have to be careful."

"Well, is this Bob guy okay?"

"I only knew him as a student, but I think he'll be okay." He added, "Tanksley won't pay good, but you need experience before you can get a good job."

"Thanks for everything Mr. Dart." I smiled.

"Good luck out there."

I'd rented my house out. Packed. Told everyone I was going long haul, gonna see the country. One last night to celebrate, I'd be leaving in the morning for my new job.

I'm Out a' Here

But for a hiccup...

June 1980
Eureka, California

I got picked up for drunk driving.

Bobby and I were sitting at the Vista, celebrating how I had such balls to become a trucker. He told anyone who would listen how his sister was leaving tomorrow to become a long haul truck driver, and how cool was that.

"She's going to write a national best seller about it!"

"Is that right?" The bartender played along. "Well, I expect a signed copy when it comes out. When you leaving?" He asked.

"Tomorrow!" I said.

"My fucking sister is going to drive a truck all over the country!" Bobby repeated to the barmaid, who shoved in next to him to refill her drink tray. "She's going to write a book about it." He slurred. "Have you ever read her poetry?"

"Bobby. Stop." I nudged his shoulder with mine.

"What? Can't I be happy for my sister?"

"This one's on the house." Kent, the bartender, set a full glass in front of me.

"Be happy a little quieter," I said to my brother, emptying my glass and picking up the full one.

"I'm just so goddamn happy you're doing this, Margot. I didn't think you were going to make it, for a while."

"I know."

We sat there talking loud, fighting to hear ourselves over the juke box, with two or three draft Budweiser's lined up for each of us on the sticky bar, the crowd getting rowdy. Bobby lit another Camel, and I swiveled my stool to watch the pool games. Billy and his deck hand, blindsided me, gave me pats on the back. Billy shook his head, "You be careful out there, now," he said. "Kent," he yelled, "Me and Ron here need a refill. And give another one to my girlfriend." He pointed to me. Ron was already back at the pool table, concentrating.

My brother had gone over by the door, to sit with three girls who worked picking crab. One of them shouted to me, "Hey, that's all right, man, you go for it!"

The Vista Del Mar was a local's bar. Walk in and be recognized. Guys came in from pulling green chain in the mills. A fisherman's bar, located one block from the docks. Been called a biker's bar. Twenty-five cents a glass for draft Budweiser. It was the kind of place where we frequently went outside to pee because someone would have thrown up all over the toilet.

We closed down the bar and, apparently, Officer Manos had followed me, lights blinking, all the way home. I didn't notice him till I'd started down my driveway. Despite my protest that I could walk to my house from the car, he hauled me off to jail.

I knew Officer Manos as Jim, who sang tenor in high school choir. I sang alto, but I'd never talked to him. He was shy. I was the first-string quarterback's girlfriend. But I knew who he was. Growing up in a small town, we all knew who we were. At the time, I felt thoroughly humiliated that Jim had arrested me. Many years later, I wrote him a card, thanking him for arresting me because that night planted the seed which changed my life. I'm glad I wrote him that card, because he died young, in his fifties.

At the jail, being so hammered I couldn't say the last four letters of the alphabet backwards, they booked me and threw me in the drunk tank where I sang as loud as I could until I finally passed out.

Terrible place. So uncomfortable. I had it all to myself. Concrete floor and walls. Brightly lit. Empty wooden benches. No one to talk to. Twice, that I can remember, they asked me to be quiet, so I sang even louder. I finally sat down in the corner I guess, because that's where I came-to when the lady woke me to tell me I was being released.

51

Walking home from jail, early the next morning, reeking of stale beer, I laughed at the audacity of having spent the night in jail. Me! Unbelievable!' Bobby was the one who slept in the drunk tank, not me.

In that last week before I was to leave for my new adventure, I'd almost chickened out. My other brother, Terry, thought truck driving was the absolute worst idea anyone could ever think of, and since Terry was the good brother, this shook me up quite a bit.

"All that vibration's terrible for your ears." With worry lines visible on his forehead, he continued: "And the noise. You can write about absolutely anything, Margot. Why risk going hard of hearing?"

I never had an answer for Terry. I just knew he was right.

But Bobby wanted to celebrate and my mother, who'd been through hell and back because of me, gave me a big hug and said, "Go," which is what I needed to hear.

But now I had a DUI to fuck with.

A few phone calls, and I learned California offered a diversion program called Lucky Deuce, which would erase my DUI if I didn't drink and went to their meetings for 12 weeks. Plus, due to a backlog, California allowed DUI arrestees three months before they had to enroll in the program. I had three months before the DUI would show up anywhere.

I could still leave today, if in three months, I came home and ran through this Lucky Deuce Program. I concocted an emergency. I would pretend my brother got in a terrible car accident. Tell the company my family needed me. I'd come home, run through this Lucky Deuce program, and be back on the road by January.

DUI resolved, I packed up my 1967 Rambler, drove south through the *Redwood Curtain (*what Humboldt County locals call the border between us and the rest of the world) and seven hours later arrived at the Sam Tanksley Trucking terminal in Santa Nella, a few miles north of Los Banos, California.

I followed Miguel, the mechanic, out to a huge white truck with red and blue stripes painted around its middle. Being a cab over, I wouldn't have trouble seeing over the engine, because I'd be sitting right beside it.

I grabbed the steering wheel and pulled myself up into my seat.

"Fire it up." Miguel had climbed in the jump seat (the passenger seat) and closed his door.

I started the engine and pointed to a gizmo I'd noticed on the floorboard. "What's that?" The little black thing looked exactly like the handle I pulled to start my lawn mower.

"That's the cruise control. You've never used one?" I shook my head, no. Miguel, my test proctor smiled. "When we get up to 55, you pull it up and turn it. It sets the speed so you don't have to keep your foot on the pedal."

"Oh. That's great."

"Your air is right under the seat."

I felt the knob, pulled, and my seat rose. I pushed it in, gauged my distance to the pedals, pulled it out again, and settled on my seat height.

"Don't worry about parking. Just let me see you back up before we pull out onto the freeway."

I found reverse, checked my mirrors, released the clutch, and inched backwards.

"Okay. That's fine. Don't worry about your leg. You'll get used to it." Miguel could see my leg shaking because the clutch was so strong.

"Turn right out of the parking lot. Then up the on-ramp to the freeway."

I waited. No cars or trucks. I pulled clear into the opposite lane and my rear wheels cleared the corner by a mile. "Boy, right turns are easier in a cab over."

"You learned in a conventional?"

"Yeah."

"A cab over will be a snap for you. You can see so much better."

I turned left to enter the freeway and the gears shifted up like butter. "This is so much easier than a 5x4."

"A 5x4! I've never even driven one of those. But, this trailer is empty. Shifting is totally different with a load." Miguel's calm presence felt the opposite to Dick Dart. "Do you have a handle for yourself?"

"I thought I'd call myself Sunny Avenue."

Miguel smiled. "That's good. We're Shirley Temple."

"Shirley Temple? What's that?"

Miguel grinned, but I didn't feel belittled in the least. "Shirley Temple is Sam Tanksley's handle. If someone calls out on the CB to a Shirley Temple, it means they are calling you, unless there's another Tanksley truck right there."

"I don't even know how to work the CB."

"Don't worry. It's easy."

My driving test consisted of two on-ramps, two off-ramps, a few miles of Interstate 5, and another short stint of backing up in the humongous empty parking lot.

The engine in neutral and still running, we both jumped out of the truck. "You'll do fine," Miguel said as he rounded the front of the cab and pulled gloves from his pocket. He put the gloves on over his greasy hands, pulled himself up into the drivers-seat, and backed the truck into its space behind Tanksley's shop. I waited.

Miguel smelled like soap. Skinny, maybe part Mexican, I wondered about his hair, a clean brown shoulder-length shag cut.

Walking with him back to the terminal I asked, "Who cuts your hair?"

"My wife's a hairdresser, but we separated a few weeks ago."

"Oh, sorry." I paused. "What do you think of this Bob guy?"

"Your partner? I don't know him. I mean I know who he is." We reached the mechanic's bay. "But, I think he's a safe bet."

We stood next to the huge bay where the mechanics work on all the trucks. "There are a lot of jerks out there." Miguel warned. "You'll be fine as long as you're careful."

"I will be." I smiled a goodbye and walked into the lounge. I recorded the mechanic. The first entry, my book had its beginning. A black, six-inch square journal with over 300 pages. Small enough to fit in my purse and big enough to last.

I'm hired. Bob had called dispatch and would be at the terminal in an hour. I sat waiting in the driver's area, a linoleum floor with folding tables and chairs, full ashtrays, and candy machines. I picked up a greasy *Road King* magazine, the cover ripped off, and started thumbing through the pages.

I hadn't a clue what reality would bring, but my imagination filled in the blanks with the Rockies, the Great Plains, loading docks, and the trucking culture I imagined to look like Dick Dart, blustery, huge, and with a kind heart.

Bob, Partner #1
Loading lettuce.

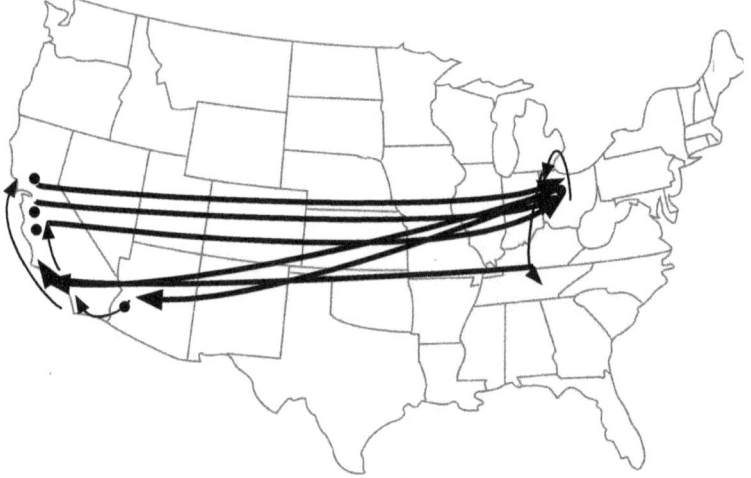

July, 1980
Salinas, California

Bob put a helping hand on my back end as I climbed into the truck.
"Don't."

"Oh, come on." A narrow and pointed voice. "I was just helping you."

"I can do it." I frowned as I swung up into my seat. At 28, 5'4" and about 125 lbs, getting into the jump seat took a four-step plan: Pull, step, swing, sit. Right hand pulls. Right foot steps. Swing (with gravity's help) into the seat and sit. If I timed the sit wrong, or the umph to my swing lacked enough propulsion, my 125 lbs would hang in mid-air, and I'd have to swing in again with greater force.

The driver's side was easy. Just grab the steering wheel and pull.

As Bob walked around the passenger door, the inside latch scraped his arm, tearing his thin white T-shirt sleeve. Through the dirty windshield,
56

I watched him continue around the cab, his head down, neck pink. Sweat stuck his shirt to his belly providing a clear visual of his nipples and belly button.

At sixty plus, Bob, in a suit and tie, could have passed as a wall-street banker. His tall, lanky, body looked fit, and with plenty of gray hair, people might have found him handsome. "Retired air traffic controller ... Sold cars in Redding before I took the truck driving class ... Cheapest course in the country I'll bet."

The drivers had separate storage compartments, accessible only from the outside. Second seat's storage compartment, on the passenger side, held my five gallons of granola, peanut butter, jelly, bread, tuna, mayonnaise, Tab, toiletries, about five changes of clothes and my tennis racket and balls. My sleeping bag, flashlight, boom box, tissues and wet wipes went up in the truck's second-seat sleeper compartment, which was behind the jump seat and above my outside storage compartment. First seat stored all his belongings on the driver's side, both inside and out.

We arrived at the loading dock in Salinas to find a line of trucks waiting. "Oh, crap. We're going to be here all day." Bob rubbed his forehead like he had a headache.

Blonde wavy hair and a plaid shirt got out of the truck in front of us. He looked like he might know something. I jumped down from my seat and was blasted by the heat and engine noise outside our idling, air-conditioned cab.

"Hi. Is it always this busy here?" I joined the blonde in the shade by his truck.

He lit his cigarette. "No. But it looks like we're going to be here all day."

"What's going on?"

"They're staging a dock strike. Boss screwed one of the workers so now no one's gonna work till they settle it." He blew his smoke away from me.

"What happened?"

"Fork lift broke down. Boss said it was the guy's fault, told him he had to use the pallet jack."

"What's that?"

"You new?"

"Just hired."

"A pallet jack is a like a fork lift on the ground and you push it around. Go on up there and take a look."

"Thanks. Too hot, though." I said, and walked back to our air conditioning. I reported to Bob.

"Crap."

Bob decided to re-work his logs, to show me driving since June 19th. Driving alone, he'd been driving way more hours than the law allowed.

"I make four per cent more when I drive alone and the company makes another seven percent. Everyone wins." Bob explained. "They won't let us drive alone for too long though. Afraid we'll get caught, or get in an accident. If we get caught, we have to pay our own fine."

First seat got paid 14 per cent of the load. Second seat obeyed first seat and received 11 percent. We never knew how much a load would pay, they just sent a check wherever we requested. I had my checks sent to my mother, since I intended to save as much as possible. If I needed money, I could request a com-check, pick it up at the next terminal, and that amount would be deducted from my paycheck. Tanksley employed about eight hundred drivers to run four hundred trucks, give or take. We shipped produce from west to east and dry freight from east to west.

Late in the afternoon, the repaired forklift loaded our lettuce and we headed out of Salinas in rush hour traffic. Already behind schedule, and now in bumper-to-bumper traffic, I had to pee.

"Here. Use this." Bob pulled out a plastic bottle from under the seat and held it out to me. The opening was at the end of a long curve.

"That's impossible, Bob."

He pulled over on the shoulder and kinked the cab, making a kind of "V" with the trailer.

"No one will see if you do it by the tires."

Fucker.

I shook my head. What was I doing with that guy? Was I nuts?

The Doghouse

Not the sleeper, please.

July 1980
Interstate 80

"Got any kids?" I asked Bob as we climbed the Sierra Nevada.

"No. Never been married." Bob took his eyes off the road and leered at me. "Ya know, *we* couldn't get married because I don't want to have kids."

"Oh. Right."

We talked for another hour, and on the uphill climb through the Sierra Nevada, Bob asked, "How 'bout I buy you a steak dinner? I know a great place in Boomtown."

"No thanks, Bob. I'll eat what I've brought. I can take a walk and stretch while you eat though. You go ahead."

"Aw, come on. Don't make me eat alone. I'm buying."

"No. Please, Bob. I want to eat my own food. And I really want to take a walk." *And I don't want to eat with you.*

Bob pulled into a gambling casino/steak house in Boomtown outside of Reno. There was a 20-foot-high neon lady in a bikini with blinking lights offering us a martini. The olive lit up green when she closed her eyes.

"It's not safe out here for a girl. Where are you going to walk?"

"Around the parking lot. I'll be careful. Please, you go ahead."

Bob locked the truck and walked away. "What time should I be back?" I called, but either he didn't hear or didn't answer. I set my watch for a half hour.

A parking lot. I walked to the edge, sat cross-legged on the pavement behind a Cadillac, and poured a pint of milk over a small Tupperware bowl full of granola. A littered field. Windowless stucco houses a hundred yards beyond. Suddenly a rat scurried out from the parking lot and off

59

into the stubble. I ate my apple and enjoyed the warm, dry breeze. The scent of my red delicious apple, mixed with the smell of tar, the far-off sounds of car doors, gambling revelers, even music, conjured up my imagination about all that would come. Bob would be manageable. I was lucky to be here.

When I returned, Bob wasn't at the truck. I didn't have a key, so I passed through the smoky, liquor and sweat smelling casino looking for him in the restaurant but he wasn't there either. I cased the slot machines, the card tables, the bar. No Bob. When I returned to the truck, there he was, pacing.

"I could leave you here and the company wouldn't say a word. I don't know why I waited."

Wow, he's really mad! "I was just here and didn't see you."

"I don't have to wait for you, you know. If you don't show up I can consider that desertion and leave."

"I went inside to look for you. You didn't give me a time to be back. I never thought you'd be done eating this quick. I'm sorry."

"You have to be here next time or else." Bob's neck was bright pink. "I'm not going to eat by myself. I just went in there to wash up. I've been waiting here for almost thirty minutes."

You're lying out your ass. I looked down, contrite. "I'm sorry."

"Well, don't do it again." He climbed back in the driver's side and I wondered when my turn behind the wheel would begin.

Three hundred miles later, outside Elko, Nevada, I finally got to drive.

I couldn't tell whether I was going uphill or downhill by looking at the road, which was why I needed to "drive by the seat of my pants," know-my-throttle, listen to the engine. An amateur watched the tachometer. Even going down a slight grade, especially a long one, felt ominous because the truck picked up speed so quickly. Pumping brakes would catch them on fire so we only used five pounds of continuous pressure, which was a feeling, not a dial I could watch. These trucks had no Jake brake (engine brake), which would have helped to keep downhill speeds under control.

I drove twelve hours straight, from outside of Elko to Rawlins, Wyoming, where the company had a terminal that refueled and maintained the trucks. We stopped on the shoulder before exiting, because Bob only allowed me to point our truck straight on the freeway.

The twelve hours, or 600 miles, breaks the law by two hours. We recorded in our logs that we traded the driver's seat every five hours. *Why don't we just fucking drive what we log?*

Standing out in the parking lot, I felt wobbly, vibrated, and had trouble seeing clearly. Further out, I leaned against a telephone pole in the seedy, outskirt of Rawlins and got pitch on the back of my sweatshirt. I already had grease on my pants, maybe from the parking lot back in Nevada.

Hiding in a shadow, I wrote in the dim street light, hoping Bob would think I was in the bathroom, and give me a longer break. Since Boomtown, our relationship had taken a turn for the worse. I got my first trip through Wyoming down on paper.

Coming across Wyoming, Bob stuck his head out of the sleeper. "Turn that radio off. I can't sleep with it on."

I turned off my boom box.

"And don't reach back here for anything. I like to take all my clothes off."

"Snap the curtain shut, Bob, so I won't be tempted."

"OK, but then I can't get any air." Five minutes later he unsnaps the sleeper curtain, breathes on my neck. "Don't use the CB. They'll follow you when they figure out which truck you're in. We don't want them to know you're here. And you don't know how to use it anyways."

"Is it really hard? Could you teach me some day?" I tossed out the sarcasm without thinking first.

"Why are you so damned uppity?"

Little Iodine crossed my mind, what my mother used to call me. I looked at the road and said nothing.

"You'll bring all the trucks around us, damn it. They'll watch for you. When you pull into a rest stop, they'll be right behind you. You don't want that. You'll see. I know what I'm saying."

"Ok, Bob."

He jerked his head back into the sleeper.

Pitch dark now, sudden light from the terminal's lounge caught my attention. Bob had walked out the door. Moths swarmed the light above him. I pulled my sweatshirt off the sticky telephone pole. Break over, journal stuffed in my purse, I walked toward the truck. Happy for my turn in the sleeper.

I bounced and jiggled in my sleeping bag. The engine roared. Maybe I dozed. To get air, I opened the six-inch metal cover and stuck my nose toward the fresh air that zoomed by. I flopped from stomach to back to side, so grateful for the time-off and the privacy, if only in a 4x 12 foot cubicle, bordered by our luggage compartments, a pegboard wall, and the red plastic sleeper curtain.

Out of the sleeper five hours later, I watched Nebraska's cornfields go on forever. We probably crossed the Platte River a dozen times.

"Why won't you eat in truck stops?" Bob asked.

"I'm saving money. Eating from a grocery store is a lot cheaper. Plus it's a lot healthier."

Bob decided to eat lunch in a rest stop. He stopped off at a 76 truck stop to buy some "fixins."

"Hey Bob, can I get a key for the truck? That way, I can wait for you inside it. And I wouldn't have to ask every time I want to get into my stuff. Sorry I fouled up like that back in Boomtown."

"No. I can't give you a key and a key can't be made."

Further down the road, on perfectly flat land, we passed what looked like a monstrous sow bug, an over-turned trailer.

"What do you think happened, Bob?"

"He probably swerved to miss a car that pulled in front of him."

"What do you mean?"

"That's what cars do. They pass, pull in front of you and slow down. I blow the horn when they do it. Makes me mad as hell."

We drove another 900 miles to a rest stop outside of Indianapolis. There were fireflies and mosquitoes everywhere, including all over our windshield. Bob got out his little cook stove and I cooked a vegetable stir-fry for both of us in front of a deep red sunset. Bob's mood improved.

Cincinnati was only a few hours away.

For all of our non-stop rush, twelve-hour shifts and peeing on the side of the road, we arrived two days early. Bob wanted to get the load off and get loaded again immediately, make more money. Kroger's loading dock opened at 6:00 a.m. We arrived at 4:00 a.m., got in line, and then Bob wanted me to take a nap in the sleeper.

"You go ahead, Bob. I'll nap on the doghouse if I feel like it."

"No. Women come up to the truck. If they see a woman in here, they'll keep bothering us."

That doesn't even make sense. "I don't want to sleep. I'll read. You go ahead."

I couldn't bring myself to get trapped in the sleeper with Bob in the truck and not driving. The doghouse, the two seats plus the padded area above the engine between the seats, served as the second driver's sleeper while parked in situations like this and officially, belonged to me. Totally comfortable, probably because I'm short, the doghouse offered a much cooler temperature. I could see out, get a breeze through the window, and I didn't feel claustrophobic. There was not enough room, even for me, to sit up cross-legged in the sleeper.

Neither of us got in the sleeper.

The gates opened and we waited for our turn to back in, one at a time, while the rest of the drivers watched. An inside loading dock, built long before the invention of a 52' trailer, the parked trucks were mere inches from each other and backed in at a severe angle to the dock. This warehouse was intended for trucks half our size. Bob paid a dockworker to back our truck in.

Our load was hot and some of our lettuce had spoiled. The temperature gauge had mal-functioned. The refridgeration unit had buzzed away, a nauseatingly loud, continuous noise, but it hadn't been cooling anything. Bob insisted he checked the inside temperature at every stop, but I never saw him open the rear doors even once. I thought about tattling on the lying son-of-a-bitch. See if I could get him fired.

Not only was some of the load spoiled, but much of the lettuce had cracked ribs. Cracked ribs indicated the lettuce had grown too fast, which meant the inside of the head would be too white as not enough photosynthesis had occurred.

Nine hours sitting in the truck, me reading or walking, Bob approaching a heart attack, Kroger's found a buyer for our lettuce and accepted the load. Shortly after that, dispatch instructed us to wait in Indianapolis, Indiana. We didn't need to call back for thirty-six hours. This load of lettuce paid $1775 to Tanksley. I made $195.25.

Indianapolis
Albert

July 11, 1980

Motel 6 in Indianapolis charged $8.00 for a room. First Seat was responsible for the second-seat's motel room, and Bob wanted me to sleep in the room with him. Not in the same bed, he assured me, standing in his underwear, beer in hand. His motel room door was wide open.

"I'm not paying more money for a separate motel room."

"Ok, I guess I'll sleep in the truck."

"That's stupid."

"Can I have the key to run the air conditioner? I won't drive anywhere, I promise."

"No. It will use too much fuel. They track our fuel usage and we can't use the fuel for air conditioning."

"That's bullshit." I muttered, walking off toward the motel's office.

The company only required Bob to pay for one room. Sixty-six degrees was a hot day at home, so this 87-degree heat with 97 per cent humidity was killing me. Luckily, a woman driving alone in another Tanksley truck pulled in next to ours. She readily agreed to split the cost of the room. Bob spat a white globule on the cement.

At 45 or 50, Darlene had bleached white hair and decayed teeth. She sat comatose on her bed, staring at a re-run of *Mork and Mindy*. After a shower, I put on clean pajamas and stared at the TV from my own bed (*A Love Boat* re-run). I ate peanut butter and jelly, a Baby Ruth, and drank a cold Tab. We made no effort at conversation and I conked out before *Love Boat* ended.

The best night's sleep I'd had in five days, I prepared for a full twenty-four-hour layover in Indianapolis. After granola and milk, I collected tourist info, a map and a bus schedule from the front desk. The bus stop was three miles down the road. At 9:00 a.m., the heat and humidity already had me sweating. But as I got out on the straight stretch into town, a couple pulled out from the motel and offered me a ride. Grateful, I hopped in the back seat and watched the three miles to the bus stop whiz by. They took me all the way into town. No air conditioning. They didn't mention the heat, so neither did I.

I planned a tour of the children's museum to start, and they dropped me off right in front. Right off, I noticed the clean streets, I think because so much garbage and filth littered the warehousing side of town. I could see three statues from where I stood. Bronze, oxidizing to green. Like Greek or Roman history pictures. An ornate, concrete building stood on each corner the likes of which I'd never seen in California, much less in my small home town. Huge buildings. Carved looking jobs. And down the street, a huge red brick building sat with window after window lined up in a row, and above the windows sat concrete curly-cue bearded gargoyles.

The post office building, on the corner opposite the museum, reminded me of the huge hat box where my Mom kept her "Jackie Kennedy" hat, a wide-brimmed black velvet monstrosity complete with a veil. She'd bought it to wear to my Aunt's funeral and wore it with her "nun shoes", black things with thick heels and laces that we'd laughed about ever since they went out of style. Missing her suddenly, I decided to buy a post card inside that monstrous hat box of a post office, but while the floors were marble and the ceiling was entirely mosaic, no one thought to include post cards in the decor.

I toured all three floors of the children's museum, a gray building, all cracked like an old man. Ten-inch moths, giant centipedes, four-inch cockroaches, a bird-eating spider, toads, turtles, frogs, a 1930 Maserati, Zulu thumb pianos, Egyptian mummies. I bought a post card, told Mom I loved her, and mailed it directly from the gift shop. Reluctantly, I decided to leave the museum's air conditioning to hop a bus headed for the zoo.

Hot, sweaty, stuffy, miserable wet air, and not quite noon. No one seemed to care. I arrived at the zoo's entrance and immediately, a white

66

policeman approached and rolled down his window.

"You sure you want to go in there?"

"This is the zoo, right?"

"Yeah. You meeting someone?"

"No, why?"

"Well, this ain't exactly a white neighborhood. Might be better to come back when someone's with you."

"The zoo isn't safe?"

"You'll be safe once you're in, but out here ..."

"I'm only here for the day," I interrupted. "I'll be gone tomorrow." I kept walking toward the entrance.

I could see him shaking his head as he rolled along beside me in his cop car, all the way to the entrance, before driving away. With cars on less than a quarter of the parking lot, no one standing around with guns in their pants, I didn't feel too threatened. I paid and walked immediately to a piece of shade to record our dialogue before I explored the zoo.

My God. The animals lay in cement prison cells, looking like they had the flu. They looked hotter than I felt. Steam rose off feces, the foul smell nothing like barn manure, but more like rot, or sulfur. Where did they even feed these shit-covered monkeys? I couldn't believe the black bear in his cramped cement cage. I didn't think he could even walk. His fur was half gone. No wonder the parking lot was practically empty.

Outside the zoo's entrance, I saw a tree-shaded bike trail along the edge of a green park. *I'll find a spot, take in the breeze, and record this pitiful zoo. Maybe I'll write a letter to the Indianapolis City Council, get that off in the mail this afternoon.*

The breeze amongst the trees helped. I sat, but whoa! The ground crawled with red ants. I looked for a bench just as the mosquitoes struck, so I took off walking. No further than sixty yards into the park, a black fellow slowed his bicycle, road alongside me, and talked in some jive language I didn't understand. *If he starts to get off his bike, I'll kick the bike onto him and run.*

Was the policeman right? I'm really not supposed to be here? I turned around and headed back to the zoo's entrance and the bus stop. He didn't follow. Perfect timing, the bus arrived and I boarded.

Filled with black people, I purposely walked further down the isle than the first available seat, to surround myself with more black people than ever before in my entire life.

Downtown, I had an hour to wait before catching the bus, which would drop me off three miles from the motel. Too hot outside, I went in the cafe directly behind the bus stop for some air conditioning. Packed with black people, I stood at the counter waiting for a vacant seat and ordered tea. Lipton's arrived in a coffee mug, barely lukewarm. It looked like dirty water.

A black man about my age approached almost immediately and invited me to share his booth. He offered his orange juice and grateful, I ignored the hideous tea.

"What you doing here, girl?" he started.

"I'm waiting for the bus. I can't handle the heat out there and I don't want to walk anywhere else." Milk chocolate brown skin, a shorter, natural looking Afro (nothing processed, greasy, or stick-out) and no comb stuck in it. He wore used black slacks, a silky dark shirt with dark gold checks, no t-shirt and flip-flops. He was clean and his teeth were white. I only looked at him because we were across the table from each other. Gorgeous.

"You in a black restaurant, girl."

"I know." I raised my chin a notch, looked down my nose a bit. "Is this gonna be ok?"

"Just don't see a white girl come in here is all. Where you from?"

"California." I rocked back, preparing to leave.

"Is that right!"

"Northern California. Rural. Hardly any black people at all. A policeman at the zoo told me to be careful today, because I was white."

"Yeah, well, what you doin' out here?"

"I'm a truck driver." *How cool is that.* "We delivered yesterday in Cincinnati and now we're laid over here till we get our next load. What's your name?"

"Albert. Yours?"

"Margot," I pause. "With a t."

"A t?"

"It's French. My Mom was born in France."

A guy approached the table. "Is that you, Albert?"

Albert laughed. "Hey ..." Then I couldn't understand another word. The guy looked directly at me the entire time. He left after about a minute.

"You got family?" Albert asked.

"Three brothers. All older." I answered and another man walked up.

"Hey, Albert," he said and again, I couldn't understand what they talked about for another two or three minutes, while the guy looked directly at me.

"That feels weird," I said, tipping my head to the man just leaving.

"They just want to get a look at you, is all. You don't have to wait for no bus, ya know. I could take you back to your motel."

"I don't know." I loved his white teeth, the full lips, the whites of his eyes. Too thin, but I loved his smooth skin. I glanced at the waitress, and then looked at the woman in the booth behind Albert. Both women sneered, blatantly stared at me. I focused on Albert.

"Hey, I'm not going to do anything, just give you a ride is all. I promise."

If I get my own groceries, Bob can't make me eat in truck stops. "I *would* like to do some grocery shopping." Heads turned as Albert held the door and we walked down the block together.

A big '60s red Ford Fairlane. Albert's car sat higher in the front than in back. The car was so wide that Albert couldn't have crossed that distance to touch me even if he wanted to. We rolled the windows down and Albert started the engine. It roared, loud, like there was only half a muffler. No air conditioner.

I imagined a gun in the glove box. I figured I could open the door and roll out if I needed to.

"Tell me about your family," I sat up cross-legged on the bench seat.

"I got seven brothers and sisters."

"Whoa! Are all your brothers and sisters as good looking as you are?"

"No." He rocked back and laughed. "No one is ugly, but I'm the good lookin' one." Still laughing. "Ever since I was born, I been good lookin'. Even my Momma's friends have gone after me. Once I went with a white school teacher."

I didn't ask what that meant. "What about your parents? What do they do?"

"My Pop died when I was nine. Momma raised us up doing whatever she could."

"Oh, that's tough."

We were on a six-lane road going 50 mph. Everyone I saw was black and if I looked out my window, I'd see them gawking.

"Wha'd you do before you went truckin' girl?"

"Well, I taught high school for a year," and added, "before I got fired."

"No, not you! Why'd you get fired?"

"Oh, it's a long bullshit story,"

"Go on, girl."

"Well, I agreed to coach the tennis team, because no one else would. I didn't even know how to coach or run a tournament."

"Youse a tennis coach?"

"They promised I didn't need to do much. The team just needed an adult. 'They're so good they'll win the championship without you,' the principal said. And they did."

A car swerved in close and veered away, the driver staring.

"I got pissed because some of my students ... I taught English," I explained. "But my students who were in choir didn't have robes because the school wouldn't pay for them. And here I was, coaching tennis on courts that had brand new windscreens installed. The only wind screens on any tennis court in Humboldt County. Three thousand dollars so fifteen kids would never have wind blowing their tennis balls around. And thirty kids couldn't have choir robes."

"That's raw," Albert put his elbow out his window and drove with one hand. "So what happened?"

"I wrote a letter to the editor about how unfair it was. The worst part was, at the spring awards banquet, I got booed."

"Girl, that's some story." Albert suddenly crossed the double yellow lines *and* the three lanes for on-coming traffic. He parked next to a cyclone fence.

I continued talking as if nothing unusual just happened. "But now that I'm a *unique woman truck driver who's gonna write a best seller*," I fake chuckled, "everyone will be asking me to speak and I'll end up getting an honorary doctorate from somewhere."

Albert wasn't listening. He was looking off through the fence. Ant-sized people played softball a hundred yards in the distance. "Just want to watch my cousin," he said out the window. "Just want to see how it's going, is all."

Cars whizzed straight at us. I imagined someone pulling up in front of us. *Maybe he nodded to someone in the cafe. They've done this before. They know I can't jump out in this traffic, and there is nowhere to run if I did. If there's a gun in the glove box ... I better start carrying a screwdriver in my purse.*

Not a single person knew where I was or how to find me. Even I didn't have a clue where I was. Would Bob report me missing or think 'good riddance'?

"I better get on with shopping and get back to the motel." Extra casual and all nonchalant I continued. "Bob is expecting me and I don't want him to call out the National Guard."

"Who's Bob?"

"My driving partner."

Albert started up and pulled back into traffic. At a nearby Kroger's, I stocked up. More tuna, apples, bread, coke, and milk. The fruit looked lousy. In California, we got to touch ours. Shrink-wrapped fruit, I'd never seen it before.

We headed back to the motel. "I've never talked to a black person before," I began. "You're the first."

"Lordy, girl. You been missin' out!"

"Where I come from, everyone's white. I've never seen so many black people as I have today. Not in my whole life."

"And now you searchin' 'em out." He grinned, like he knew something.

"What do you mean?"

"You attracted, honey."

"Curious. I don't know about attracted."

"White women are attracted to black men."

"Oh really?" A bit snide. "Why is that?"

"Cuz they both been kept down," Albert's elbow is back out the window.

"Nobody keeps me down." I'm serious.

Albert laughed. He had the best laugh. Deep down in his throat.

"White men and black women. They gotta be tough. Black women were forced to make it somehow, cause their men had to run."

"Yeah, I see."

"They're stronger for it. The white woman and the black man can't be strong. If they do, they be beaten or dead."

I recognized the road leading to the motel and knew I was virtually home safe. Relaxed, I risked "I think the attraction is as much to do with sexual fantasy and forbidden fruit as anything."

"It's ok, girl. I's just talkin' straight with you."

"I got afraid when you pulled up to the fence. Bob really couldn't care less if he ever sees me again."

"I figured you was scared. Was you really an English teacher?"

"I couldn't have made that up if I'd tried."

Albert fidgeted, wiped his hands on his pants. In front of the motel room, two white people stared at us. All the cars had white people inside. Albert cracked his knuckles, said he best be going. I thanked him several times, eager to get into the room and write it all down. I told him how much I enjoyed talking with him, got my sack of groceries from the back seat, and waved goodbye.

Showering off a day full of sweat, I sat down to record everything. "I did it!" I wrote. An hour later, my left hand cramping, ink all over my little finger, I decided to make up with Bob because tomorrow we would be back on the road together 24/7. I knocked on his door. He threw it wide open, wearing only his boxer shorts. I closed my eyes.

"Can I buy you a beer?" I asked, and turned away to hide my face. He was so white. His skin sagged. He stood on shapeless legs covered with blue veins. Brown age spots covered his hairless chest.

"I've got three beers left in the ice bucket." He turned to get me one.

I popped open the Budweiser he handed me and walked to the shade of a huge maple tree. Green grass covered the ground. Nothing sounded better than a beer in the shade. Except for a beer in the shade without Bob.

Bob, dressed, drank one with me while I downed the last two. He took off with my money to get a second six-pack and some bug repellent. I picked through my groceries and chose tuna and apple for dinner. I fed the mushy brown apple to the ants that clamored by the thousands at the dumpster.

Mosquitoes spoiled the soft breeze and cool shade that evening. No one else dared to be outside with them. I wouldn't be enclosed in a room with Bob, who brought back a 12-pack. He swatted at mosquitoes while I sprayed bug repellent on both of us. We waved our beers around swooshing mosquitoes away. Bob spouted on about the layover, the wasted time, losing money, and how the motel maid ought to be fired.

I pretended to listen but daydreamed about Albert, sipped my beer, and drifted back into the past, Bob's chatter a constant hum somewhere off in the fields, or up in the maple tree behind us.

Chapter (12) **Shift Happens**

My Three Brothers
are somebodies

When I was little, I used to stand beside my Mom while she sat at her dressing table. She'd spread red lipstick around her mouth, blot it with tissue, and click the lid back on the tube. She didn't even use the mirror.

"Bobby always has to be the big show off, Margot." Mom would inhale her Kent cigarette, and start taking her curlers out. "Just a god damn jazzbo."

"Yeah, he's a jazzbo," I would agree. I had Mom all to myself when she got ready to go out for the evening, maybe because she didn't put her dress on till last.

"Empty this for me, honey." She'd hand me the ashtray. Hold her cigarette. "What are we going to do with him?"

"Spank him. Make him go to his room." Cigarette butts and ashes belonged in a special waste can, so they wouldn't accidentally set any tissue on fire. A heavy green glass square, we never let the ashtray fill all the way up. I'd set it carefully back on her dressing table, which had a glass top that could crack. She'd take a big swallow of smoke, ash her cigarette (two pats), and let it rest in the groove where the cigarette belonged.

She'd get her earrings clipped on and check her bright red nails to see if they needed any filing. I'd watch those nails shine through her curls when she finally scrunched her hair around.

Dad would be greeting the babysitter downstairs.

"Zip me up." Mostly, I remembered the dark blue silk dress, probably because the material had maroon velvet paisley designs that were stiff compared to the silk. It had short sleeves and a boat neckline. I'd stand on my tiptoes to get her all zipped up. Even though she wore perfume, I smelled her Kents, and could have picked her out blindfolded.

I'd get the quick hug and kiss at the door as they left, my brothers off somewhere in the four storeys of our house. They never waited at the door to say goodbye like I did.

When I was eight or nine, Bobby's best friend was killed in a small plane crash. Mark's dad was flying the plane, and he died too. Mom and I were standing in the sun porch of our humongous house. She'd learned the news less than an hour previous, had told me, and was crying. My Dad walked in, took one look and said, "What are you crying for? You didn't even know him."

"Four kids in four years," I overheard Mom talking to her friend. "That son of a bitch."

I felt sorry for her because Bobby was always doing something awful. Daniel broke stuff, and she didn't like all his talking. We had a live-in maid, and Terry was good, but still, I just wanted her to be happy.

Daniel, my oldest brother, really did jabber away non-stop. Daniel's childhood story involved drilling a hole through his fourth-floor bedroom into Dad's bedroom closet, intending to bug Dad's phone. Unfortunately, he missed the closet by six inches and put a half-dollar sized hole in Dad's bedroom ceiling. Daniel taped a white plug over it but unfortunately, left the white plaster dust on the maroon carpet.

Daniel always got caught. I thought Dad sent Daniel away to school because he breathed too loud at the dinner table, that's what I remember, but if you ask Terry, he'll tell you Daniel got sent away because he tried to bug the phone. Mom always said, "If there's one cow pie in the pasture, Daniel will step in it." We called Daniel cube because he was more than square, which was Bobby's idea to begin with.

Mom told us Bobby created art by reaching in his diaper and drawing on the walls. He was climbing out of his crib at six months and because he'd fall on his head, he got nicknamed Beezie, beezer being another name for a human head.

Wild. That was Bobby. I remember when he got to drive Dad's Volkswagen the week Dad was out of town. Bobby took the hubcaps off and reversed the wheels so they were on back to front, making them sit out from the wheel arches.. To be a jazzbo, I guess. He never got to borrow the car after that.

Mom nicknamed Terry *Little Lord Fauntleroy* after the children's story about the charming endearing son, who, because of his kindness, got rich. We jut called him moneybags.

Me, she called *Little Iodine.* "Iodine is a prankish conniving little girl who is forever at odds with her parents and all authority figures in general." I have no memory of conniving or being at odds. Mostly I remembered wanting to play with Terry, but he never allowed me in his bedroom, where I wanted to roll his marbles along the baseboards with all his friends. Terry converted the empty wine cellar into a game room and I wasn't allowed in there either.

I played a weak second fiddle to Terry who, in college, received one of eight scholarships from the Whitney Museum of Modern Art. They gave him an all-expenses paid quarter in New York City, a loft in Manhattan, a private painting studio, access to workshops and visiting artists, and an all-inclusive pass to every museum and art function. He was the first student to be accepted from California.

As a musician, Terry practiced so much on the piano he injured his wrist. Said he was too high on a chord change to stop. His classical compositions were so full of emotion they made me cry.

But you'd have to be his sister, or a close friend to hear those songs. The public got to hear his reggae band, the Heart Beats. The Heart Beats sang original songs telling everyone to "love themselves." They did some published songs, but mostly the band members composed original music. "My Heart." (Love yourself). My favorite song was called "Halleluiah Herb" which he composed for a movie about marijuana in the 70s.

I'd never been big on the *love yourself* message. When I was drinking and dancing, sure, I loved myself and everyone else, but sober, mostly I felt guilty, bad, not good enough, lonely. It felt as if, like, by just hearing it, I was supposed to be healed. But, I was their biggest fan. Always there. Up front and dancing. He rarely put me on the guest list, though.

"This is our sole income, Margot. If we put you on the guest list, pretty soon we'd have to put everyone on the guest list." I thought he was ashamed of me. It never occurred to me how much Heart Beats seven members struggled to make ends meet.

I always called Terry first with health or finance questions. I admired his talent and brains, but we never got close.

Bobby was another idea altogether. Bobby carefully cracked walnuts in half, cleaned out the nut, wrote "Sorry! No Nut!" on a slip of paper, glued it all back together and then threw it back into the bin at the grocery store. One time, he made a rubber mask of himself, like a president's head or a monster mask, and answered the door wearing it on Halloween. "Who are you?" the kids would ask. "Why, I'm myself!" he would answer.

Bobby made peanut men with pipe cleaners and peanuts in the shell. Little downhill skiers, cowboys, doctors with little glasses, tricycle riders, monkeys, bikers with beards on motorcycles. He'd leave them on grocery shelves, or tip the bartenders with a little bartender one, or perhaps leave one on your steering wheel or hang one off your shirt collar if he could get away with it.

That was Bobby. Me, I couldn't tell a joke to save my life.

When we were kids, Bobby spent his whole allowance on a sewing machine for me that really sewed, and a pencil box for my pencils. It wasn't just me, either. Bobby gave away all his money or, unfortunately, he would lose it. He couldn't take care of much. Lost all his teeth before he turned twenty-five. Then, drunk, he flushed the false ones down the toilet. They broke in the pipe somehow, and he went without for a few years.

Bobby held the Junior Olympic record for the 50-yard breast stroke because he swam the entire length under water. The next year, they ruled the swimmer's head had to remain above water. Could be he's still in the record books. He was a gymnast too, competed on the rings, a perfect iron cross, toes pointed, flips. Even better, he was a high diver. Half twists, full twists, forward or backward, straight in with hardly a splash. His most famous dives were off the cliff at the Ravencliff Summer Camp for boys in Southern Humboldt.

I loved his swan dive the best. A giant leap out like he would take off flying, an arc down and he'd enter the water with hardly a sound.

Mom thought his cartooning was too adolescent, wanted him to develop some aesthetic. Make fine art. All the time, whether he was watching television eating, or talking, he had a pencil, doodling some cartoon. My parents talked about a possible career for Bobby with Disney animations, but he never made it out of junior college, just took the money they were sending and didn't go to class.

When Bobby hugged, I felt wrapped in the softest cotton. Like resting. Like safety. Like being loved.

I wanted Mom's love. I had it, but it just didn't look like what she gave Terry. It wasn't enough. I wasn't enough. Even when I was enough I wasn't enough.

My brothers were all somebodies. Even Daniel, for all the shame we heaped on him, went off to rewrite a *Survival on Land and Sea* manual for the Naval Institue Press. He taught survival swimming to sailors and wrote the *Naval Aviation Water Survival Training Program, Instructors Manual*. And before that, he was a navigator on Naval airplanes. I'd trust Daniel with my life, and evidently, so would the Navy. Daniel was charged to follow protocol to the last nano-second should the president determine we needed to drop a nuclear bomb. I think they made a good call on that one.

Daniel left home after high school and never came back. He got religion. I don't think anyone calls him cube anymore, back in Florida, and I'm glad of that.

Maybe I'm too loud. I don't know. I never wanted to be a nurse. I tried teaching. Failed at marriage. Seemed like my brothers used up all the good ideas. Maybe I could become an author. Another reclusive Emily Dickenson.

People might have thought I was running away, going truck driving, but I didn't care. My truck driving book project was the absolute first independent choice I'd made in my whole life. That people-pleasing spin in my head was finally quiet, and knowing who I was, at least relative to Bob, drunk now sitting next to me, was a snap.

Hopefully, I'll measure up to my brothers some day. Amount to something more than an embarrassment, more than the town's mental patient.

I swallowed the last swig of beer, put the empty can back in the case, and opened another.

Margot, relative to Bob, you're an angry bitch! Ha ha!

You're just drunk, Iodine. Shut the fuck up. Tonight I'm happy.

Apron Strings
If you cut 'em, they bleed.

When I entered the six grade, Mom started divorce proceedings with plans to marry her lover. The divorce took four years because my Dad argued that Mom committed adultery and my Mom argued, "You would too if you were married to yourself." I don't remember a single word spoken about the vodka.

In the end, we four kids had to go before the judge. "Do you want to live with your Mom or your Dad?" the judge asked. Secretly, I wanted to live with my Dad, but Dad would be OK without us and I was afraid Mom would lose it if we didn't live with her. She'd already tried to commit suicide once.

That awful night, Bobby sent me to my room because I was too young to watch.

"Shut your door." He waved me away. But I left the door open just a crack, pulled a large Butterfinger from my candy drawer, and started nibbling the chocolate off the crunchy peanut-buttery insides.

"No!" I heard Mom answer Bobby through her sobs.

Bobby's words melted together. I couldn't understand him, but he sounded like the policeman on TV who talked a person out of jumping off a skyscraper.

Bump. Thump. They'd fallen on the floor. Daniel paced the hallway. I saw him open Mom's door and heard Bobby say, "We're OK, Daniel. Just close the door."

Maybe a minute more (I'd finished the Butterfinger), Mom's sobbing quieted. Her door opened and I heard Bobby tell Daniel. "I got 'em."

I stuck my ear towards the door. Bobby continued. "I got her fist open and the pills went all over. She let me pick 'em up."

"Is she laying on the floor? Maybe you could get her into bed." Daniel wanted to help, but knew Mom would have fought him.

"I did. She spilled her drink on herself."

Quiet. Nobody walking away. I peeked out, and both Bobby and Daniel were listening at Mom's door. Bobby opened it, closed it. "She's asleep."

I closed my door. Got a Hershey bar, and climbed into bed. With the crunchy buttery candy packed in my teeth, chocolate melting on my tongue, I sucked on the sweet comfort till sleep came.

When the lover decided not to divorce his wife and ended the affair, Mom tried again. And another time, Terry held Mom by the pool doors while Bobby got the car keys out of her hand. I think they escorted her to her bedroom. There were more times. It happened after a phone call once. And then when the airplane pilot instructor affair ended. I never helped with Mom's suicide attempts. Usually, I just went to bed with a Butterfinger, my favorite.

Mom drank too much, but we never told. In fact, years later, the counselor suggested the next time I see my Mom, say to her, "I don't like it when you're drunk." He said I had to use the word drunk, I couldn't just say "drinking."

Unfortunately, the next time was Thanksgiving. Quietly, I said "Mom, I don't like it when you're drunk." She left the kitchen, went to her bedroom, and my stepfather escorted me out the door.

Smirnoff was Mom's brand, drunk by the fifth. No ice. Around dinnertime, she'd start with "Your Dad always had to be the big fish, Margot. I've spent my life in the smallest ponds." By *Kojak*, Bobby and I would be reminding her of her pilot's license, her poems, and she would recite the one great poem her professor thought she should publish. "I don't care about publishing," she'd say, and look off somewhere beyond the TV. "He wrote his life on the head of a pin," she'd recite, "then slowly down the shaft ... Down round, round down, he missed the point as he passed on down."

My uncle told stories about Mom having a string of boys following her around through high school. Then the war took all the young men. Mom said she worried she'd be an old maid, that's why she married my father. Said she never cared about a mink coat, Christmas parties for two hundred, a live-in maid, swimming pool, airplane, and the travel all over Mexico, which she said was another small pond.

If we didn't live in the biggest house in town, then it was the second biggest, which must have been what being a big fish was all about. Mom drank back then too, but after the divorce, she'd be stupid by six o'clock.

My junior high friends will tell you my mom was their favorite. We were a pack, us kids, maybe ten of us. My big house was the favorite hangout, partly because it was so big and had a swimming pool, but more because Terry might walk by. And my friends loved Terry's friends. They loved when his band practiced at our house. When Terry wasn't there, we listened to Bob Dylan records. We could stay up as late as we wanted on sleepovers, and we had big boy-girl parties at our house too.

Mom would take us to Moonstone for beach parties. We'd roast hot dogs and marshmallows. We'd skim board the entire day or watch the boys play touch football even as the sun was setting.

I knew my friends' mothers. They were nice enough, but couldn't hold a candle to my mom. She made me proud. The way she dressed, what she'd say, the way my friends liked being around her.

Parties, charm and happiness on the outside, drunk on the inside. We never told. In high school, we never brought people over to the house after five o'clock.

As a tenth grader, I started going with the quarterback, and in my junior year, mom re-married. Daniel and Bobby weren't included, only Terry and I attended the wedding.

I loved Ben, her new husband, an architect. He painted my bedroom lemon yellow with a fat orange stripe going up one wall. Cobalt blue stripes separated the yellow from the orange. My Mom bought new bedspreads and curtains. The drinking continued, but no one had to be carried to bed.

No more frozen turkey rolls for Thanksgiving either. Poppy, her Lhasa Maltese, got to come back in the house, washed, clipped, and combed. Mom and Ben started building a gorgeous house overlooking the ocean. Drinking after five, but it didn't really matter. I was with Aaron, the quarterback, and I was in love.

I-65 Through Kentucky
The rest stop could have been TV.

July 14, 1980

At five in the afternoon, dispatch finally gave us our load: *Life* Magazines. Pick them up in Nashville for delivery in Los Angeles, San Francisco, and Sacramento.

"They don't pay us for deadheading, you know." Saliva hit the steering wheel. Bob wiped his mouth on his sleeve. Driving empty, for six hours, did seem unreasonable. From Indianapolis through Kentucky and into Tennessee. "And three deliveries," Bob gunned the engine, jerking the tractor into tenth gear. "We'll lose money on that too."

I'd never been through Kentucky. Green. In July.

"And making us wait all day to get our load, some dispatchers like to do that. Give their friends loads right off. Some guys pay the dispatcher to give them the good loads." Bob's cheeks pinched into his nose.

On the jump seat, every bump in the road shot through my spine and into my headache. The driver's side was air cushioned, but the jump seat was hard as a rock, thus, "The Jump Seat." Out my window, the landscape bloomed in chartreuse, emerald, lime, even jade. Fresh, against sky like an ice-blue topping. Steam rose up out of the tobacco fields. Well, some of the fields were corn. I think it was silage. I saw soybeans occasionally, and hay.

But I only smelled air conditioning, because only a fool would roll down the window. And not just because of the heat. The engine was damn loud. Always.

I loved the horses, especially when they grazed inside white fences, the ones with two white boards going around the acres like little railroad tracks up on edge. Even without the horses, I loved the fences. Lots of them sat way back from the freeway and looked like establishing shots for *National Velvet*.

The sun set. I hadn't had my turn to drive yet. I'd sat there taking the bumps for five hours.

"There's a rest stop down the road a ways you might want to see."

"Why?"

"It's pretty well known. A lot of truckers stop there. There's always a party going on. Want to stop?"

"I don't care." *This could be good.*

"There's usually women there too, if you know what I mean." Bob smirked.

I didn't respond.

"It's quite a scene. You really ought to see it. No telling when we'll be back."

"Can I drive after this rest stop?"

"We'll see."

Bob passed the Southbound rest stop, took the off ramp and headed back north on I-65. His chin pushed forward with purpose.

"The party doesn't get going till midnight," Bob announced "We're early. There should still be a place to park." Bob parked in an open space just past the restrooms. Five prostitutes hung around the drinking fountain. A few more were sitting at picnic tables.

Bob was out of the truck in a flash and off to the restroom.

My God, all that skin! Are those women wearing mosquito repellent?

A trucker approached the picnic table. I could see his belly hanging below his old gray t-shirt. Holes around the collar and sleeves. I couldn't see his face under his cowboy hat, and his boots were white, with heels, pointed toes, and curly-cues.

A woman got up and walked with him back to the parking lot where I saw him open the passenger door, and push her behind up to the seat, his hand under her short black skirt. Her earrings dangled to her shoulders, and I worried if she didn't take them off, they'd get caught in her hair when she leaned back. Or maybe she'd just lean forward.

All of the women at the drinking fountain held cigarettes between long painted fingernails.

Twilight over, the mosquitoes swarmed under the rest stop lights. Maybe Bob was doing it with a woman in the bathroom stall, because I couldn't see him anywhere. A pair of truckers drank beer about ten feet from the women at the drinking fountain. The man with the belly hanging out joined them, and the woman he'd hired joined her friends. The truckers laughed, and then the shorter one made his way to the picnic table. He talked to the same woman, the one with the earrings, and she got up and walked with him ... to the same truck! He shoved his hand up her short black skirt and followed her into the truck.

Then a woman by the drinking fountain joined the three men, who supplied the beer and I watched all of them smoke. Parking spaces filled up with trucks, leaving empty spots in between.

Bob came back. I put my journal away and headed to the bathroom. Two more women, one with ratted straw and the other with hair dyed coal black stood in front of the sink putting on eye liner. Both wore tight short skirts and tight, low-cut t-shirts. The ratted straw lady had huge boobs, so large I thought they might fall out. She had rolls of fat and fat ankles. I could see the collarbones on the black-haired hooker and flashed on a joke about women with two fried eggs. I peed and got back to the truck. Bob sat in the driver's seat catching up his logbook.

As I closed the door, Bob announced, "We'll sleep here tonight. You can have the sleeper and I'll take the doghouse."

"I'm not sleeping in the sleeper. It's too hot." *Never in a million years, Bob, would I get in the sleeper with you in the truck.*

"Roll up the curtain. That's what those ties are for. We'll leave the windows down."

"The mosquitoes will kill us, Bob. I don't want to put the bug shit on and then get in my sleeping bag but I'll take the doghouse if you really want to stay here." *It would be worth it just to watch the night away.*

"You can't take the doghouse. They're going to knock on the door all night wanting to know if we want some business."

So sick of Bob, my tone came out like venom spitting a hard straight line, eyes boring right into him. "Ok, I'll take my sleeping bag and sleep outside."

"You can't take your sleeping bag outside. It's not safe." I watched his arms flailing about and enjoyed his misery, my power to incite him.

"Watch me, Bob." I pushed past him, grabbed my sleeping bag, yanked it out from around him and was out the passenger door. "I'll be fine. I'm going to the far end over there." I pointed. "Nobody is down there. Nobody will know I'm there." I started walking.

I got down to the far end. As soon as I turn off my flashlight, the stars lit up. But mosquitoes covered me as soon as I stop walking. I'd forgotten the mosquito repellent. I had to go back and I didn't have a key.

I knocked on the driver's side. Bob opened the door, and hopped out smiling. "I knew you'd be back." He walked around to open the passenger side door. I climbed into the sleeper, dug into my stuff and grabbed the repellent. Out of the cab, I walked away before he had a chance to start up with me.

Back at my end of the rest stop, I imagined all the strange bugs that would surely crawl in my bag as I lay down on the hard ground. I tried to focus on the stars. The party of truckers and hookers was far away and I couldn't imagine any of them coming down here. The night was warm, and smelled a bit like pesticide because I was lying next to a cornfield. I worried that ants would crawl in my ears. If something big got in my hair, I didn't think I could stand it.

In the dim light, I saw a flashlight point at me from far off. It swung with the gait of a man. First thought, someone saw me walking here and was coming to rape me. Ridiculous, but my heart pounded. I'd be trapped in my sleeping bag if I didn't get out and run, now. The light came directly at me, came closer, then in my face, blinding me. The light shut off. Bob.

"I can't let you sleep here. It's not safe." Bob laid his sleeping bag down next to me. "I can't *believe* this!" He screeched.

"I *won't* sleep next to you." I screeched back. "If you're going to sleep out here, I'm going back to the truck. Give me the key."

"This is ridiculous."

"Then let's leave. I'll drive."

"You can't drive at night on this road. And you don't know how to get to the plant."

"I can drive *and* find the *Life* Magazine loading dock." I spat. "If you won't give me the key, and you won't leave here, I'll go to another spot. You can't sleep next to me."

He threw the key and it bounced at my feet. "I'll sleep out here, then."

I let him.

Every space filled. Trucks no more than an arm's length apart. Our truck had a 'portable parking lot' —a car carrier— on one side and a North American Van line parked on the other. Our side mirrors practically touched. Four truckers stood in front of my truck swallowing beer and blabbering, forcing me to walk past them to get to my door.

I tried to swagger like a dyke. I threw the sleeping bag over my shoulder and acted like I always carried a sleeping bag around at rest stops. Like maybe I'm just airing it out and it's none of your business.

"Hey girlie, girl, who you ridin' with?" One says.

"Maybe she's ridin' alone." *What if the key sticks and I can't get in the truck?*

"You want some company?"

"Thanks, but no thanks," my voice filled with tough-girl-don't-fuck-with-me.

I got the driver's side unlocked, got in, but my shoelace got stuck when I closed the door, and I was so scared I unlaced my boot and just left it there rather than open the door again. My heart pumped. I put my hand on it and pushed, to help me breathe through the clot in my throat.

I stared at the bathrooms, where now I saw a lone boy. A teenager. Skinny. He leaned against the wall, smoking under the light and the swarming mosquitoes. I wondered whether he was a trucker, waiting, while his partner did a little business, or whether he hoped a trucker would come along for him, and would want him for a little business.

Once my breathing slowed, I moved back in the sleeper and tried to relax, grateful to lay on top of my bag instead of getting inside with all my sweaty mosquito repellent.

After a bit, I felt my head ache. Getting to the food in my storage compartment meant getting out of the truck again, so I didn't eat that night. I didn't want to risk turning on the sleeper light either, so I didn't read, I just laid there, thinking.

What makes Bob so repulsive? He actually means well. He wouldn't hurt me. He was no different than ... how many other guys?

A woman knocked on my door until I stuck my head out the window. She was way tall, barely had to look up to see me. Her dark skin shone smooth in the moonlight and for a moment, I thought she smiled when I said no thank you.

Finally, I went to sleep.

In the morning, Bob opened the door with his own key. He never asked for mine back and I didn't offer.

Peas Canned Before You Were Born
Brown Lettuce

July 15, 1980
I-40 Oklahoma

I-40's white concrete reflected into my eyes. I stared out the passenger window. Flat, varied browns and greens. We crossed the Arkansas River, moved into Oklahoma. A high overcast glared on the freeway. I couldn't figure what grew out there, but people were taking care of it. Their houses, tractors and barns dotted the countryside. I saw a sign, *Sequoyah National Wildlife Refuge.*

I inhaled a huge breath of air conditioning and shouted over the engine. "What's that, Bob?"

"That big refuge? They made it about ten years ago. Want to help the birds."

"Want to stop?"

"No. They probably don't allow trucks." Bob zoomed past the exit. "I hear they get Monarch butterflies down here. Supposedly they're developing crops or something. Food for the birds."

"Sequoyah, I think that's some guy who made an alphabet. Do you know what tribe?"

"Cherokee. This is Sequoyah County, sweetheart."

I watched a field of wheat float by. I wanted to put my headphones on, but knew I'd offend Bob just when I'd taken steps to get along.

We vibrated across a huge water source. Curious, I got out my road atlas. "Eufaula Lake. Bob, this is huge!"

"Biggest lake in Oklahoma. Actually, it's a reservoir."

"Want to stop?"

"We've got about two hours till we hit Oklahoma City. We'll stop at the terminal there."

"Doesn't the white road hurt your eyes?"

"I don't let it bother me. You'll get used to it."

Oklahoma City had the biggest Tanksley terminal. Huge bays for truck repairs. Clean showers, laundry facilities, clean lounge. "Most people get their mail here," Bob reported. "You might want to too. It's safe here, and we'll go through here a lot."

We fueled and headed out. No showers, no laundry. Bob pulled off the freeway just out of town into the Flying J truck stop. "Let's have a steak."

"Bob, I can't. I'm way constipated."

"Okay. Have a salad. I'll have a steak."

"I can't do it, Bob. I'm sorry." They serve brown lettuce in truck stops. Instead of vegetables, they should say 'peascannedbeforeyouwereborn'. I watched his lip curl up and his nose bend down over it. "I'll walk around the store while you're eating. If I find some fruit, I'll come join you."

Bob slammed the door and took off.

There must have been a hundred trucks in the lot, at least three rows deep. Suddenly, I was afraid to walk between them. Even with the engines off, the refrigeration motors drowned out everything else, like footsteps. Maybe I had a hangover of fear from those men at the rest stop, who knows, but I took the long way around, circumvented the rows, walked next to the stubbly field, down the sidewalk, past the fuel pumps, and finally into the store, which adjoined the restaurant. Maybe the walk did it, but I softened toward Bob, bought some Metamucil, and decided to eat with him. I found him in a booth, eating a hamburger.

"Maybe I'll get a hamburger." I slid in across from him.

"Now you decide." He put two French fries in his mouth and continued. "Can you get it to go? I'm about finished." He mopped his catsup with a gob of fries and stuffed his mouth.

"Okay. I'll get a Coke. I've got some tuna I can eat in the truck."

My turn to drive. 360 miles later, we pulled into a rest stop outside Tucumcari, New Mexico, at midnight.

Bob climbed into the driver's seat. "We're going to keep driving. To make up for lost time," he yelled.

I was being nice. What was he mad at now?

I bounced around in the sleeper. Maybe three hundred miles east of Flagstaff, I climbed back into the jump seat about an hour after sunrise. Flat forever was out the window. Scrub brush. Small trees. Compared to Humboldt County, the entire country looked flat, with small trees, and a constant blue sky.

"Let's take some time off in Flagstaff, Bob."

"We'll make a pit stop is all. Get some breakfast."

"Let's stretch, walk. We can hit some tennis balls."

"No. I want to get the load off in L.A. so we can get up to San Francisco."

"The L.A. load isn't even due till Monday, Bob."

"If we get both Sacramento and Frisco loads off on Monday, we can get another load and head straight out."

Maybe he's taken Benzedrine.

Truck stop for breakfast, sponge bath in the women's restroom, and we got back on the road. I drove from Flagstaff to Barstow, which looked like "the bad lands" in a western movie. I wanted to hear what my Mom would have said about this dry barren landscape, and flooded myself with missing her. Thought I might call home when we got to L.A.

Bob jumped behind the wheel after we refueled in Barstow. He was nervous. Sweating.

"Did you sleep okay?" I asked.

"I always sleep okay."

I thought he was following the truck in front of us too close. He seemed extra mad. Climbing the grapevine on I-5, south of Gorman, at about three o'clock, the cars whizzed past. We had more power than the truck in front of us, and kept gaining on him, until we were riding his bumper. We'd lose our power if we backed off the accelerator, but if we didn't slow down, we were going to ram him. Suddenly, Bob pulled left into the line of cars. A pickup in our blind spot swerved and lay on the horn. I grabbed the chicken bar. We swerved back into our lane.

"Crap."

We lost our power and crawled up the grapevine.

An hour later, on eight-lanes of freeway, bumper to bumper traffic, Bob pulled out the map, intending to locate our exit.

"Let me look at the map. I'll direct you."

"No. It's too hard for you." He slammed on the brakes. Honked the horn. Shifted. Tried to unfold the map and spread it across the steering wheel.

"Bob," I raised my voice. "We've been on duty for twenty hours. Reading the map while driving on a crowded freeway, lost, is how accidents are caused."

He didn't speak.

"Please pull over!" I yelled.

"You are the most uppity person I've ever met. You've caused me more frustration than anyone I've ever met!" he screamed. "Oh, shit! You just made me miss our exit." He pulled over to the shoulder and idled there, intent to study the map.

"Let me drive, Bob. I can handle this traffic. Or at least let me read the map!"

"You are so damn snippity." He threw the map at me. I got to look, but he demanded it back before I could plot a route.

He signaled, and without waiting, drove right back into the stalled traffic. Car horns honked like a choir. We inched forward. Bob took the next exit and drove along a frontage road to a dead end. We had to back up for a hundred yards before we could turn around, only to re-enter the traffic jam fifteen minutes later.

Miracle, they accepted our load when we finally got there at ten o'clock on a Friday night, three days early. The loading docks in San Francisco and Sacramento weren't open on weekends, but Bob headed north after unloading. He'd been driving since three that afternoon.

Another seven hours, we went off duty in Los Banos, where I checked into a motel, on my dime. The next day I walked up to Tanksley's terminal to talk to the manager.

"You can ride with Bob or quit," the manager said, and turned back toward his desk. The conversation was over.

92

Miguel
Little Iodine

July 16, 1980
Santa Nella, California
(Los Banos Tanksley Terminal)

Miguel walked out of the mechanic's bay, his overalls covered in grease but smelling like soap. His hands were clean. Even the fingernails. His hair fell in the shag haircut, perfectly. We stood in the shade.

"Bob's terrible."

"Did he try anything?"

"No. He's harmless that way. He's mad that I won't eat with him."

"Why won't you eat with him?"

"Restaurants are too expensive." I paused. " I'm saving money." Miguel didn't say anything. Then I admitted, "Bob said he would buy."

"He just didn't want to eat alone."

"I know. But I couldn't ever get away from him. He controls everything I do."

"What do you mean?"

"Is it true that second seat can't have a key to the truck?"

"He won't let you have a key to the truck? How do you get into your stuff?"

I left out the part where I got the key from Bob. "He comes with me. And then he stares at all my stuff." I frowned.

"That's rude. But at least he's harmless. You're not going to quit are you?"

"Not yet. I'll make another round with him. But, how are you?" I looked at his face just then but he was looking at me so I looked at the pavement.

"I'm doing okay, but my kids are fighting and Sophie isn't sleeping very good."

"How many kids do you have?"

"Two. Sophie is eight. Mateo just turned five."

"Oh. Do they live with their Mom?"

"No. They live with me. Mom takes them during the day. Cindy's living with another guy. It wouldn't be good for the kids to see that."

"I'm sorry. That's hard."

The other mechanic walked out of the bay, looked at us, did an about-face and walked back inside.

"My break's up."

"Thanks for talking to me, Miguel."

"See you next time. Hope it goes better for you." He turned his back and I walked into the air-conditioned lounge. It must have been a hundred degrees in the shade.

Underneath, *Little Iodine* laughed in my ear. *You're a snob*, she whispered.

Am not, I fought back.

But *Little Iodine* laughed louder. *You could have eaten with him*, she hissed. *You're a snob.*

I felt bad. Ashamed actually.

Santa Nella, California
Vladimir and Igor

July 16, 1980

Back at the motel's pool, I chose a lounge chair about three down from Vladimir and Igor, who talked away in a language I didn't recognize. I greased up, popped a cold Budweiser and called out, "Where you from?"

"Czechoslovakia. We are so lucky to be here."

" Oh. Were you in an accident?"

"No. In 1968, remember when the Russians took over?"

I looked blank.

"We were lucky to get out. Igor here, he got out of Yugoslavia by swimming across (something) to get into Switzerland. Me, I walked out."

"I can't imagine. I've lived my whole life in one small town."

"You are so lucky to be born in the United States. Best country in the world. We are so happy to be here. We will do good. Be good citizens of your country."

"Do you miss Czechoslovakia?"

"Oh, maybe a little. But New York City is our home now. We are very grateful to live in United States."

I drank beer under the scalding sun, dipped in the pool, and napped. I ate a dry turkey sandwich in the motel's restaurant, too tired to walk across the street for a decent meal.

"Where is your home town?" Vladimir would talk and then translate for Igor.

"About 350 miles north of here, on the coast."

"What did you do there?"

"Married the high school quarterback. Used to teach."

Vladimir asked lots of questions, making it easy for me to touch the details. "How'd you get to be a truck driver?"

"Oh, that's a story." I began.

Columbus, Ohio
Marie

July 18, 1980

Bob and I drove into San Francisco Sunday evening, and I got to sleep on the doghouse. No arguments. We unloaded at 6:00 a.m. and Bob let me pull out of the loading dock.

Right off, dispatch gave us a load of bell peppers and lettuce to pick up in Salinas, headed for Columbus, Ohio. Bob let me drive to Salinas, which involved a few freeway exchanges and traffic. We watched the trucks back into the loading dock, waited three hours for our turn, and Bob backed in straight after considerable gee-hawing. I wondered if I'd ever learn to back up.

Bob took the wheel out of Salinas.

Terry was so right. Constant vibration and noise. Spreading my sleeping bag out in the sleeper, I hit my head on the roof. Bounced right up there. I hadn't slept yet when the truck was moving. My arms kept flying off the bed.

Then I got to drive.

The sunset out on the salt flats colored the sky from orange to red to blue to purple. Simple, but vast. Black silhouetted mountains. The skyline looked drawn with a sharp pencil. Stars already up in the purple. A cloud to my right, crescent moon at eleven o'clock. We could have been on another planet. A large group headed to the Black Hills in South Dakota parked next to us. Graffiti written all over their bus protested the mining of Uranium.

Bob gave me space. I talked more. He allowed more break time. I let him buy the steaks. He cooked. I caught up with my journal. We finished the dinner of steak and potatoes. Break over. Movin' on.

Bob let me back up and park in the Rawlins, Wyoming terminal. The clutch took strength to push but my leg didn't cramp from pushing it again and again as I continued to over-steer and miss my spot. These big rigs don't have power steering. My arms tired quickly, steering at zero miles per hour. I broke a sweat, but finally backed in okay.

Maybe someone talked to Bob about my complaints in Los Banos. Or maybe he tried to put me off the truck and was told, "Ride with her or quit."

Since I got more rest time, I cooked dinner for us again, in the same Nebraska rest stop. Pork chops. Bob made a beer run. The rain began. Water splotched my writing so I put my journal away. Thunder cracked. Lightning struck in the distance. Rain came down harder until, six feet back under the shelter, still being pelted with rain, I watched a double rainbow over the cornfield across the way.

We drank too much. I slept on the doghouse.

In the morning I met Ramona, a ten-year old Syrian girl whose family left Iran thirteen months previous. Her mother scooted her out of the bathroom but in a bit she was back, watching me sponge bathe. Her family liked the Shah, she told me. "Don't call the Ayatollah '*Ayatollah*,' he doesn't deserve it."

I followed her out of the restroom and saw a car full of people waiting for her. Ramona, a roundy-round, as my mother would say, with dark eyes and hair that "used to be long." She crawled into the back seat of the beat-up old sedan. The door slammed on a chorus of voices, Arabic I imagined, and with a failing muffler, they sped from the rest stop.

A flat tire outside of Davenport, Iowa, but with two sets of duals (eight tires) under the front of the trailer, we drove to the terminal in Indianapolis before getting it changed.

A whole day off after unloading in Columbus. Bob let me use the truck sleeper instead of paying for a room. He gave me his key as if to say, "I won't bother you."

About a mile down the road, teenagers partied at Swimland. I spent the day by the pool, showered, and ate a hamburger for dinner. An exploratory route back to the truck, I passed a volleyball party, private tennis courts and kids on bicycles. Next to the truck, in the bowling alley's lounge, the TV spilled light on the bar and its few customers. *Loveboat* again. One more beer before bed in Whitehall, white suburb of Columbus.

At sunrise, as I was dozing, suddenly the truck bounced, like someone was climbing up the door and looking in the window. I held my breath. I hadn't shut the sleeper curtain and I knew my legs were visible. I didn't move. After what seemed like an eternity, I got my wine opener, which resembled an ice pick, and lay rigid, preparing for the break-in. When he smashed the window, I would sit up and strike his arm when he tried to open the door.

After five minutes, or maybe thirty seconds, the truck stayed still again. I peeked out to see an old red truck pulling out of the lot. Probably siphoning fuel. Never intended to break in.

Another free day. I took an hour's bus ride through abject poverty. Not one white person. Then, right out of the history books, stood a grand and pompous courthouse. More oxidized bronze statues. Even the capitol's walls had paintings with elaborate quotes of liberty and justice for all. Have any of those black people, living in such close proximity, ever been in the capitol? Do they have equal access to the public swimming and hot showers I used? How in the world do we untangle this mess, right this wrong? Back to the pool, I swam and showered. So easy for me, all white with a tan.

The next day I met Marie, a produce vender on a street corner, who struck up a conversation as I peered over her oranges.

"I've been married three times," she tells me. "You?"

"Just once. Almost twice."

"What happened?"

"Long stupid story."

"Oh, I got those too." She laughed. "Won thirty thousand in the lottery once."

"Wow!"

"My second husband gambled it all away. Just saved enough out of it to pay my bills is all." She laughed.

How could she laugh about that?

Closing down, she invited me to her brother's house.

Marie locked her stall. "I'm married to Mike now. We sell this fruit. Going on five years."

"So, how do you get all this produce?" I asked her as we were walking the few blocks to her brother's house.

"We pick it up at the warehouse. I got lots of regulars 'cause they know I pick out the best." Marie walked with a slight limp. "My brother works down under."

"Australia?"

"In the coal mines." She laughed again, a laugh as round and full as apples. "He likes it because it's cool down there and the job pays good."

Marie turned up the walkway to her brother's house.

I couldn't tell Marie, whose first wedding was done up with fake white roses wrapped around a trellis and tied with crepe paper, that my Dad ordered a helicopter to fly Aaron and I away from our wedding reception. That I came from country club stock, golfing, airplanes and advanced degrees. Why hurt her feelings, make her feel small?

Her brother's house needed paint. We went in the kitchen, and Marie made a beeline to the sink. "Want some lemonade? I made it fresh." Marie got out the dish soap and tub. She stacked the plates in the tub and turned on the water. "They give me the old lemons. I always have lemonade." She poured two glasses, gave me one, and took hers back to the sink, where she began cleaning up the dirty dishes.

Marie reminded me of Santa Claus, all rosy-cheeked and happy. I didn't want her to feel bad about herself, about her meager little life. I didn't want to hurt her feelings, burst that bubble she walked around inside. I watched her clean up her brother's mess, happy as a clam, and while I felt sorry for her, I told her I wished I could be as happy as she was.

But later, laying on the doghouse, vibrating away with the engine running the air conditioner, I puzzled over why I didn't hesitate to tell Albert that I taught high school and coached tennis. That my mother was born in France. That I was writing a book. With Albert, I said what I thought, tested him with questions that poked our boundaries, came

100

away feeling touched. Why did I share with Albert, but with Marie, I believed our differences would crush her? I hadn't detected a single fragile bone in her body, yet I silenced myself down to the slightest nuance. I didn't even compliment her generosity. I acted like it was normal.

I wouldn't have washed my brother's dishes if you'd paid me.

Palm Desert

Butch and Wally

July 18, 1980

Dispatch gave us Lennox Air Conditioners right out of Columbus for delivery in Phoenix and Palm Springs. Bob, impatient, started the truck up immediately, causing oil to splatter all over my open suitcase. He would not drive me to a grocery store. We rushed off without warming up the engine only to learn that the Lennox air conditioning plant wouldn't load us until 5:00 a.m.

"Bob, I think someone may have siphoned fuel out of our tank the other morning."

Bob produced a sawed-off broom handle and stuck it in the fuel tank. "We've got plenty." He climbed back in the truck and slammed the door.

"So what did you do on your layover, Bob?"

"Crosswords."

He didn't ask what I did and I didn't tell him.

I slept on the doghouse. Bob kept the sleeper curtain snapped. We loaded first thing in the morning. Bob drove.

And then we ran out of fuel.

The CB came in handy. Right away, another truck stopped to help us siphon fuel from our refrigeration tank so we could reach the next truck stop.

Bob wouldn't give me my turn to drive. I wouldn't talk. Tension so thick it cut through the engine noise.

Interstate 17, from Flagstaff to Phoenix, had a six per cent grade for about eleven miles and I got to drive it. At sunrise, the colors —shades of reds, oranges and browns— changed constantly. Rocks worthy of photographs.

Clear blue sky. One eye watched the speedometer, the tachometer, and the road, while the other eye gazed on geology formations I knew nothing about. The sunrise set those rocks in light like I'd seen in the movies. Twice the transmission popped out of gear but I jammed her back in, just like a truck driver. With the load of air conditioners pushing me, I kept the steady five pounds of brake pressure on for the entire eleven miles.

In Phoenix, Bob let me call the plant for directions. I drove through the heavy morning traffic, overshot the left turn at a huge intersection, and almost hit the stoplight on the sidewalk. Three crowded lanes of traffic on all sides and I'd stopped every one of them. Had to back up. Correct my angle. Not a single car honked but instead, patiently watched their morning's entertainment. Bob quietly directed my correction. Humbled, grateful for his patience, sweating, I drove the rest of the way to the loading dock without further complication.

Onward to Palm Springs, where Bob chose a Motel 6 fifteen miles outside of town and I registered for my own room. We started our layover together by the pool. He talked about his forced retirement from air traffic controlling, his training as a controller in WWII. We even discussed the possibility of renting a car and touring the homes in Palm Springs.

"How about we go grocery shopping?" I asked.

"No. The company has spies everywhere to watch for illegal movement of the truck."

Bob passed out beer to the four Chicanos by the pool and opened another for himself. He attempted conversation with loud one-word questions and pointing. Finally, he left after knocking down the pool equipment while putting on his shoes.

Beer drinking began around 10:00 the next morning, and Bob received me in his underwear when I brought him the TV schedule he requested. I groaned, rolled my eyes, about-faced, and left him standing in the doorway.

Instead of the Chicanos, two construction workers, Butch and Wally sat by the pool. In 114-degree heat, Butch, Wally and I chatted like friendly neighbors, cooled off in the pool every few minutes, and Wally had a stream of jokes that kept us laughing. When Bob banged the latch against the cyclone fence, our three heads jerked to the right in surprise. We watched

Bob approach, stumbling a bit until coming to a stop beside Butch. He announced to me, who sat on the other side of Wally, "You can't go with me in the morning. The plant is on strike. There might be violence." He burped. "Excuse me. It's not safe for you to come along."

I rolled my eyes for Butch and Wally's benefit. "I'll lock myself in the cab, Bob."

"Margot, you're not going."

"It's my right ..."

"You're not allowed." Bob dove in the pool and swam away from us, pitifully drunk.

I set my alarm, and at 5:45 a.m. I walked out to discover Bob had already left, even though the Lennox Corporation didn't open till 8:00. I called personnel to state my case, thinking he'd left me. I waited. Butch and Wally wished me good luck. I got a peck on the cheek from each of them. They were off to hammer nails in the 114-degree heat.

At noon, Bob finally returned to the motel, our truck still loaded. "Dispatch says to drop the load in L.A. now. Let's go." After I loaded my stuff on the truck, Bob drove back to the empty, barren, Lennox plant in Palm Springs before we headed off to Los Angeles to drop the load. I wondered if dispatch threatened him to fire him because I'd complained, but that seemed pretty far-fetched.

"The company is instigating these long layovers for us."

Really, Bob? Wow. They must really hate us!

"You're a spy. You're on my truck to observe my driving habits."

That's creative, Bob.

On and on, Bob shot his mouth off, waving his arms around the cab. All the way into L.A., timed to his voice inflections, Bob jerked the wheel back and forth. He spit on it, and I entertained myself watching to see if any spit would reach the windshield.

"Do you know how to get to the Lennox plant?"

"Of course I do. Who do you think I am. I should never have taken you on. Did you tell dispatch I'm taking whites?"

"You're taking whites? I didn't know that!"

"How else would dispatch know? You're a liar, Margot. You'll never be a truck driver. No one could stand to ride with you. You're a snob."

"No I'm not. I never told dispatch anything. I only said you left me at the motel. That you said the plant was on strike."

"How could they accuse me of taking drugs, then? Little miss uppity-thinks-she's-so-hot." He stammered like he couldn't think how to finish me off.

"Maybe, Bob, just maybe, since we drive twenty out of twenty-four hours a day, they put two and two together."

"That's what truckers do. I cut down on our driving because you couldn't handle it. I drove because you didn't know how." On and on...

I ate while we unloaded, but Bob stomped around watching the forklift driver.

Without calling dispatch, and without eating, Bob took off driving again, north on I-5. He looked like a cartoon character, face leaning over the steering wheel, speeding up with our empty trailer, shifting down waiting to pass, jerking the wheel to pull into the fast lane, shifting up again, building speed, shifting down again.

At 11:00 p.m. Bob slammed his truck key down on the counter in front of an empty, dark Los Banos office, and stalked out.

I took the key and walked around while Bob loaded his car with all his stuff. When he finally drove away, I climbed in the sleeper and didn't wake till the sun hit the windshield around nine the next morning.

Miguel came out from under a truck, saw me leaving the office, and waved me over.

"Bob quit!"

"I heard. What happened?"

"I drove him crazy. They're giving me a new driver."

"That guy in the lounge needs a second driver. Sorry, I can't talk now. I'll put in a good word for you. Don't worry." He walked back to the truck, down the ramp underneath the cab, and disappeared.

In the lounge, I could smell the man's body odor despite the barbeque potato chips he stuffed in his mouth, which he neglected to close.

I started having regrets about losing Bob.

Kent Partner #2

Bo

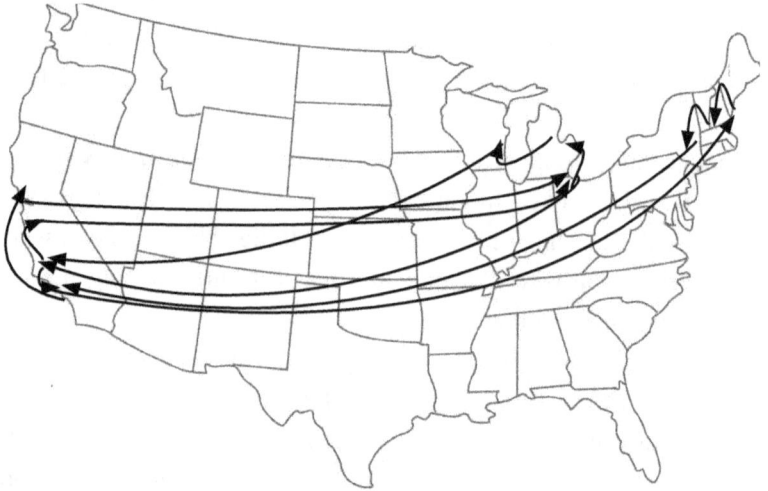

July 25, 1980
San Jose, California

I got Kent.

Thirty-five but looked twenty. Claimed at eighteen he could still pass for twelve at the theatre box office. Small understated his size. I guessed a hundred pounds. He claimed ninety-eight and told me one time a guy tried to make him clean the toilet in the Nashville Tanksley terminal.

"Why?"

"He didn't want to clean it. Said I made the mess, but I didn't."

"What'd you do?"

"I got outta there and reported him to the office. But they blew me off. That's what they do."

"That's what they do?"

"Yeah. To *me*. They would help *you* if someone bullied you. They don't care about me."

Probably accurate, I thought, as I watched him pull out of Tanksley's parking lot with his leg fully stretched to depress the clutch, leaning over the steering wheel, nose and chin tied for the lead.

Kent's tiny nose came to a perfect point, a symmetrically perfect triangle under two black dots, called eyes. Lacking color, he had thin straight hair. His conservative haircut exposed pinched neck muscles, two distinct tiny sausages traveling up his long skinny neck to above his ears. He had a small head.

"You married?" He asked.

"Divorced. You?"

"Yeah, but my wife filed for divorce six weeks ago, two weeks after our anniversary." Kent thumbed his nose like it itched.

"How long you been married?" I asked.

"Just past ten years. Got two kids too. I don't know what I'm going to do. She wants me to move out."

"Boys or girls?"

"Girls. Angela and Holly. Six and eight. "

Kent's load belonged in San Lorenzo, on the East side of San Francisco bay.

"I need to be home. It's like they're growing up without me."

I noticed that Kent watched the rear-view mirrors and signaled just like Dick Dart taught us. An entire car can hide in a truck's blind spot, and will stay there, if the driver doesn't know better. So truckers watch the mirror, note the color of the vehicle approaching, and wait for it to pass. If we need to change lanes, we signal and wait, giving any hidden car a chance to get out of our way.

What a relief to be rid of Bob's erratic lane changes. Bob would pull into the fast lane when a car was merging onto the freeway. That's bad. The merging car has to make way for the truck's presence by speeding ahead or waiting for it to pass. That's the rule. Pulling out into the faster lane, creating a huge blind spot on our right, endangered everyone, especially if we're tired, or angry. That was Bob.

We delivered Kent's load of chemicals without a hitch, only one wrong turn and a quick detour to get back to the dock. Unloading immediately, into a clean warehouse, we got our papers signed and drove to San Jose, to an empty gravel parking lot Kent used for his layovers on the west coast.

"I usually just read," he said, then pointed. "There's a Motel 6 over there if you want. It's not too bad."

It looked decrepit. "I'll sleep on the doghouse. I don't mind. Want to get something to eat?" A Denny's restaurant stood next to the Motel 6.

Seduced by a poster advertising live music, I asked the waitress, and she gave us directions to the *Country Store,* just three blocks over.

The band, called Pace, played hard rock and roll. The *Country Store* lacked 'country'. Three bars, neon lighting, a disco ball, waitresses in skimpy outfits with little round trays, and thousands of square feet full of young, identical, magazine-beautiful white men and women.

The place smelled like cologne and looked like money. Women dressed to the nines. Lots of black clothes accented with shimmering tinsel. Cleavage sporting silver pendants. Stilettos. Men with hairy chests and gold necklaces. My jeans, work boots and striped top looked as alien as my free-form uncombed hair. Kent wore a collared shirt and sat, immediately disappearing into his chair.

"Wanna dance?" I asked Kent.

"No way." Kent recoiled, shaking his head, stopping me with the palms of his hands.

At a buck fifty a beer, I drank three. Kent nursed one. No one would ask me to dance if I sat with Kent, and I couldn't sit at another table while he sat there, so I got up and danced by myself, as if I couldn't care less about all the shellacked ladies dancing with their gyrating men and practically having intercourse on the floor.

Kent waited. We left before eleven and walked the three blocks back to the truck. Only an occasional street lamp. Empty littered lots. Structures with no windows, or windows boarded up. No stars. Smog, which smelled like fast-food grease. "That's the first time I've ever been to a "singles bar," Kent offered as we climbed into the truck.

I kept the window cracked, listened to the freeway off in the distance, and slept soundly. I never heard a peep from Kent.

We spent the day cleaning the truck. Reading. I walked, but I never got beyond the asphalt and litter. No green lawns or trees. But kitty-corner, down the street and around a corner, I found *The Good Times Lounge*, advertising nightly music and dancing. Around dusk, I talked Kent into checking out that lounge, maybe have a beer.

We left before ordering because Kent squirmed and whispered to me it wasn't a safe place.

"Just one beer?"

"No. Let's go."

I thought about letting him go alone, but suspected he might be afraid to walk by himself. We left, ate at the same Denny's, and I ordered the same hamburger and fries.

"That's a black bar. We weren't welcome." Kent had ordered a Coke and fries. No hamburger.

"I thought it was okay."

"You didn't see their faces."

"They looked fine to me. There were what, four people in there?"

Kent didn't reply.

We walked across the street and crawled back in the truck. I spread out my sleeping bag on the doghouse, propped my pillows, and read alongside of Kent, who read in the sleeper. Around nine, I felt too visible with the overhead light shining down on me. I invited, knew Kent would decline, and headed back to *The Good Times Lounge*. About twenty black people stood in line outside the door and a small crowd milled around the entry, talking and laughing. A few men leaned against the wall and smoked.

The huge security guard greeted people as we all funneled inside and I got an ear-to-ear smile with open palms directing me through the door. I bought a beer for a dollar and sat down.

I saw two white women and no white men. The age group ranged from 21 to 65. People wore suits and ties or jogging clothes. Some women wore formals, long satin emerald green, a full-length red strapless gown, even a Cinderella dress with a huge full skirt to the floor and puffy sleeves. August. Were they going to some special event? A reunion? Plenty of women and men wore work clothes. Even blue mechanic's overalls. Some men were dressed in loud print pants, slippery paisley shirts opened to the fourth button, and others wore those two-inch block heels. Plaids, not so much, but a neon green shirt, and a neon yellow shirt, both with basketball players at the hoop. A few black clothes, and browns, but only visible to someone taking inventory. The full gambit of hair: processed, natural, long, short, bald, bleached or straightened. Fat people, thin people, old or young, and they all seemed to be dancing together. Seemed like everyone talked to everybody.

Afraid my purse would get stolen when I set it down to dance, I'd leave it at my table and watch nervously from a few feet away. Soon though, an older woman pointedly looked at me, threw her purse over her shoulder, and went on the dance floor. I smiled a thank you, and shouldered my own purse.

For the first hour, this hip, slick and cool, all processed and groovy jive-ass guy planted himself at my table. I thought I'd have to leave soon, because as much as I shined him on, he stayed and acted like we were together.

"Are you with this guy?" A big beautiful black man tapped my shoulder.

"No."

"Would you like to dance?"

"Yes." I shouldered my purse.

He wore jogging sweats, tennis shoes. A big smile. He was the best dancer I'd ever seen. Centered in his hips, he moved even better than my ex-husband. Light on his feet, subtle rhythm, head resting not bobbing. He took his time. Easy with his focus on me. Nothing pushy. Comfortable. Really, regardless of age, weight, dress, or stereotype, I thought everyone looked good on the dance floor, but Bo stood out special, maybe because he was so big.

Leaving my beer on the table in order to dance, when the bar shut down, I came out sober.

"I'll give you a ride home." Bo walked me outside. "I'm parked just around the corner."

"So am I. I don't need a ride, but thanks for offering."

"Well, come see my truck. I want to show you my truck," he said.

110

Bo had a red, cherried-out '51 Ford pickup. I got in and he drove me around the corner.

"Youse a strawng woman" he said as I unlocked the passenger side of my truck.

I wanted him to kiss me, but suddenly everything felt awkward and I worried Kent would poke his head out of the sleeper at the exact wrong moment. "Thanks for a great time," I said, relieved that I was sober enough to get in the jump seat on the first try.

"My pleasure." He waved goodbye.

Kent popped his head out of the sleeper to say hello and good night, while I crawled in my sleeping bag.

As I listened to the cars speeding by on the 101 freeway, street lights blotting out the stars, I fully sensed that esoteric notion of being "in the moment." Right now, I could smell the parking lot's oil, and in this moment, I didn't care if I ever got married or started a family. I didn't care about amounting to something, or being enough. I didn't care that I'd gone crazy. Or that I'd been fired from teaching English. Or that I didn't have any friends. I liked being completely alone, right now, with no one watching me. No one to approve or disapprove or care if I went to a bar and met a guy like Bo, who asked me the same old question.

"Aren't you scared?"

Which was such a weird question to me, because I felt so safe. All the time, people would say to me "Be careful, it's dangerous out there," and I'd think, *not near as dangerous as where I've been.* Maybe I'd remember that Easter Sunday, I must have been all of twenty-three, so lonely, when I drove to the top of Fickle Hill. I sat there watching the city lights, the stars. I couldn't understand why I kept living alone. Why I didn't just end it all, take some pills. And I knew then the only reason I kept living was so my mother wouldn't have to feel bad because I killed myself. Now that's a place to fear. Give me a Columbus ghetto any day.

Out here, I could protect myself. A foot stomp started at the shin and scraped all the way down. My whole hand on a cheek to get a thumb in his eye. A knee to the balls. Or run.

What defense did I have in my house from wanting to die?

Indianapolis
Holly and Angela

.

August 3, 1980

Saturday night we finished loading five pick ups of produce in Fresno. We were bound for Kroger's in Cincinnati, again. Kent planned to push hard to Indianapolis, his home town, where he would visit his kids and get his divorce situation under control.

I didn't ask how he was going to do that, but I appreciated his distraught mood over Bob's anger.

We hit a rainstorm on I-40 in New Mexico. All the "four-wheelers" pulled off the freeway, parked bumper to bumper under every underpass and, east of Albuquerque, they were parked on blind curves.

The CB chattered away. "White Ford *pick-'em-up truck* parked on the curve at mile marker 248." ... "Yellow Ford sedan at 215. Watch out. Her rear is hanging out."

Me: "A red car just pulled in front of me and slowed down. I almost hit her!"   "Where are you at, sweetheart?"

"Going east, just coming up on exit 170 to Carnal ... or Carnool C-A-R-N-U-E-L."

"What's the mile marker."

"Uh ... can't see it. Too much rain."

"Got a handle?"

"Sunny Avenue."

"Where you headed?"

"I gotta drive. Can't talk. Sorry." The chatter continued, much of it about Sunny Avenue, which truck she was in, where she was headed, and won't she stop soon and have dinner.

Kent spoke up, "I saw your tennis racket. You think you could teach me to play tennis?"

"Sure! I'd love to! I coached tennis several years ago. I'd much rather play than bounce the ball off a backboard."

"My Dad is a tennis coach in the Virgin Islands. I haven't seen him since I was three and he's coming to visit the girls in September."

"Great. I'll show you what size grip you need when we stop in Oklahoma. Sure hope I get some mail."

I did get mail. Two letters from my Mom. Her roses were blooming like gangbusters, the California sea lions were honking in Trinidad Harbor. Terry's band, The Heart Beats, packed Trinidad Hall and they had to turn people away. She and Ben danced and stayed out way too late but had a great time. The weather had been crisp, and she bought a new sweater. Barbara, her neighbor, was knitting both she and Ben *Kaffe Faucett* originals. Remember, Ben knew Kaffe in Carmel? She missed me and loved me.

Kent got back down out of the cab, thumped the tires, checked the refrigeration, and listened for air leaks before moving out. Onward across the plains. That white freeway hurt my eyes, so I retreated to the sleeper to be jostled there instead of in the jump seat. I didn't care about the flat landscape, devoid of shadows at high noon and already logged in my memory.

In Arkansas, we switched places. "I'll be getting off the truck in Indianapolis. Where do you want to layover? Motel 6?"

"No. Is there public swimming someplace I can walk to? I'm happy to sleep in the truck." I didn't want to pay for a motel.

"Yeah ... I was wondering," Kent stopped in mid-sentence. I waited. I didn't feel like helping him ask whatever he was wondering about.

"What do you think about ..." long pause, a shift to tenth gear, he checked his mirrors, "Do you think you could ..."

"Spit it out," I said in a harsh tone, instantly regretting it.

"Well, if you're going to hang out at the pool, would you consider taking care of Angela (8) and Holly (6) while I talk to Darlene about the divorce?"

"Darlene? That's your wife's name?" He nodded. I thought a moment. "I guess I could. Do they know how to swim?"

"Not really. But they're real good. They won't give you a problem at all. I'll call Darlene in Nashville and see what she says. Maybe a couple of hours?"

"Okay." What else could I say? The guy needed time with his wife.

I'd babysat a few times when I was a kid. The money wasn't worth it. I went through all the cupboards and ate anything good. Never got asked back.

Aaron and I had wanted kids. We talked about having five of them. Boys. Have our own basketball team. After we separated, I worried I'd never have kids. I quit taking birth control pills. I figured I'd use the rhythm method and if I got pregnant, well, at least I'd have a child.

I daydreamed about me and my daughter being best friends. Me being with her, hanging out with her, loving her, doing right by her. I'd tell her everything. No secrets. I'd listen when she told me stuff. I'd be there for her.

The rhythm method must have worked pretty good, but secretly I believed I couldn't have kids. Too masculine. I wanted to go truck driving, not open a hair salon. I never wore dresses, make-up, jewelry. I liked work boots best. And baggy pants. I hated tight pants. What woman bought a house without a man? Would rather mow the lawn than mop the floor? Hated to cook. Couldn't sew. But thought backing up a huge semi was fun, and unloading it was healthy.

Maybe I was never meant to have kids.

From Nashville we turned north and drove straight up I-65 to Indianapolis. The Kentucky green, the chestnut horses and white fences lured me out of the sleeper and onto the cement jump seat. How much could it cost to add air suspension to the passenger side?

Darlene agreed to let me babysit Angela and Holly at the pool the afternoon following our arrival. Kent dropped them off with a satchel of towels, lotion and sun hats, but no food. The kids were cheerful, easy, and practically entertained themselves. I could rest, and best of all, Angela wanted to comb my hair. I went to the front desk where they sold bathing caps and goggles and I lucked out. They had hair pins. I bought two packs. Holly gave my hair a good go. Angela spent most of the afternoon twirling and pinning my hair. She put me in heaven.

"I'm hot," announced Holly.

"Me too," I said and Angela chimed in, "Me too."

"Take out these pins, you guys. Let's go swimming."

We stepped in the pool and sat on the stairs. Kids splashed around us but neither child wanted to join them. After getting both kids up to their necks in the cool water, I asked Holly to go back to our towels and watch while I took Angela to the deep end. I promised Angela I'd turn around the moment she didn't want to go any further. We made it all the way to the end of the pool, Angela traveling hand over hand along the edge with me treading water behind her.

By the time we met Kent for dinner, Holly was hugging me and Angela was talking non-stop to her father about what a great time she had, how she got to comb my hair and I took her in the deep end.

I slept, hung out at the public swimming pool, walked, read, and wrote home for the rest of our layover. We finally picked up pork and beans in Cincinnati headed for Los Angeles.

Los Angeles
Ray, Mike, and Doyle

August 10, 1980

Back on I-40. Kent sulked. Miserable over his divorce, remorseful for not having been home enough and not making time to be with the kids.

"Can you go to counseling with her?" I suggested.

"I'll ask her when I get back." Kent didn't talk much. He spent most of his time off in the sleeper.

Finally, we took twelve hours off in Flagstaff. The sky looked thick, like a bucket of blue paint. My mother would have said azure or cerulean. The scent of pine trees saturated the air, which felt crackly and dry. Gorgeous mountain peaks created a postcard backdrop for the tennis court. I opened a new can of balls, swung, and they popped off the court and slammed into the fence like gravity didn't count. I adjusted quickly, but had it been that long since I'd played?

Altogether, we had six new balls and six flat ones. Kent didn't want to waste his three new balls, so we set those aside. He didn't want to practice dropping the ball in the same place. He didn't want to practice a level swing. He hit the nine balls all over the courts, and then retrieved what was on his side of the net.

I ran around fetching balls and lobbing them back towards his feet. Once I got him to try picking up a ball between his foot and the racket, but he didn't want to practice that either. Within fifteen minutes, we were both too hot. I didn't even have the energy to use the backboard.

I kept trying to suck in more air. At seven thousand feet, no wonder we were the only ones on the court that afternoon. Why would they even have tennis courts at that altitude? Torture. We gave up.

I talked Kent into coming with me to *The Museum Club* that night, and dancing to Gopher Broke, a country western band. Oak plank floor, pine railings, antlers. Tree trunks held up the wood ceiling. Huge wood beams, horseshoes on every wall, and a gorgeous cherry wood bar with big mirrors behind the bartenders.

I pushed, but Kent wouldn't take the dance lesson offered before the band started up. My first attempt at swing, I danced all night with the same guy, who swung me around as if I knew how to dance. Maybe all the beer clouded my perception, but I felt we could have won the contest had there been one.

Kent sat all evening, shoulders slumped, hands in his lap, half a beer fermenting on the table. I felt like telling him to just leave, he was dragging me down.

In the morning, Kent drove and I took aspirin. Finally, we did laundry in the Barstow terminal, and plotted our route into Los Angeles. Kent called his brother in L.A. who was getting married in the morning, and suddenly I got to deliver the load by myself!

At 6:00 a.m., I backed in but didn't stop in time and hit the dock pretty hard. No damage, except to my pride. The dock workers acted like they didn't notice. Five hours later, my truck was empty. I unloaded most of it myself using a pallet jack. Not a popular idea, because the men on the docks made their livelihood lumping (unloading trucks). A lumper waits around for his turn, makes a deal with the driver, who then pays him out of his own pocket. It's a job of hoping for enough work, waiting for a turn, and finally, either getting the work or heading home. Unloading took me so long that eventually, several lumpers came around to help me finish it off. But I kept that extra fifty bucks for myself. I wanted the money and I'd never see these guys again, so what did it matter?

I chose a huge parking lot surrounded by motels and restaurants for my layover, and soon enough, more trucks started pulling in. Tony, an older trucker with a thick Irish accent, invited me to have dinner, which was sizzling away on a barbeque right beside his truck. Ray, Mike and Doyle, three electricians staying in the adjacent motel, joined us. They chatted about Utah, and Tony said stuff about the salt flats but I barely listened. Exhausted, I left the party early, to sleep forever in a still truck.

The next morning, after a hot restaurant breakfast, I grabbed my novel and journal, paid the *Queen's Inn* for the use of their pool, and planned to do absolutely nothing on a balmy warm Tuesday in Southern California.

The electricians were already parked by the pool, sitting under an umbrella.

"Come join us." Mike called to me. I pulled up a chair, sat in the sun next to their umbrella, and broke out my lotion.

"How come you're not working?" I asked.

"Hunting season opens next week," Mike answered. "We've wrapped it up here, and now we're going out to the range to practice before we leave tomorrow."

Doyle laughed. "This is why we come out here at all. To shoot this range."

"I thought hunting season opened in September or October," I said, still looking at Mike.

"That's with guns. We're bow and arrow hunters." A pause. "In Idaho," Mike added. Mike was so handsome I felt embarrassed just looking at him.

"Really! Bows and arrows. You can actually hit something? What do you hunt for?"

"Deer mostly. Whatever we can find. Why don't you come out to the range with us this afternoon, see what it's like?"

"I'd love to!"

Mike and I sat in the back seat, practically touching. I could feel the heat coming off his leg. I didn't look at him even once. The only car in the shooting range parking lot, Mike and I got out and walked behind Ray and Doyle through the entrance, a rusted gate in a cyclone fence with a warning sign posted beside it.

Laid out like a golf course, dusty bushes lined a brown path to a target or a deer statue. Nothing green in sight. Mike and Doyle kept score of the arrows that hit and missed but Ray walked along in silence. The two blabbered away about tips of arrows, distances, or how much creep was in the string. I listened to half of it and noticed how Ray, a good fifteen years older than the other two, kept silent.

To thank them after the last target I said, "Can I buy you all a beer?"

"We don't drink." Ray said. "We're Mormons."

"Oh! From Utah. I should have guessed. I'm sorry."

"It happens all the time. So, do you drink?" Ray asked.

"A little. I just wanted to say thank you, is all." Ray was driving us back to the motel. Mike and I rode in the back seat again.

"So, do you dance? ... I mean, I don't want to go dancing," I back-pedaled. "I'm just curious ... if you don't mind my asking."

"We dance," Mike laughed. I felt my face flush.

"But we don't smoke or drink coffee." Ray said. "Not good for you."

"I don't like coffee at all. I drink tea."

"We don't drink tea either." Ray said. "And we tithe ten percent each year. It's the best insurance there is." Ray continued. "Mike here made his pilgrimage to Indiana for two years."

I thought Ray didn't like how Mike and I were acting so friendly. "How old were you?" I asked Mike.

"Nineteen. Best experience of my life, carrying the word."

"Really?" My attraction to all the muscles, tan, and sandy blonde hair didn't exactly shatter, but the thought of Mike going door to door with pamphlets and praising Jesus threw a wet rag on my imagination.

"We can give you *The Book of Mormon*." Ray again.

"No, but thanks." I felt embarrassed, like I'd been caught. Sex, muscles, and a tan, that's what I wanted. Don't give me religion.

Cincinnati
Alone

August 15, 1980

A friend of Kent's brother dropped him off at the truck. We loaded up cantaloupe and headed for Cincinnati.

My fifth stint on I- 80. I knew the shifts over Donner Pass by heart. We dropped all the way down to fifth before we got over the top. Fourth if we got stuck behind a slower truck.

Nevada, Utah, Wyoming, Nebraska, Iowa, Illinois, Indiana. Whenever irritation welled up at Kent, the victim, all I had to do was remember Bob, and I calmed right down.

Kent got permission for me to deliver the load alone, so I dropped him off in Indianapolis and drove the last two hours into Cincinnati by myself. To shut down the truck, I picked a strip mall parking lot, signaled, but pulled into the drive-through bank lane next door by accident.

Hideous! I couldn't go forward, I was way too tall and would hit the overhang. Even if I knew how to back-up, which I didn't, I couldn't go backwards into six lanes of traffic, and thousands of frantic cars. I couldn't slip over to the mall parking lot because of a three-foot retaining wall.

Shit. Fuck. What am I going to do?

Thank God the bank was closed. I got out and walked behind it. Their empty parking lot was way too small. Back in my truck, I broke into a sweat, swallowed, and backed up a bit. Cars honked and roared around my trailer. I backed up another two feet but yanked left when I should have eased right. Put my butt straight out, almost to the median.

Honk! Honk! Honnnnnk!

I pulled forward. Cars shrieked by. I wanted a drink of water. Cotton mouth, like my tongue had swollen. I didn't have any orange cones to put out. I couldn't back out of this mess.

To the right of the bank's low overhang, was a skinny driveway. I took a second look at the parking lot. It was my only choice. I squeaked through the narrow uncovered driveway, made it into the parking lot, and thought of Dick Dart hollering at me from the jump seat months ago.

"You don't ever have to hit anything if you don't want to. You can always get out and look ... Grab the bottom of the steering wheel when you're backing up. Take it left if you want the trailer to go left. Take it right if you want it to go right."

But the thing about these huge trucks was, going forward, if you turn sharp enough, the cab may be going forward but the trailer will kink up and actually go backward. Right off, I kinked the trailer in the wrong direction. I nixed driving up the curb onto the bank's walkway. A chain link fence walled off the extra six feet of bushes at the end of the lot. The dirt hill opposite the walkway was not an option. At least no one was honking.

I backed up, trying to get the trailer kinked the other way. Pulled forward a few feet, backed up a few feet. Eased forward again till the trailer started to kink wrong, backed up a little more, then forward again and so on. I thought about the bank having to tear down their overhang. I thought about getting fired and wondered if I'd have to pay for my own way home. Even if I did turn the truck around, how would I make the corner around the bank-lane without hitting its roof?

My 64 or 188 or 200,000-point turn may have qualified for the Guinness Book of Records, except I didn't have a witness. Still, I should have counted. I made it around the overhang of the bank's drive-thru lane and never hit anything.

I never once felt my legs or arms cramping until they started contracting about twenty minutes after I parked in the strip mall lot next door and shut down the engine.

Finally, after my arms and legs relaxed, I had no one to tell. A knuckle-biting, emotional thriller unsurpassed in my driving experience, and not another soul on the planet cared.

Chicago
Wrong turn

August 20, 1980

I paid a guy to back me in. I didn't try to lump my own truck. Lumping had to work like waitressing, where we always remembered who tipped and who stiffed. I didn't want to get caught being a cheapskate at Kroger's in Cincinnati.

Dispatch gave us a load of baby food to pick up in Sturgis, Michigan. Kent was waiting for me in the Indianapolis terminal.

"How'd it go?" I asked. He loaded his stuff and jumped in the passenger side.

"She had my stuff packed in boxes. Told me to get out."

"What about counseling?"

"I didn't ask about that. She just wanted me out."

"Where will you go now?"

"I don't know."

"But didn't you talk to her?"

"She wouldn't talk to me"

I backed off. "I'm sorry, Kent."

"She just told me to get out, and then she left."

I couldn't see any tears, but he was sniffling.

We deadheaded through flat, lush green Indiana. Thick steaming fog lay on the bog beside I-69. Flash flood warnings. Severe thunderstorm warnings. Warm and humid. Late afternoon, the Loch Ness Monster should have risen up out of the bog and sucked us in. The perfect setting for a Steven King novel.

Kent was losing it.

"How are Angela and Holly?"

"I didn't get to see them. They were at Darlene's mother's."

"Oh, that's terrible. Couldn't you even take them for an afternoon?"

"Darlene wouldn't have let me."

"You mean you didn't ask?"

"You don't understand!" Kent sulked. "There's nothing I can do."

Five hours later, we arrived at the baby food plant. Kent told me that Darlene had left him at their house, without a car, no way to move his cardboard boxes, and had to take a taxi back to the terminal.

I didn't bother telling him about the drive-thru bank fiasco.

In Sturgis, a Tanksley truck pulled in soon after ours, with a full load of baby food and claimed their rear axles were overweight. They asked the company to take off a few pallets. The dock workers pissed and farted around waiting for a decision. We couldn't load until their situation got resolved. Kent paced the loading dock with his arms crossed. When a dockworker offered him a cigarette, he answered in a shrill pitch, "No, I don't smoke." Two hours later, Tanksley cancelled our load entirely and sent us to Chicago.

I drove. Kent, practically comatose, crawled into the sleeper.

Another three hours on I-90 into Chicago. Dispatch had instructed us to follow another Tanksley driver into the *Time* magazine loading dock. Just before midnight I finally got a hold of *High Boy* on the CB, who picked us up just east of Chicago. I followed him into Chicago's industrial zone, passing *no trucks allowed, low bridge,* and *maximum clearance* signs while we took turn after turn. The maze we navigated to reach that *Time* magazine warehouse would have baffled a cartographer.

Having unloaded at 6:00 a.m. and driven the four hours back to Indianapolis to pick up Kent, I'd been on duty for eighteen hours, albeit with a considerable wait in Sturgis. When Kent threw himself into the sleeper that morning, and shut the curtain, I didn't suggest he get behind the wheel. Nor did I suggest he drive out of Sturgis.

Time magazine Inserts, which were rush orders, got loaded immediately upon arrival. Trailer seals, to ensure no one tampered with the load, were affixed to our lock. We signed a document stating our departure time was

0100 hours. We had to be in Los Angeles fifty-five hours later.

Terry, aka *High Boy*, directed his question to Kent. "Do you want us to lead you back to I-90?" Terry's truck was headed for Portland and still being loaded. We would have to wait another hour if we were going to follow Terry.

"No, I'll get directions." Kent walked off, presumably to call dispatch, ignoring Terry's partner, who had gotten out of the cab to be introduced to us. Davey, a plump, blonde female, used the restroom, and climbed back in their cab. A black man and white woman partnership.

"Kent, maybe driving would take your mind off your problems."

"I'd probably kill us. Run us off a cliff if there was one. You drive."

I rolled down the window, remembering Dick Dart's advice. "If you can't pull over and nap, roll down the window."

Heat and humidity wafted into the cab. I needed a wake-up blast of cold air, but did a few neck exercises and waved my arms around instead. I had paid attention to my driving on the way in to Chicago, not where *High Boy* was leading me.

Kent returned. "I got the directions."

"You sure you know how to get out of here?"

"Yes, let's get going." He didn't have his arms crossed, but he used that high-pitched tone, which I took to mean, *Don't fuck with me. I could go off the deep end.*

"Are you okay?" I asked.

Kent, sitting in the jump seat, didn't answer. He was looking at the floor, rubbing his jaw, something I did after I ground my teeth too hard in my sleep. He looked pinched, the deep creases between his eyebrows and across his forehead suggested a headache. I worried he might break down right there in the jump seat. I pulled out of the dock.

"Left or right?" I asked at the first turn.

"Uh ... left."

Our headlights shined into pitch black. No signage. Three choices lay in front of us. Two rights, one a severe curve going downhill, the other just a ninety-degree corner. 1:10 a.m.

"Which way?"

"Uh ..."

"Kent. Which way?"

He just stared ahead.

I had no map. 51' between trailer axles, a minimum 15.6 feet of clearance required, and a catatonic first-seat driver.

I called Terry on the CB, who, now almost loaded, agreed to come around the left turn to lead us out of our predicament. A wet breeze brought in distant road noise. A dog barked while we waited in silence. Kent rolled his window down too and the dampness moved through our truck. Terry rounded the corner, passed us. We followed him down the pitch-dark sharp turn. An on-ramp, we traveled maybe fifty more feet to see a big yellow *Low Bridge* sign. Cars zoomed by us in the dark like there was no tomorrow.

Why hadn't there been a *No Trucks Allowed* warning? Did some prankster cut down the sign?

We took the first exit. Garbage-infested ghetto. High-rise tenements. A huge dirt field on one side of the street. Fast food and liquor on the other side. The whole place stunk like rancid grease. Eighty degrees. One hundred percent humidity. 1:30 a.m. People everywhere. Crowds of teenagers. There must have been 200 people out there.

We followed Terry a few blocks down the street but then I had to stop at a red light. He pulled over to wait, and immediately a gang of kids hammered off the lock on his trailer and opened the doors.

"Terry!" I yelled into the CB. "You're being robbed!"

I lay on the horn. Ran the red light. Barreled directly toward the back of his truck. Kids were grabbing Terry's suitcase and then I saw Terry, pistol in hand, running back to his trailer from the cab.

Those kids dropped the suitcase and scattered. Immediately our two trucks drew a big crowd. I couldn't find even one white face. Terry stuck the gun in his belt. Collected his suitcase from the field. I rolled up my window, as did Kent, and watched the teenagers circle Terry. I worried, watched, slunk down in my seat and leaned in closer to the doghouse so I couldn't be easily seen. Terry walked to the back of his trailer with a crowd following him, put his suitcase back inside, and closed the trailer up. Two night security guards arrived to protect us until the *real* police came. The security guards stood in the street, with backs to our trucks and arms spread out. A blockade that stopped no one. No one guarded our other side, the side with the field of swarming kids.

Us three white folk never got out of our cabs.

We waited for the real cops, who wrote up the report. Terry's trailer seals had been broken. His trailer was dented. Kids did it. No one was hurt. Nothing was missing.

The police attempted to escort us safely out of the area, but within ten minutes, they had us facing a different low bridge. Around a right turn, down a wide gravel road, our second attempt to gain freedom brought us to a weight limit problem. At that point, because we couldn't squeeze under another low bridge to the right, I had to back around the intersection on my blind side.

The passenger side mirror provides a shot of the trailer during a blindside back up.

"Kent, what's it look like? Am I going to hit anything?"

Kent rolled down his window and stuck his head out. "I can't see anything. It's too dark. But I think you're good."

Both policeman got out of their vehicle. One stood at the back of the trailer and one stood up closer to me. The officer directing at my window took directions from the officer at the back of the trailer and relayed them to me. And my policeman, in order to see the rear policeman, had to stand further and further away as we backed around the corner.

My guy yelled "cut it ... right ... enough ... straighten her out." But I could barely hear him because cars zoomed through our path, ignoring him, many with boom boxes blasting vibrating bass music. On TV, my policeman's waving arms might have been funny, but to see him directing traffic that insulted his efforts gave me pause. What would he tell his family about this night, if he even made it home? Did he, a black man, have compassion for those drivers? Did he forgive them for being rude?

"Right! Cut right," my policeman yelled.

Finally, after I waved a grateful thank you, we made it to I-55 south.

"Someone ought to require advanced training certificates to drive trucks in Chicago," I said to Kent, at 3:00 a.m. Amped with adrenalin,
126

I couldn't doze, much less sleep, bouncing around in the sleeper, arms flapping unless I laid on them.

I drove, and thought of my grandmother's wedding crystal packed away back home. I thought of the silver dinnerware I'd inherited. The huge house I lived in. Our housekeeper. My college education being paid for. I had baby sitters, healthy meals cooked for me, lectures at the dinner table, new clothes every September, vacations to Mexico in my Dad's private airplane. Those kids probably didn't have heat in the winter or air-conditioning in the summer. And I was afraid of them. Heart pounding afraid. Adrenalin rushing afraid. The black and white divide right there, churning away inside benevolent me.

Kent drove the eight hours to Oklahoma City and I flopped around in the sleeper. As I lay there, vibrating along with the engine, thoughts surfaced. Those kids were together. They weren't in their rooms suffering through that crushing weight of loneliness. Some of them would go on to college. Some would work in factories or become truck drivers. Some of them would go to prison, sure. And there were some teenagers back in their homes, alone. Either happy or sad. But had they been white, I wouldn't have hesitated to get out of the truck. I would have forgiven their actions because they were kids. I might have considered them as individuals, like I treated my former students — all white — but each deserving respect, and time and attention from their teacher.

For the rest of the trip we rotated from behind the wheel to the sleeper and back, with quick stops for meals. We hardly spoke. Like driving alone, but with time off lying flat and vibrating.

"She's going to put my stuff at the Tanksley terminal," Kent finally said. His pancakes had arrived and he was dumping syrup over the glob of butter melting on top. We were outside Oklahoma City, at the 76 Truck stop, which I knew well enough now to recognize the waitresses.

"Can you rent storage space?"

Kent scowled. "I'm trying to save money." Then he gulped too much water and coughed so hard, he got up from the table like he needed to get to the bathroom and throw up.

I could tolerate Kent okay, and while he was in the bathroom, I finished my Number 1: scrambled eggs, bacon, and English muffin.

We made our delivery with four hours to spare.

Kent stayed with his sister-in-law, and I spent my layover with Monte, a truck driver parked next to me in the same L.A. lot. An older gentleman with kindness in his light blue eyes, peppered-gray hair to his shoulders, a ruddy complexion and tattoos on both arms. We introduced ourselves over lunch. He beat me at a game of miniature golf. We walked. We watched TV in his doublewide sleeper. From top to bottom, decked out in red tuck-and-roll, the whole sleeper looked spotless clean and smelled like mint air-freshener, which hung from the ceiling.

Monte told me a story about stealing trailers. A load escorted the entire way from Florida to New York City. A load he didn't want to know anything about. "So what's your story, girl? Why are you out here?"

"I almost got married," I paused. "For the second time. Things started to go wrong ..."

"Whoa! Back up! Start at the beginning!"

So I did.

Robin Thought I'd Do It

What if I hadn't?

August 22, 1980
Los Angeles, California

Sitting in Monte's sleeper with the TV sound turned off, light from the screen switching from bright to dark, I told Monte about my family. About growing up in a small town, trying to fit in, about Terry being Mom's favorite, and Bobby, my black sheep brother. Monte pressed for details. It took me an hour just to get to high school.

"I married the quarterback of our high school football team."

"You weren't a cheerleader were you?" Monte interrupted.

"I was, but that's another story. Aaron and I met a few months before my fifteenth birthday, and shortly after, he gave me his little gold football, our high school's official symbol for going steady. The football hung on a long chain to just above my navel. All the players gave footballs to their girlfriends. Carol wore Aaron's football the previous year.

After we'd been together for about a year, I asked Aaron, "Why'd you pick me?"

"Well, Cathy wouldn't do it," Aaron fumbled. "Robin said he was pretty sure you would."

"He said that to you?" Monte's eyebrows practically touched his hairline.

"He did. After I'd *done it.*

"God." Monte frowned.

"Aaron was warm and fuzzy. Kind. Soft. Dear, actually."

"Let me get this straight. You lost your virginity when you were fifteen?"

"Yeah. If I tell anyone I say sixteen."

"You ever been around a bunch of fifteen-year olds? They're just little kids!"

"My mother caught us one time. My bedroom was about a mile from the kitchen. Nobody ever came to my room, but Mom walked in suddenly, saw us, turned around and walked out. We never talked about it, but she made me an appointment with a doctor so I could get on birth control."

"Okay. Go on."

"Aaron was handsome. Over six feet, muscular and with lots of wavy dark hair. He made friends easily." I thought for a moment, "I guess I just tucked myself under his arm."

"When I turned eighteen, Aaron proposed, and a year later my mom orchestrated a blow-out wedding at the country club. My Dad rented a helicopter for our getaway."

"No shit!" Monte handed me a Coke. "Here, keep talking. This is good!"

"The helicopter landed on the country club's lawn, flew us five miles back to the airport, and we took off for a skiing honeymoon in Ashland, Oregon." I gulped down some Coke. "During college ..."

"Are you a college graduate?"

"I am." He asked a string of questions. I told him all about my college career, the twenty-five hours a week working at Bank of America, and the parties.

"Dresses were required at the bank, and at the college, students were protesting the war, staging sit-ins, wearing greasy long hair and burning draft cards. Did you do any of that?" I asked Monte.

"Naw. I was running loads then, making lots of money. But I'm legal now, I swear."

"I didn't protest either. I was getting grades and money, being married and partying after football games."

I talked about my married life, all the football, scouting games with Aaron, partying with the coaches, football on TV all day Sunday and Monday night.

"Jesus. That's a lot of football."

"We even studied for Pigskin Picks, a contest about the local games that came out in the paper every week."

"Were you happy doing that? I mean, did you want to?" Monte asked.

"I don't know. It's just what we did. I never thought about it."

"Jesus." There was silence. Monte reached over to the cabinet at the end of the bed. I could see his leg was stiff so I tucked my feet under me to give him more room. "Keep going." he said, pulling out an embroidered pillow to put under his knee.

"Okay, tell me if you get tired."

"Girl, this is better than TV!" Just then another semi pulled in our parking lot. He parked perpendicular to us, blocking our view, which seemed unusual.

"Why'd he do that?"

"I don't know, but I don't want to get trapped." Monte scooted down into the cab, fired up the engine, and pulled around to park parallel to the other truck.

"Maybe he thinks Denny's is a better view," I offered.

"You cold? I could turn on the heat."

I smiled. "No. But turn it on if you want. It might help your knee."

"Nah. I'd rather use a blanket." Monte crawled back in next to me and waited.

"Aaron's circle of friends grew. Work colleagues, all the coaches, city league basketball players. I started getting left behind, and when Aaron finally would come home, I'd give him hell. Didn't take him long to stop coming home."

Monte nodded. "I know how that goes."

"Yeah?"

"I been there. Never again." Monte looked like an old man just then, with dead eyes.

"You been married?" I asked.

"Never got there, but I lived with a lady once. She gave me too much hell. I split. Never saw her again." Monte rubbed his knee.

"Pain?" I asked.

"Got arthritis in 'em or something. Keep talkin'."

"I was twenty-three when Aaron and I separated. Shortly after, two weeks I think it was, the junior high school's librarian moved in with him."

"That's raw," Monte frowned. "I'm glad you got rid of him."

"Yeah, maybe, but all those people, all that partying, they were all Aaron's friends. Suddenly, I had no one."

"You'd been somebody else's girl, and then your world turned upside down."

"I didn't have a clue. I felt so humiliated but I wouldn't admit it."

"I been on my own since I was fourteen." Monte yawned. "I like my life enough, I guess. I meet a lot of interesting people. How about chapter two at breakfast?"

"Okay. It's the first time I've really told the whole story to anyone." Stone sober, I slept deeply in all that spotless tuck and roll, curled up next to a father figure. I didn't care. I felt safe. He didn't touch me.

In the morning, we walked across the parking lot and six lanes of traffic to eat at Denny's. I talked on. Monte listened.

"I got a teaching job, a crazy mixed-up paperwork deal where I was working half-time for the community college and half-time for a high school. The junior college required that I be enrolled in the masters program, so I signed up for that too. Plus, I started playing the piano and writing poetry.

"You play the piano?"

"Not much. Mostly, I was trying to fill time."

He paid for his steak and eggs and my veggie omelet. We set out walking.

"I started going to the Vista Del Mar, the VD as we called it." Monte laughed at that. "A fishermen's bar. Pool table, juke box. Guys coming in from pulling green chain at the local saw mills."

Monte nodded.

"The teaching job lasted one year and I flunked out of the masters program."

"Ouch."

"In a small town, nothing's private."

"Yeah."

"Embarrassing, losing my job like that."

"We all lose jobs, kid." Monte offered.

"Yeah." I kept talking. "So, deciding to chill, I bought a round trip ticket to Maui. After I rented a room, the pseudo *"landlord"* rented my room to another guy. No place else to go, I had to share my room with that guy. Mr. Fucking Landlord totally suckered both of us, so for revenge, I stole all his clothes when I moved out. Kept them a week and then dumped them on his porch."

"People have been killed for less." Monte shook his head, put his arm across my shoulders and relaxed it into a gentle squeeze. We walked along beside six rows of traffic with lights and left turn lanes. Engines idling, top forty hits blaring out car windows. We turned into a strip mall parking lot.

"It sounds horrible saying it out loud."

"We do stupid things, honey. That's how we get smart."

"Okay. So I'm in Hawaii, and I hardly made it to the beach. I never even went snorkeling."

"What did you do?"

"I worked as a bookkeeper by day, and at night I took a job as a cocktail waitress thinking I'd meet people. The bar was set back off the main drag and though it was really beautiful with a huge old tree, nobody came in. I served a few locals who sat there and got plastered listening to Hawaiian music, but mostly I watched these gargantuan cockroaches scurry across the bar, through the cherries and pearl onions."

Monte and I stepped into Waldenbooks. "I need a few more novels. I'm almost out." Monte said. "Let's find the thrillers ... and I want a few westerns."

"Okay. Then let's check out the historical fiction," I teased, "for the college graduate." I didn't feel afraid of Monte knowing me. I loved how he asked me questions, pulled everything out of me.

Monte bought *Salem's Lot* by Stephen King and two westerns. I bought *The Monkey Wrench Gang*, by Edward Abbey and a detective novel, *Last Bus to Woodstock*, by Colin Dexter.

Coming out of Walden's air conditioning, the heat blasted my face when Monte opened the door.   I started right in. "I did meet Gary, though."

"Where were we?" Monte asked.

"I'm in Hawaii."

"That's right. Okay. Continue."

"Gary introduced me to opium, and right off I knew I couldn't ever buy it. I'd be one of those women you see in pictures, fucking any fat old man for another toke on the pipe."

Monte burst out with a belly laugh. "Kid, you've seen too many movies."

"I loved that stuff." I noticed out the corner of my eye that Monte was starting to limp. I slowed my pace. "I remember sitting on the floor in my bedroom, totally euphoric just watching a huge cockroach crawl under the rug, actually creating a moving hump the size of a marble, a boulder, walking across the room. You ever smoked opium?"

"Yeah, I liked it, but it put me to sleep. Cocaine was the perk that came with my job. Always had plenty. Burnt my nose out, once. I don't do it anymore."

"I never liked cocaine that much. Made me stand up, pace. I talked non-stop on that stuff. And I got headaches."

"Huh."

"I slept good on the *Big O* though."

"The *Big O*?" Monte's crow-feet wrinkled.

"Well, that's what Gary called it." I chuckled. "That stuff gave me such a flood of contentment. My body would go so soft. Totally limp out. If there was a problem in the universe, it wasn't mine. I've never had that kind of relief, before or since.

"Not that Gary was a bad guy, but did you meet any good guys in Hawaii?"

"I guess not." I stared at the pavement while we walked. The heat bothered me, felt hotter than eighty in the shade. "Let's go in there." I pointed to a small ice cream parlor with a few tables. The checkered floor stuck to my shoes and the air reeked of sugar. Monte ordered a piece of pie. I got chocolate ice cream. We sat next to the wall, back in the corner.

I broke the silence again.

"The worst part about Hawaii, this tubby guy with no discernable I.Q. started hanging out with me at a concert. I liked his smooth tan skin, his almost non-verbal presence. I was grateful to be with someone, anyone. Then, it became apparent that I was either going to have consensual sex or be raped. Too much beer, he was way large. He took my arm and steered me up an alley. Afterward, I got away as quick as I could."

"Shit, that pisses me off."

"Could have used opium that day. Did you do a lot of drugs?"

"Yeah. But not any more."

I waited, but Monte didn't say anything. He finished his pie. I worked on my ice cream and said, "Sure were a lot of drugs in Hawaii. The day of my flight home, the red-eye out of Honolulu, a fellow hitchhiker gave me a large chunk of mushroom, which I ate in two bites. An hour later I couldn't pack for all the laughing. My roommates packed for me and got me on the plane, to Eugene, Oregon instead of Eureka, because I figured I'd have an adventure hitch hiking. Everyone else was doing it. Besides, you never know who you might meet, right?

"So, who'd you meet?"

"Tom."

"Of course. Tell me about Tom."

Los Angeles
Monte

August 23, 1980

Monte brought two glasses of water back to the table for us. He sat. Slid a glass to me. "To wash down my pie." He drank half the glass. "Okay, I'm ready."

"Tom was short, stocky, had wild blonde curls. Funny. Tom was already standing on the ramp entering I-5 when I walked out there. His pack was stashed in the bushes, and he asked me to hitch with him because he'd have an easier time getting a ride.

"Duh, as they say." Monte interjected.

People came in, got their ice cream cones, and left. Nobody else sat at the tables. "Turned out he was headed to Eureka too. We got one ride the whole way, but it was a pickup so I got the cab and Tom had to sit in the bed. We stopped to eat in Cave Junction, half way, and I offered to switch, but he said he was fine. Then, he had no place to stay so I offered him my house and, of course, my bed.

"Of course."

"He stayed a whole week, waiting for a room in his friend's house to become available. He was broke but wouldn't take any money. I thought we'd keep being friends after he moved to his own room, but he didn't come by. So I decided it was because he didn't have a car. He had told me he was shy about using the phone. I went to his friends' house twice and both times they said, "Tom's not home," like I was a bill collector or his probation officer. I just stood there like a dumb ass on their porch, pretending it was no big deal.

"I really liked him, Monte. I thought he liked me too. To this day I have no idea what I did wrong."

"You probably scared him off, wanting a friend so much."

"My worst fear," I looked at my empty bowl, "was being alone."

"What you resist, persists."

"Tell me about it ..."

My eyes stung and watered just then. "God, I've never said all this before. It sounds so sordid. I'm such a loser." Monte reached across the table and touched my hand. "Remember that landlord in Hawaii, the one whose clothes I stole?" Monte nodded. A racking sob came out, "I slept with that asshole." Tears ran down my cheeks. "I can't believe myself." My breath caught like hiccups out of control between sobs. So dramatic. Embarrassing.

I saw the counter lady staring.

Monte handed me a wad of napkins and stood. "Let's get out of here."

We walked back to his truck, Monte outright limping. He fired up the air conditioning. We crawled in his sleeper and leaned against the red, tuck and roll backboard. I took a big breath and sighed.

"So I got home." I sniffed. "I had plenty of stories to tell in the Vista. I'm like, *everything's fine couldn't be better*. I'm tossing back beers and playing pool, laughing. Pretty soon, Monte, I really believed I had a great time in Hawaii."

"Everyone fakes it in their twenties," Monte said. "My twenties were rough. No fear on the outside, but shitting my pants carrying loads across the border. I'd hang for a few weeks at this pool hall outside of Tucson, shoot the shit with everyone like I had it all together."

"Boy, I can relate to that. Monte, you ever have kids?"

"I don't know. And I'm not proud of that fact either. That woman I told you about, she was pregnant when I left her. I got so mad, I hit her one night. That was the end of it for me. I never wanted to hit a woman again. That's when I hit the road, instead."

"Oh. God ... for your whole life ..."

"What I got myself into, no woman was ever gonna wait around, with me leavin' like I did. I'd be gone for weeks, maybe a month. Couldn't call home. Had to wait for a call to come, wait for my load, for the signal." Monte saw my confusion, "that it was safe to cross."

"You never got caught?"

"Nope. Ten years ago, I turned myself in. Got tired of watchin' my back every time I turned around. Got a lawyer, and he got me eighteen months and probation. I was just a runner. Small time. I didn't know nothin' really."

"Heroin?" I didn't want it to be heroin.

"Mostly. And cocaine. I'm totally clean now. Got off probation three years ago. And I don't use. Don't even drink. Prison helped me kick all of it."

I fluffed one of his pillows and lay down.

"So anyway, you got home from Hawaii and then what happened?"

"I found a job as a secretary for a woman who wanted me to create a library catalogue for her German language books. She fired me after I couldn't figure out how to do it!"

Monte bellowed. We both laughed hard, so hard that Monte farted, and then we really let loose.

Finally settling down, the weight of life temporarily expelled, I snuggled into Monte. "I quit a job as a bookkeeper for a plumber that stored his bills in my right hand drawer and paid one or two of them every once in a while. I quit a dishwashing job at a greasy lunch diner that was too hot. Customers stuck their cigarette butts in the mashed potatoes. The floor was so thick with grease, I left my shoes on the porch when I got home.

"Finally, I took a job working mornings for Eureka City Schools. The job required a mess of paper work and the monitoring of students. Except there were no students. Businesses were supposedly mentoring these students, but there were no participating businesses. I was supposed to recruit businesses and students to this program, which had been receiving state funds for a couple of years. The program would be evaluated in three months."

"So you got paid to sit like a duck."

"Yeah. I was stuck in a room with no students to interview, and no idea which businesses to recruit. I'd send call slips out to arbitrary students in business classes, but no kids ever showed up.

138

"But really what I'm doing, Monte, is going to the Vista, thinking I'm gonna' get a man. And every time I brought one home, I swear, Monte, every time, I believed it was the beginning of something wonderful. In the morning though, we mostly skipped breakfast and said goodbye." I wiped my nose on my sleeve. Monte handed me a Kleenex and I blew into it. "That went on for two years. I'm a total fuck-up."

"Well, you've certainly fucked," Monte lifted his arm and put it around my shoulders. "But you're not a fuck-up. It's not like you've hurt anyone else." He held my shoulders as we sat in his sleeper watching the city of angels drive by, a sea of concrete, motorcycles, and colorful cars, the air conditioner humming along, the engine vibrating the cab.

"You got cookies in here? It smells like chocolate chips."

Monte reached into his cabinet and pulled out a white bag of bakery cookies. "Didn't smell these last night?" he teased.

"Well, I did, but I didn't want to ask." He gave me the bag and I took two.

"It's life experience, honey. Would you have rather been a housewife, with snot-nosed kids, watching TV, waiting for something to happen?"

That got a weak smile out of me.

My voice hurt. "That mall has a theatre. Want to see a movie? I'll buy."

"Sounds perfect. I'll buy the popcorn," Monte answered.

We watched *Coming Home*, starring Jane Fonda. And I thought I had problems.

We headed back to the truck. "Did you go to Vietnam?" I asked.

"Nah. Too old by then. Never served. Hungry?" We ate dinner at the same Denny's where we had breakfast. "When do we get to the part about your second marriage?" Monte asked after we'd been seated.

"You're such a good listener."

"Like I said, better than TV, girl. Can your voice hold up?"

I drank my glass of water. "Here goes." I started. "I finally got a man."

The Best I Knew How

Was worse

August 23, 1980
Los Angeles, California

"I'd taken on a second job waitressing on the dinner shift at a popular restaurant."

"While you were in the business thing at the school?"

"Yeah. Three weeks into that job, the chef asked me to marry him ..."

"Oh honey, no."

"Yes. A cokehead and I paid for his habit. Pathetic. We drank at the bar after the restaurant closed, then moved on to his friend's house to do the illegal drugs. Night after night. Jeff always had to have the last word. He talked over everyone else, was right all the time," I sighed. "I liked waitressing. It was an Italian Restaurant. Made good tips."

"So what happened?"

"I just acted cool, like everything was fine. But about a month into it, I wanted out. I hated wasting the money, but desperately wanted to believe we were moving to Wisconsin, that I was starting a new life. I watched our plan turn to fantasy, and stuffed it. Made myself sick. But I hung in, all the way to the wedding night. I would have married him before admitting I'd fucked up."

"But you didn't marry him."

"I would have. That's the horrible part. I would have married him instead of admitting I'd made a mistake."

"Why *didn't* you get married?"

140

"The night of his bachelor party, he got so loaded, they piled him into a truck to get him home. Apparently he came to, didn't want to quit partying, so he stepped out of a moving pickup and fractured his skull."

Monte's eyes bulged. He gasped. "Makes Aaron sound like a saint."

"That night, maybe it was two or three in the morning when I got the call, I actually looked up and thanked God I didn't have to get married."

My tears started up again. "I never cry. I can't believe this." I wiped my face with a napkin. The waitress delivered our check and hightailed it out of there. Didn't even ask Monte if he wanted more coffee.

We sat there over empty plates, stomachs full of hamburgers and fries. I still had half a milkshake.

"You're not the first to sell your soul for a man, kid. Want to take a break? Are you all right?"

"It gets worse."

"How can it possibly get worse? This is crazy!" Monte picked up the check, paid, opened the door for me.

"I might as well get the whole thing out." I said.

We walked back to his truck in the twilight. With store lights against the purpling sky, smooth pavement under our feet, I took Monte's arm. The air, a Southern California balmy stereotype, lifted the spring in my step. Maybe the cool evening helped Monte too, because he wasn't limping.

"Go for it." Monte had a look of rapt attention, sitting back in his sleeper, familiar with our seating arrangement.

Out came an abbreviated version of going crazy, trying to revolutionize teaching, prevent WWIII, Napa State Mental Hospital, the isolation, depression, suicide attempt, and when I finally finished, around 1:00 a.m., with getting hired on as a truck driver, Monte said "That's a story worth telling, girl!"

Again, I made a beeline to my truck, a quick change into pajamas, and settled in for the night in Monte's truck. "You okay?" Monte said.

"Yeah. I think I feel better."

"Sleep safely." He reached up and snapped off the light, patted me on the head, and rolled over. Within minutes, he started snoring.

"I'm grateful to you, kid." Monte said the next morning. "You've given me a weekend to remember and I much appreciate it. "

"So, you live a life on the road, that's it?"

"Still runnin' I suppose. Maybe someday I'll settle." I waited, but Monte didn't continue. Finally, he said, "I'm much more interested in hearing about you than tellin' my sad tale.

"What are you runnin' from?"

Monte scratched his head. He looked toward the dumpster at the far end of the lot. Finally he said, "Loneliness, I suppose. But I've made peace with myself." He looked back at me. "Don't need to stir it up any. There'll come a time, I promise, Margot, when you'll be more interested in listening to others than tellin' your own tale."

Brake Failure

In a rain storm

August 24, 1980
I-40 Arkansas

Monte, gone. He'd played out the nurturing father like a champ, but I couldn't imagine any daughter ever told their father everything I had revealed to Monte. Certainly not *my* Dad.

I shook my head, even smiled at the dirty, bug-ridden windshield, about to be liberated from all its crap. Just a little bit of soap and water and the light would shine through again. Monte wasn't soap, and I didn't feel clean exactly, but the whole weekend felt to me like dark chocolate with the tang of salt-water caramel, a mouth full of joy, but no desire for a second helping. That bitter-sweet taste of the past acknowledged, losing its power, maybe I was done with my poor choices.

On the road again, Kent and I picked up a load of tomatoes in San Diego due in Windsor Locks, Connecticut in a week.

A full moon over the desert, I could have driven without my headlights on I-10 all the way to Tucson. To my right and left, rocks and sparse vegetation cast long shadows on the flat land. Nothing moved that I could see, but plenty of nightlife had to be out there. Snakes. Spiders. Wile E. Coyote.

After Kent drove to Las Cruces, I got behind the wheel and watched the sun come up on I-25 to Albuquerque, through towns called Hatch, Truth or Consequences, and Elephant Butte. Gray became yellow became brown. How did people live in such rocky, flat, barren land? Yes, the sky goes on forever and I saw signs for water —Elephant Butte

Reservoir, Caballo Lake—next to a town called Oasis, but I couldn't live there. These folks lived in mobile homes, extreme heat, dust and little gray bushes. Other than the blue above, where was the color? How do they live without color? Give me mountains, ocean, redwood trees, year around greenery and wood houses.

Kent climbed out of the sleeper. "The vibrating gives me a headache." He plopped down on the jump seat. A few minutes later he said, "My back hurts," and climbed back in the sleeper. "I don't want to drive." He snapped the curtain shut. He looked like a little monkey pacing a tree branch.

We traveled through big blue New Mexico skies. On through flat, windy, brown Texas plains, where the sky turned gun-metal gray. In Oklahoma City, I got a letter from my Mom. Her roses were still blooming, she gave two flats of lobelia to the neighbor, Ben was finishing the copper sculpture in the bathroom. I took a shower, ate another hamburger at a new truck stop, dozed, slept a bit. Rain showered down all around us.

West of Little Rock, Arkansas, the CB became all a-chatter with the news of what lay ahead. Flash flood warnings, the whole state on high alert, possible evacuations. The sky looked dark, the color of smoke. Lightening cracked a hundred yards to our left. Rain a few miles ahead, clearly visible. Thunderheads. For 180 degrees, the sky blotched up like an abstract in grays from steel to charcoal. Rain angled down from rumbling shadows. Lightning split apart the smooth slate color, a perfect brilliant contrast. The rain came in spatters. Above, black clouds took shape like gods. Like Dad was up there with his mouth wide open, laughing at me. I tried to remember what Dad looked like with his mouth wide open. Did he rock his head back when he laughed? I couldn't picture it. All I could see was his face looking down at me with that half smile, like *I gotta have patience, she's just a girl.*

The clouds. Powerful, magnificent, gorgeous. And then we reached the rain. Ran right into it, like a wall.

I'd never seen rain like this, even though I lived in a rain forest, where we got at least forty inches a year. This rain wasn't pouring. It was hitting us. Whole glasses of water thrown at the windshield. Garden hoses thumbed to create maximum impact. An army of henchmen sending the king's limitless onslaught of water across the windshield. The wipers were useless.

Cars were parked on the shoulder or huddled together under overpasses. The CB hollered out, "Ten inches of rain in the last two hours." Sheets of water and gusts of wind hit the driver's side, and even though I had slowed, the truck was slowing still. I applied the fuel, but we continued to slow down. I looked at the gauges. We weren't hot, and the tachometer demonstrated my request for speed.

The air pressure gauge was dropping steadily. Our mechanical brake was kicking in, shutting us down because we had a leak in our air brakes. As I pulled to the shoulder of the freeway, Kent jumped out of the sleeper.

"Why are we stopping?"

"We've got an air leak." The rain stormed down on us so loud we were yelling. I pulled to a safe stop. Thank God we weren't on a hill.

"Oh great. We'll have to get a tow back to Oklahoma City."

I got on the CB. "Sunny Avenue here." I yelled. "Is there a Shirley Temple out there?"

A hoarse male voice answered through lots of popping and static. "Haven't seen one, Miss."

"Our brakes went out. We're on the shoulder just past mile marker 117 going east. We're going to need a tow."

Male voice: "I'll see if I can rouse someone for you, Miss. I be going east. I'd stop, but I'm ahead of you, up at the 135-yardstick."

"Break!" Sounded like a tenor voice. Younger.

"Backin' out." hoarse man.

"I'm coming up on your back end, Miss," the tenor chirps. "At the 110. You need some help?"

"Brakes are out. I need another Tanksley driver to send a mechanic. We've got terminals in Oklahoma City or Nashville."

"Miss, you be in the middle of nowhere. No mechanic is comin' out here in this rain. You gotta wait."

"Oh, no."

Another voice. "Break."

Tenor "Go ahead."

"They're talkin' about closin' the road. Gettin' rescue teams out here to pick up the stranded."

"10-4. Miss, maybe I can get you going again. I'm coming up on your back door now."

In the rear-view mirror, I could see a Roadway semi pulling over. "Kent, get your jacket on. This guy's pulling over. I don't want him to think I'm alone."

In the deluge of rain and wind, both Kent and I got out of the truck.

"Where's the leak?" Big Red, the tenor voice, looked fit. He wore a long rain jacket and a ball cap. Work boots.

"Can't hear anything with all this rain." Kent pretended we'd been listening for the leak.

The Roadway driver found the leak right off. We were lucky. It was the brake pot on the outside passenger side of the tandem axle, right next to where we were standing, the first one he listened to.

"Bleed the service brake," he called over the rain. I ran back to the cab and drained the air out of the brakes.

Squatting under the trailer to keep from getting thoroughly soaked, I watched *Big Red* disconnect the emergency and service brake lines from the leaky brake pot, which released the last of its compressed air with a weak pop and then a sigh. Kent got back in the truck. Rain, like rocks, pelted the pavement around us.

"Hand me a penny," he shouted to me.

I scurried up to the passenger window, where Kent was watching in the rear view and told him to hand me my purse.

Really wet now, I hunched over, scooted back under the trailer and handed *Red* the penny. "Give me another penny," he yelled over the rain. I did.

"Got a dime?" *Red* sat on the pavement and water bubbled up on him like he was a rock in a rapid. The water reached above the soles of my waterproof boots, but my butt was still above the river. *Big Red* looked like a drowned rat.

"What are you doing?" I handed him a dime.

"If I plug this line, the air can't get to this pot and leak out." He pushed

146

the coins around with his little finger trying to lodge them in the service line just right. "I've gone five hundred miles like this. You'll make it to Nashville if I can get this dime in right."

Moments later he hollered, "I think that'll do it. Fire it up. See if you've got air."

I had air. I ran back to report the success, crawled back under the trailer, smiled and gave him a big thumbs up. "Thank you so much," I shouted.

"Just watch her, but I think you'll be okay," he yelled back.

Still under the trailer, the engine running, the rain pummeling the pavement, I got my wallet out to pay him but he was having none of it. "My pleasure, ma'am. Out here, we got to help each other. That's what we do."

I looked at him. He was smiling. He tipped his ball cap, crawled out and ran back to his cab.

One dime and two pennies. The air didn't leak out, so the mechanical brake didn't kick in, and we drove two hundred miles further to the Nashville Terminal to have it fixed. The rain in Nashville reminded me of a November deluge in Humboldt County. Nothing so drastic as what we'd just driven through, but not by any means a drizzle.

Showered, in dry clothes again, I climbed in the sleeper, chastising myself that I didn't invite *Big Red* to a truck stop for a meal. Never in my life had I met someone so generous. My mind wandered as I vibrated and flopped around in my sleeping bag while Kent drove. I couldn't imagine my Dad sitting in the rain fixing some stranger's truck. The truck and the sleeper and all the noise falling away, I wondered if Dad had ever operated on anyone for free. Dozing off, I couldn't think of a single time I'd ever helped another human being. I'd never even shared my candy. And then sleep actually came to me in a moving truck.

Bugs

Did anyone else care?

August 25, 1980
Practically Everywhere

North on I-81, through the Appalachians, the sun finally came out. Emerald and lime. Lots of new yellow. Pale blue sky streaked with white. I wanted to roll down the window, inhale, but didn't want to go deaf, lose my hearing like Terry predicted. Tanksley trucks weren't high-end, and the engine noise, along with the vibration, was sure to prove what I already knew: Terry was always right.

Maybe I'd get to drive back this way through those glorious oranges and reds some day, like in a fall calendar picture. Wouldn't be this year, though, as I'd be back in Eureka beating my DUI rap.

The bugs this trip. My God. All over the windshield. Not fifty miles out of the terminal in Moriarity, in Oklahoma City, and again in Nashville, insects covered the windshield. A bug graveyard. The big ones splatted out yellow, big as a quarter. They dried on like paint.

Back in New Mexico, a gargantuan June bug with antlers sat in the path to the restroom. He spread his wings, shiny brown plastic looking things. I backed up, but he didn't take off, so I made my way around him. Inside the stall, creatures hid in the shadows. Anything could have attacked, or dropped off the ceiling and I'd have had no warning. I saw a two-inch June bug on every other concrete block, and drip-dried to get out of there as fast as I could. In the light by the sink, those two-inch June bugs turned out to be metal bolts. I should have known better since they were lined up so evenly, but still, back in the truck, the fear sat in my chest, stuck so hard in my craw that I had to drink water. And that was nothing compared to what I saw in Virginia.

At a rest stop, a huge spider, about a foot above a fountain, stopped me from getting a drink of water. Finch-yellow with a black network inked on his back. Big as a half-dollar. He was sitting, with claws for legs, in the center of his muscle-bound web, and I knew if I stuck my head under him, he would drop down in my hair and kill me, or worse, I'd rise up into his net of ropes and booty of dead flies. Get it all over me. I could see myself screaming, trying to bat the sticky web off my head, the spider getting on my hand, scurrying up my arm. Way too much imagination, but I decided to go thirsty. I wouldn't have touched him, not even with a stick.

"How about we take 86 to 87, Kent? Smooth out the ride for a bit."

"No. It's a toll road." Holding the chicken bar, he was literally pulling himself up off the seat anticipating each pothole, trying to minimize the jarring to his back.

"Why not? Dispatch will reimburse us."

"They'll take forever to get me a check. We'll have to stop at every tollbooth. I'll start driving in Maryland. I know the way."

"I don't mind paying the tolls and getting reimbursed. You're practically standing as it is, Kent."

"*No. You* can't get reimbursed. *I* know the way," he screeched.

"Kent, I'll give you the money. You can pay me when you get reimbursed."

"*I said No!*" He screamed, as my mother would say, like a smashed cat.

From the corner of my eye, I could see him stretching his neck out, rolling his shoulders as if to put his voice back in its box.

Later, driving towards the evening sun, staring straight at it, my eyes didn't hurt. The sun was red. I wondered if kids made red suns on their kindergarten pictures, if parents told them the sun was really yellow, just covered with smog, which smelled like dollar bills.

Kent took over after sunset, and with the jump seat not being air cushioned, I figured I'd save my back, lie flat, bounce in the sleeper.

Several hours later, Kent brought us through Windsor Locks into the Kroger's warehouse, where we slept till 6:00 a.m.

New York City
Gassed Tomatoes

August 30, 1980

Our tomatoes didn't ripen over the trip. Kroger's refused the load. Picked too early, the tomatoes were hard as apples. Dispatch sent us to Hunt's Point in the Bronx, New York, to get rid of our green tomatoes. There, a wholesaler would gas the tomatoes to make them turn red and then sell them, but not to Kroger's. I wondered if I'd ever eaten a gassed tomato.

After writing down dispatch's directions, I got to drive in New York City. We drove under train tracks casting a dark pall on all the concrete in the late afternoon. Clutch in, clutch out. Clutch in, clutch out. I listened to the hiss and pop of the trains' electric wires, in spite of our own loud engine. Drove through the smell of rotting fast food, liquor, and saw a dead rat in the gutter, a dead dog left in the street. Rolled up the window. Clutch in, clutch out. Listened to the engine, the air conditioner.

We arrived at the warehouse, where, in the left turn lane, we got in line behind five or six trucks, out on a six-lane street. The truck in front of me threw fast-food wrappers out his window. On top of that he emptied his ashtray.

Prostitutes lined the warehouse, maybe five of them. An hour later, still idling, the air-conditioner dripping, I watched a stark-naked woman walking down the median, approaching our truck, at 3:00 in the afternoon, in sweltering heat. Barefoot. Her eyes at half-mast, she bent her elbow and waved at us like a president's wife, palm open, hand rocking back and forth as if to include everyone.

She was beautiful. Full body, coffee colored, smooth skin around generous curves, big hips, big boned, bouffant hair without the ragged ends. I didn't watch her in my rear-view mirror, but put my head in my hand, because I saw the little girl inside her, covered in opium, dying of loneliness, begging to be seen, all hope nearly extinguished.

We finally entered the warehouse, a weedy dirt courtyard with open concrete bays on three sides. We parked in the middle of the yard, and a forklift began stacking our pallets on the dirt. The bays angled downward like entrances to underground parking, and I watched as a bulldozer drove in one, scooped up tomatoes, and backed around our trailer. He raised his bucket and poured a red and green mess into a waiting dump truck. Pig food, I hoped. Surely, not tomato sauce. Garbage strewn everywhere, I could taste the smell. Cooked in the heat and rotten on my tongue, it reminded me of the slaughterhouse on I-5 in California. Not that death smell, but just as bad. I had to pee in the weeds, and hoped no one could see.

Philadelphia

Road construction

August 30, 1980

Finally released from the low-end of American commerce, we were immediately dispatched to Bristol, Pennsylvania, for paper, a rush load due in Los Angeles five days later. Three hours after loading, tired and thoroughly lost somewhere south of Bristol, Kent and I gave it to each other with both barrels.

"You took the wrong exit." Kent screamed from the jump seat.

"You *told* me to take that exit."

"You took the wrong exit!" We were squabbling like two pre-schoolers, and suddenly I started to giggle.

"Can I see the map?" I half smiled.

"What's so funny?"

"Nothing." Another snicker pushed itself out even though I tried to suppress it. Kent threw my Rand-McNally Road Atlas across the doghouse. It hit the steering wheel and the maps came out of the leather folder, ripping from the cover. My maps, because my first seat driver didn't even have maps.

Rand McNally Road Atlas mapmakers must think no one ever needs to go north from Delaware up through Philadelphia to Bristol. Neither Kent nor I knew where we were or how to describe our location on the CB. My maps were screwed up and I no longer saw anything humorous or absurd.

Thick traffic on cloverleaf after cloverleaf, I drove until I could get away from all the exchanges, get to a more manageable freeway, something I could locate on the map. "Here! Here!" Kent would point at each freeway exit, reaching a slightly higher pitch with every exit I passed. Finally, I landed on I-95 south and took the exit of my choice to work out a plan.

"Look Kent, there's a toll road that goes all the way up to Bristol. I'll pay. Please?"

"No. It goes into New Jersey. I don't know if we're licensed for New Jersey. Take I-95."

I wanted to needle the asshole since he'd ripped my maps, but I-95 looked like a direct route. I dropped my argument and headed north on I-95. I didn't ask if he wanted to drive and he didn't offer.

We hit road construction. The detour took us through the abject poverty in Philadelphia. We idled along in bumper-to-bumper traffic. Endless blocks of broken concrete, wrecked buildings, garbage, barbed wire coils on top of cyclone fences. Dead cars in a dirt lot, papers wind-blown into more cyclone fences. Man-sized holes cut through fences. Wire sticking out like a pitchfork waiting to impale the next child who dared to walk by.

But kids were laughing and running in six-packs. An impossibly young mother pushed a stroller, toddler at her side. Boom-boxes on shoulders, adults sitting on stoops smoking, iron grates on stores, a neighborhood setting I'd only seen on television, with background music. Traffic so much a part of their daily life, no one even noticed our sixty-two feet idling by.

When we finally reached Bristol after six o'clock, the dock was closed. I shared my granola with Kent, gave him his first ever apple-and-peanut butter. With my sleeping bag spread out on the doghouse, pillow on top of my coat, I cozied in and looked through the steering wheel at the night sky. Lights from the dock blotted out the stars. We'd be ready to load at 6:00 a.m.

Another entire day without pay. For me, money didn't matter. Separation from family didn't matter. I had an adventure and a book, but poor Kent exuded hopelessness. I recognized that in this job he couldn't scrape together a living for his family, but still he drove me up the wall.

Even if I had thought of consoling him —which I didn't—I wouldn't have known how.

Oklahoma City
Kent, Mr. Plaid

August 31, 1980

Almost twenty-four hours behind schedule, I drove out to I-76 where Kent took over. We fueled at the Indianapolis terminal, but since we'd spent our layover sightseeing in Philadelphia, Kent had no spare time to visit his kids. We had to push hard to make our delivery on time in Los Angeles.

"If you phoned your kids," I urged, "you'd feel better." But he declined, and I got back in the truck frustrated with Kent's sad scenario. His was a *cut-and-run* move and later I had to admit, so was mine.

With Kent not speaking, I developed a case of the fuck-its. I made no attempt to smooth feathers. Sleep, drive, eat. Repeat. Lots of my bristling, Kent's sniveling, and no kind words at all. When off duty, each of us kept the sleeper curtain shut. Through Illinois, Missouri, Arkansas and Oklahoma, we never made eye contact. At the Tanksley terminal in Oklahoma City, the shit storm finally struck.

The fuel jockey tipped his ball cap and bowed to me as I got out of the cab. The mechanic laughed at the fuel jockey. I laughed, they whistled. We played out the scene like a TV script, me smiling, taking a bow, while Kent stomped around angrily looking like a little two-year-old. In the office, there was a message waiting for me from some driver wanting to date me. The terminal manager teased me, and our laughing wound down as he handed me two letters from my mom.

Kent asked for a com-check, but the manager turned his back and didn't wait on him.

I left the office hearing Kent call out, "Sir, I need a com-check."

I had my mom's letters and had almost reached the truck to read them, but turned sharply when I heard someone say, "You're such a little shit!"

The guy was skinny. Maybe 5'9." He towered over Kent like a bully harassing a first-grader. He was either puffing out his chest like a big dominate sage grouse, or holding his arms straight to his back pockets to resist hitting Kent. Red plaid from neck to wrist, pearl buttons, a huge belt buckle, but this guy wore a Cardinals' ball cap, a personal identity statement.

"What's going on?" I asked, all sunny and bright. Mr. Plaid addressed me while nodding his baseball cap toward Kent. "That your partner, I take it?"

"Yes." I nod back, straight up and down, like I would for my father.

"Jesus." He turned back to Kent. "And you're complaining?" He rolled his eyes. "Cry me a river."

"She keeps fucking us up." Kent backed up a step and stuck his chin out. I'd never heard him say "fuck" before. His pinched voice climbed up the scale. "She's making us late on this rush load," he screamed. "I can't make any money with her on my truck."

"I'm ready to go, Kent. What's the problem?"

"He thinks his problem is you," plaid man interrupted. "He told the terminal manager that you got him lost, made him late on two rush loads. He wants you off his truck."

I stared at Kent. I knew he had convinced himself the Bristol directions were my fault, but it didn't occur to me he would complain to the company.

Mr. Plaid turned back to Kent. "You couldn't direct your way out of a paper bag." He looked back at me. "Miss, I put up with him for three months," his thumb pointed at Kent. "Do yourself a favor. Get off his truck. I'll put in a good word for you."

A high-pitched tone came out of Kent like his ears and nose were plugged. Kent's eyes squinted shut. I thought he might have a seizure or swallow his tongue. For maybe five seconds he stood there, stiff as a board. A greasy fuel jockey came over to watch. The mechanics were

155

staring from the bay.

"You're lucky she doesn't take a baseball bat to your head, Kent." Plaid man called as he walked toward the lounge. "Excuse my language, miss."

Back in the truck, Kent driving, me in the jump seat, Kent jerked his head back and forth, looking between me and the road.

"God damn it, Margot, your sleeping bag is too big. It keeps rolling out on my feet."

"I'll stuff it in the compartment better next time. I'm sorry."

"Because of you, my pillow got all wet in the air conditioner leak." Kent's whole 100 pounds turned when he screeched at me.

"How's that?" I asked.

Facing the road, he stuttered trying to form the words. "I need your sleeping bag out of my way!"

"Who was that guy back there?"

"What guy?"

"The one who almost hit you!"

"Oh, him. That guy was on speed. He almost killed us." Kent fixed his eyes on the white pavement. "Now let me drive. You're making us late."

I hopped in the sleeper and stayed there.

Oklahoma City to Flagstaff being the flattest, smoothest part of the trip, I dozed, even slept. Kent stayed in the sleeper while I drove. We hardly saw each other until we reached Barstow, where Kent announced his decision to do laundry and have the truck washed.

"Really?" He parked the truck in the wash rack and I watched him march off to the washing machines with his box of clothes. Must be some kind of residual shock from Oklahoma City, I reasoned.

I showered, hung out in the lounge, ate candy from the machine, and started my Woodstock novel. Finally, I walked into the washroom.

"We'll go to Los Angeles first and then head down to La Mirada," Kent informed me, meticulously folding his clothes. Kent, obviously, needed help.

I returned with the bill of lading and handed it to him. "This says deliver to La Mirada first. See?"

"Doesn't matter. We'll make back a little time if we go to L.A. first."

"Kent, what if La Mirada's load is blocking the L.A. delivery?"

"No big deal. It happens all the time." He loaded his clothes into a pitiful cardboard box and began walking to the truck.

The L.A. dock was closed. We spent the night there. La Mirada, on the other hand, had waited all night for us. After that fiasco, we made the seven-hour drive to Los Banos, and announced to the office manager that we could no longer ride together. Finally, with a mutual show of disrespect, we both walked away from the truck, Kent to hide in the bathroom (I imagined) and me, to pass time with the manager. My plan was to chat him up, get him to recommend me for someone to ride with that I could tolerate.

Bob, and now Kent. Was I causing this? Was I the asshole?

Donald, Partner #3

Los Banos, California

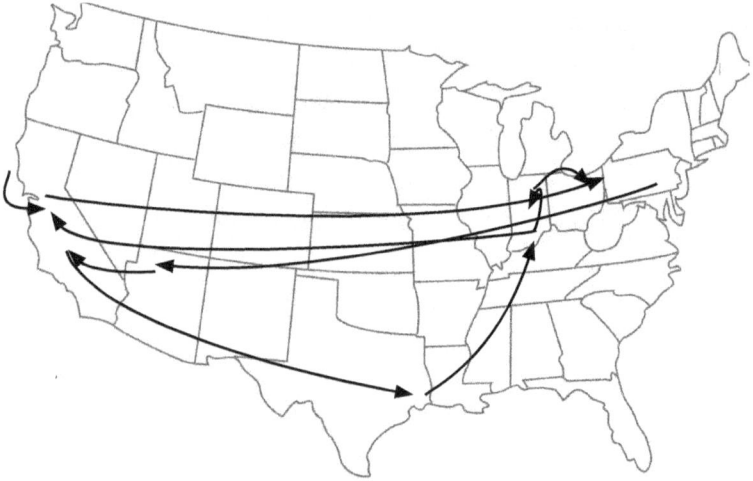

September 4, 1980

"Two down. Who's the lucky guy who gets me next?"

Miguel laughed. "It happens all the time. It's not just you."

"How are you doing?"

"I'm doing better." Miguel looked happier. "The kid's Mom finally took them for the weekend. It made a big difference. Mateo cried a bunch and I think he feels better. Sophie is sleeping again."

"Looks like she gave you another hair cut. It looks good." I smiled. "Got time for a break?"

"No, sorry. Will you be staying here tonight?"

"No. *Donald* is picking me up anytime now."

"Okay. Maybe one of these times you'll be laid over here. We can talk for more than ten minutes."

"That would be good. See you on the next round."

Donald arrived. Headed for Cincinnati with a load of produce, I piled my stuff onto his truck and we took off.

158

Donald and I took turns driving five-hour stretches, taking half hour-breaks, and logging what we drove. With few exceptions, I-80 looked exactly the same, like I'd read the novel three times already. Nevada was still desolate, Wyoming's stunted bushes went on forever, the Platte meandered more like an estuary than a river. I did enjoy the sliver of crescent moon over Illinois, and an orange and clouded Indiana sky. The only surprise came somewhere southeast of Indianapolis, a huge fresh green salad bar at the Texaco truck stop.

Donald aced the Kroger warehouse dock on the first try. When the air conditioner leaked, he adjusted something underneath it, and showed me how to do it.

Donald had beautiful blue eyes and a thinning face. When he laughed, which wasn't often, he looked like the court jester. About 5'10, Donald wore jeans and collared shirts, but he could easily have disappeared in a crowd. Two kids, married thirteen years, divorced last year. Donald told me he had a lady friend. I decided he was patient, gentle, and kind.

He ignored me. Never asked me a single question.

Cincinnati being Donald's hometown, he got off the truck after delivering our produce and I parked our truck in the same strip-mall next to the notorious bank lane. I killed thirty-six hours reading, walking, sleeping and never talked to a soul.

Rested and ready, dispatch sent us to Parkersburg, West Virginia. Finally, a new place. We drove east across Ohio, I-71 to US-35, and then on US-50. Ohio, at least from the roadside, looked entirely squared off. Divided colors of things growing or done growing. Nothing wild. Finally, on US-50, we got to rural terrain. Trees, small towns, the up down of rolling hills like ocean swells. At the border into West Virginia, we reached the foot of the Appalachians, and Parkersburg. We drove up beside a fireman polishing his fire engine.

Donald hollered out the window. "Can you recommend a motel for us? We don't load till the morning." A lot of words for Donald to speak all at once.

"I'd let you stay in the firehouse if I could, but it's against the rules."

"Oh no, that's okay." Donald put the truck in third gear, inched forward.

"You can stay at the Salvation Army, though. They don't charge anything and they're clean."

"We can pay for a room. Any suggestions?"

"Well, motel row is that way," He pointed with the rag in his hand. "You can't miss them. I've never stayed in any of them myself, so I can't say which one."

We turned left, and headed down an old narrow street. Cobblestones would have blended right in. An old brick building engraved and dated in the late 1800s. We stopped for a woman controlling the cross walk. About sixty, she wore a navy blue uniform with white armbands, cap, and a silver badge. Crisp, starched, back straight, and specific with her stop sign, she waved the grammar school children across the street, marched to the sidewalk, turned on a dime, and waved us through.

I showered in Donald's room, while he waited in the truck. When we traded places, Donald said, "Be ready by 6:00." I said, "Good night."

No refrigeration motor roaring behind me, I slept like a rock.

In the morning, we were loaded from floor to ceiling with plastic containers due in Phoenix, Arizona. Food-storage, wastebaskets, cutlery, plates, sandwich bags. I started my turn driving and barely felt the weight pulling on my throttle.

We drove down I-74, cut over to I-64 and headed south on I-65 to the Nashville Terminal. Steamy hot outside. Cool in our air conditioning. Green colors, tinged with orange. Soon, the whole countryside would be in flames of color, but I'd be home by then, dealing with the DUI.

From Nashville we took I-40 west. Oklahoma had flocks of birds. Little black guys and graceful big white ones. New Mexico's sunset looked more like a water color, all smudged together instead of the crystal clear airbrush I expected. And rabbits, everywhere in New Mexico. Seemed like I'd see more road kills, but the rabbits must have learned about *hrududil,* the cars in Richard Adams' *Watership Down.*

The sunrise in Arizona was large. Really, the change in colors stopped my breath. I actually gasped. The changes of landscape, like a slow motion color wheel moving in the orange and red range. Browns and yellows on the edges. Shadows of gray-brown morphing into burnt orange. Then rock-orange-red. And then a clay-red when the sun hit the
160

rocks directly. All bathed in a brilliant blue that went on forever. People here might think these colors and this sky were no big deal, but I'd lived in year-around green trees and under a coastal fog. Jaw dropping. That's how I'd describe an Arizona sunrise.

The rocks in Arizona blew my mind too. For miles and miles, balanced on top of each other, they created artistic formations. With the slightest imagination, a boulder became an elephant, a cliff turned into a guarded fortress, sentries posted along the rock-face, guns pointed.
Downhill on I-17 South, with only a load of plastics behind me, the truck handled more like a car. I-17 didn't have warning signs about curves, or posted grades, but Bob had warned me, and Donald spoke more than a few words. "Just because we have a light load, don't take this stretch for granted. Stay easy on the brakes."

I thought about coming back someday, and hiking in these canyons, photographing these colors. Scorpions? Tarantulas? Maybe just day hikes, or with a tent. And a partner.

"Tommy England, got your ears on?" I called to the truck ahead of me. "Tommy England, your brakes are smoking. Do you copy?" Nothing. Not even static.

Donald leaned over and flipped on the CB. The squelch static burst into the cab, loud, and both of us jerked back in surprise. I had turned the squelch knob instead of the on/off knob. Donald adjusted the squelch. "That's not smoke. That's exhaust." He stated.

"Oh. Looked like it was coming off the tire to me."

"It's not."

All through the trip, I kept embarrassing myself in front of Donald. "There's a place resting up ahead ... Want to stop? ... I'm my favorite terminal ... When we get to Phoenix, I want my Dad." He never laughed at my screwed-up words, just sat there looking straight ahead. That evening, in the parking lot of the Fandango Club in Phoenix, I spilled my overnight case out all over the passenger floor and down into the parking lot. My toothpaste bounced under the cab and I had to crawl under there to retrieve it from behind the tire. I got grease on my face, after itching my nose, which I didn't know about until late afternoon the following day.

Donald liked to hang out at the Fandango Club, a huge trucker's bar with live bands seven nights a week. I stayed in the sleeper and read. Suddenly, light filled the cab when Donald opened the door. I heard him grab the tire thumper from behind the driver's seat, and then saw his false teeth after he laid them on the doghouse. He slammed the door shut, and I leaned forward to get a good look at the teeth.

"Pay up, you son of a bitch." I heard him yell.

"I don't owe you a God damn thing."

"I'm gonna beat it out a you."

"Whoa there. Back off." A third voice. They were all yelling at once just feet from the truck. I heard more voices. Donald threatened to bash the guy's head in. Scuffling sounds.

"Pay up." I heard a voice say. Milling sounds. Grunting. A few minutes later Donald shoved the tire thumper back behind the driver's seat, jumped in the truck and put his teeth back in.

"What was that all about?" I climbed into the jump seat.

"I beat him at pool and he wasn't going to pay me."

"Uh, the false teeth really surprised me, Donald. You're so young."

"I got the shit kicked out of me a lot when I was young."

"In high school?"

"Quit when I was in the 10th grade. Niggers kept beatin' me up."

Donald burped. "One time I spent two days in the hospital 'cause niggers got me." The smell of beer reached my nose.

Had he said fuckers, or cock-suckers, I couldn't have cared less. But the N word. I felt my lip curl.

"Some white gang had just cut up a nigger and I just happened to be the first white guy around for this nigger gang to take revenge on."

"That sounds awful. Glad you made it out alive."

"Oh, that happened all the time. I've been in jail about thirty times."

"My God. How old are you?"

"Forty. No, forty-one. Fighting's just something to do, that's all."

I moved my sleeping bag out on the jump seat. He crawled into the sleeper and snapped the curtain shut. "Good night, Donald."

Donald didn't answer.

Moriarity, New Mexico

Mid-service

September 11, 1980

After six hours deadheading to Los Angeles, we loaded beans and bell peppers for a return trip to Houston, which would take us onto I-10. I backed into both produce docks, slowly, without a problem, and thanked Donald for the opportunity. At two miles per hour in reverse gear, inches or feet between me and two other semis, succeeding felt a whole lot better than serving clam chowder to dinner guests or balancing the boss's checkbook. I liked this job. The loading docks in California were huge compared to the older docks on the east coast. I wondered when I'd get the chance to try my skill at jack-knifing the trailer into the Kroger's dock in Cincinnati or Columbus.

Out in the middle of Arizona, Donald told me he'd be quitting Tanksley. He'd landed a new job driving in Cincinnati. He'd be home every night and paid for all his time in the truck. Nine dollars per hour.

"That's great!" I didn't try to turn his announcement into a conversation.

With Tanksley, I'd made about twenty-five cents an hour considering all the deadheading and waiting. I'd never figured my hourly rate if I only counted my time driving.

At the terminal in Moriarty, New Mexico, the truck was scheduled for a mid-service. Tanksley had reserved a hotel room for us. The engine's routine maintenance would be performed by the night mechanic.

To expose the engine, the entire cab is pulled up about sixty degrees. I couldn't use the sleeper. I forgot my sleeping bag, followed Donald into the motel room, and slept with him.

A forty-one-year-old man with a tenth grade education, who had

163

probably never read a book, and had false teeth. A fighter, a racist who didn't talk, and I wasn't even drunk.

Texas. Hard-core brown. Brown buildings, brown people, brown land, flat and forever. We even ate brown food in an All-You-Can-Eat steak house called the Iron Skillet, which was painted brown with dark brown trim. They sold brown leather vests and brown boots there too.

Neither of us spoke, except to order.

Using pallet jacks, we unloaded the beans and bell peppers ourselves, in silence, and made an extra twenty bucks each.

Immediately, we were dispatched to Cape Girardeau, Missouri, the company's home office. Still on I-10, after huge, brown, boring Texas, we entered Louisiana, a lush, textured, green view of swamps, trees, and lakes with bridges. A thick tangle of vines covered the trees on both sides of the freeway. An impenetrable wall of ivy leaned over the road and I could see cumulus clouds dotting the strip of blue canvas above us.

Up through Louisiana, on I-55, big white birds stood on cows. North of Tickfaw, big frogs carpeted the rest stop. Maybe they were toads, but not a single amphibian bothered to jump out of my way. I didn't see a single flattened frog. Were they migrating?

Back on the road, cotton crops mostly dominated both sides. But for other crops, why in the hell would farmers dot their fields with oil drums full of fire? Certainly nothing needed to be hotter. Must be a ton of insects out there. Our windshield sure supported that theory. I could hardly see through the yellow goo. And heat plus humidity must release something from plants because Louisiana smelled solid, like sticking my nose in the oven to check on a pumpkin pie.

We drove across Arkansas, which looked like middle America next to the exotic extreme of Louisiana. Louisiana felt like a movie set. Arkansas, a repetitive job. Like filing contract after contract alphabetically in creamy manila envelopes, Arkansas rolled us along field after field of fenced blonde rectangles. Green, often. Hot, always. Better roads too, but dog-and-cat kind of people lived here. They didn't live with alligators and armadillos roaming their back yards.

In Cape Girardeau, we picked up a dry box, a trailer hanging out two feet beyond the rear axles. With no refrigeration unit, the front end butted

164

up closer to our cab. Full of Levis and triple sealed, Donald wouldn't get home now since we were headed for San Francisco.

I didn't understand why Donald didn't get off the truck to start his new job. Maybe he had lied about it. I thought maybe since I had slept with him he'd changed his mind. Maybe the job didn't start for another month. Maybe he'd requested that mid-service in Moriarty. He'd planned the whole motel thing. No, he wasn't that smart. And I could have rented my own room.

In West Memphis, we finally stopped to clean up at the 76 truck stop. The counter person charged me two fifty to use the shower, and I waited for an hour before finally knocking on the bathroom door. Seven women, besides me, waited. Prostitutes. Could have been sisters they looked so much alike. Skinny and malnourished. Gaunt skin. Rats' nests for hair. Jewelry. Every one of them wore black. The pressure to conform prevalent even amongst whores. About the same age, same height, I outweighed each of them by twenty pounds. Dressed in my work boots, baggy jeans and a man's plaid shirt, I could smell their drugstore perfume through my own sweat. I moved in and out of the entry, because standing so close in the alcove felt like invading their space. I wondered how much they got paid for their services.

I'd had enough of waiting, when the girl in the bathroom slipped out, and I saw her let one of the other seven in the shower. I complained to the 76 attendant who said, "You're the one with the key. Just go in there and kick her out."

I did. She climbed out of the shower and started dressing by the bathroom sink. Smeared with dirt, the tiled walls in the bathroom looked like my dog had jumped all over them after rolling in mud. The shower tiles were the same, only wet, and the dirt ran down the sides like brown finger painting. Hair covered the shower's drain like a thick patty-cake, and after saturating my flip-flops, water seeped between my toes. I stuck my big toe in the mess, pushed it off the drain, and the gray water barely circled down the pipe. I had to touch the faucets, but tried to suck my body in close, away from the walls.

I kept talking to the girl while I showered, asking questions, so I could tell if she came near my stuff. In minutes, I stepped out, grabbed my towel, and as I dried off, she let another whore in the bathroom. I told that girl I'd have the rest of my shower in private. Thank God she left, as I had no back-up plan. So grateful for my work boots, I dropped my flip-flops in the garbage on the way out.

Because I didn't feel like being the bouncer of the 76 bathroom shower, I let the girl back in, but then the 76 attendant wouldn't return my key deposit because someone was in the shower. I made that poor girl put on her clothes and get out.

So I could keep my two dollars and fifty cents.

On this trip out west, New Mexico had huge dandelions in bloom all along the highway, and clump after clump of purple flowers. Good-looking horses too. New Mexico's sunsets were picture postcards, like Motel 6 artwork. I could easily see a few cowboys coming through the tumbleweeds, shooting their pistols back at the posse behind them.

Donald didn't want to deliver in San Francisco because "queers lived there."

I rolled my eyes and kept my mouth shut, but decided not to make another round trip with him. I'd had enough of Donald.

With convincing urgency, I called Tanksley explaining my fake emergency. My brother had been in a wreck. He needed me to live with him for a few months until he got back on his feet. "He can't drive. He can't cook." I explained. "He gets the casts off around Christmas."

Dispatch promised to re-hire me in January if I chose to return. I assured them I'd be back.

Stopping For Red Lights
Car camping

September 1980
Eureka, California

Trusty Rambler packed, I set off for home on a Saturday night. I reached the small town of Willits around 10:00 p.m. Highway 101 becomes Main Street in Willits with a speed limit of 25 mph. That night, I hit every red light in town. People spilled out of bars and live music floated into the street.

I had nowhere to sleep when I got home, and wouldn't be able to drink at the Vista Del Mar. I knew I'd run into people who would peg me, like I was wearing sandwich boards that said, "I went crazy. I have no friends. Look at me ... I sleep in my car." And I'd have to pretend I didn't care.

I decided to join Willits' festivities and have a last beer. Maybe I'd dance a bit too, celebrate my courageous three months on the road. I parked in a lot behind the sign advertising a live band, went in and plunked my dollar on the bar, asking for a Bud Light.

The ten people inside were shitty drunk. The floor stuck to my boots. A couple hung on each other pretending to dance. I watched the couple and ordered another beer. Then, coming out of the men's bathroom, a filthy, stumbling drunk approached me, and I remembered the fat, drunk pig who raped me in Hawaii. I high-tailed it back to my car, where I locked the doors and slept for an hour before getting back on the road.

I arrived in Eureka around 3:00 a.m. My house rented, I had no options for a place to stay. Bobby rented a small studio above the Art Center,

167

where he lived in his clutter, sleeping there even though it wasn't allowed. My Mom's home, a gorgeous architectural dream overlooking the ocean in Trinidad, entirely designed and built with no inside walls, lacked even a modicum of privacy. Ben used the loft, which could have served as an extra bedroom, as his studio. Even if they had offered, which they didn't, my high school memories of their snoring, which could drown out incoming airplanes, deterred me completely. Besides, I hadn't even told anyone I would be home, much less arriving in the wee hours.

I parked just off Wabash Street, crawled in my sleeping bag, and tried to sleep. In the morning, I washed up at the Texaco.

Terry's cabin, maybe a hundred yards from his house, was a possibility. Wool Berber carpeting, speckled gray. Black slate under the wood stove, white walls and redwood trim, I might even meditate in his calming colors, considering the forest greens and browns outside.

An outdoor shower and a porta-potty. Floor to ceiling windows. The cabin had six feet of open space around it before redwood trees overwhelmed the view. Dense with ferns, huckleberry or red flowering current, I couldn't have penetrated the bushes out there, but a bear could, and I'd seen scat out in the field on the way to Terry's garden. Easily something wild, a raccoon, skunk, or deer could wander past the windows, two feet from the window seat where I could sit, warmed by a fire in his wood stove.

Terry didn't cut forty-five degree angles to fit the baseboard around his one dividing wall, but carved a piece of redwood, which fitted perfectly. With six walls shaped into a hexagon, maybe 300 square feet total, even a crazy person had to appreciate this oasis.

By contrast, my house totaled 600 square feet, had five rooms and a hall. Walls divided each room. 3x4 windows, none of which would open, looked like peep holes placed in the exact middle of each wall. Built in 1937, my house's ceiling reached to all of seven feet. The outside had chipped white paint on the original siding. Yellowed, cracked linoleum covered every floor. Still, the fact that I had even bought a house at age twenty-four (and female) counted for something. I planned to use my truck driving money to fix up the place. I hoped to rip out the ceiling first.

I figured I had a fifty-fifty chance Terry would let me stay in his little cabin. I'd promise not to bathe there so his well water wouldn't run low. I wouldn't use his propane, and I wouldn't use much wood to make fires. I'd ask only to stay on weekends, tell him my drive to Eureka for the Lucky Deuce commitment was too long to make daily, the gas would be too expensive.

"Of course you can," Terry cut off my flood of words. "Take as much wood as you need. Showers and propane are no big deal. Have at it."

I felt like a little kid who had asked for an allowance knowing I hadn't made my bed. I felt grateful for such comfortable digs, but thoroughly diminished. Any which way to Sunday, no matter how much money I eked out of my job, I'd never design, much less produce an artistic, comfortable home out of my house.

"Try not to bend these branches," Terry edged around them as I followed him into the woods with my suitcase. "I don't want the trail to be visible from the house." I liked the idea of his cabin staying hidden too.

On the weekends, I slept at Terry's, and hung out at Mom's during the day. On sunny afternoons, I stared out at Trinidad Harbor watching captains steer their dingys from the dock to their fishing boats and back. Whales spouted, sea lions barked. Before the sun set, its brilliance coming straight at me, I'd watch the sparkles of light if the water was choppy, or a sheen of polished glass if the bay was calm. Trinidad Head, the rocky promontory sheltering the bay, would flatten into a silhouette backed with purple twilight. By then, we'd all put on sweatshirts. Mom and Ben would pour more Vodka, I'd get another Diet Coke. We'd watch the fishing boats bobbing in the swells, their anchor lights twinkling.

Other nights though, we'd see the fog bank rolling in, blotting out first, the horizon, then Trinidad Head, the fishing boats and their lights, and finally, engulfing us in wet, bone-cold gray. We'd have our sweatshirts on before three o'clock, even if the sun had been out. Seemed like wind waited till November that year.

Saturdays or Sundays, Mom puttered in her rose garden, and Ben worked in the potting shed. They'd manicure their bonsai maples, water the pots on the deck, and because it was September, Mom's famous blue

169

lobelia got hauled to the compost, one dying plant at a time. Theirs was a look-don't-touch house, a work of art.

I walked on the beaches, napped, and read.

During the week, I stayed in town. To expunge my DUI charge, the court required I attend three Lucky Deuce meetings, which I took to calling my "second chance assignment." The court also required me to attend three Alcoholics Anonymous meetings each week for twelve weeks. Signed by the meetings' secretaries, my *'second chance'* card would prove to the judge I'd completed the program. In January, my driver's license would be wiped clean of all evidence that I'd ever been a drunk driver.

I met Louise. She organized us, as a kind of an unpaid director of Lucky Deuce meetings. With two DUI's, she had an eighteen-month obligation. She managed newcomers, passed out packets of information, and in general, positioned herself as our warm and friendly greeter. She found out that I was sleeping in my car and offered me a room in her house. First, though, she had to get her three housemates to approve, but she thought they wouldn't mind getting a cut on the rent.

Turned out her boyfriend, Matthew, didn't like me —I had no idea why— and her housemates thought the house was too crowded already. Louise persisted, "only two nights a week ... strictly temporary," and they finally relented. I could sleep in the little alcove off the kitchen as long as I didn't hang out there or use the kitchen. They didn't want any rent.

That left just three nights each week to sleep in my car.

I picked all sorts of places to park. Behind Winship Junior High School, a policeman woke me around midnight and told me to move on. Same with the Safeway parking lot. Montgomery Wards, ditto. Quiet streets in quiet neighborhoods proved the best place to sleep undisturbed. Just not under a streetlight. Wake at the crack of dawn. Use the gas station out by Pierson's first thing in the morning. Warm up eating breakfast at Denny's.

Hospitals had the best public restrooms.

While lying in the back seat of my Rambler, in the town where I'd grown up, I imagined the friends I once had enjoying barbeques with each other, laughing and watching TV. I doubted I'd ever even had friends, because not a single person called me after Aaron and I separated. I'd walked into bars like the Vista, or the Vance, even the Ritz, alone. Like it was normal. Now, sober, I couldn't go to the movies because I was afraid of being seen alone.

I couldn't stretch out my legs in the Rambler. If I faced the back, my butt hung over the edge of the seat. I could manage almost twenty minutes on my back, with my legs up. Mostly, I stared at the back of the front seat.

Not drinking, I had no place to go. The library closed at eight. The hospital's receptionist asked me to leave the waiting room. In my car, I stewed over my life —in my own juices— as Mom would say.

Between bouts of feeling like a pathetic, homeless, friendless loser, I'd kick into planning speeches as the *uniquely destined woman* who rose above hardship. I'd write my best-selling truck-driving memoir and go on tour promoting my book. Everyone would marvel at my boldness, my creativity, my insight. People who went crazy had potential for greatness. I could harness my spunk, make something of myself, show everyone.

But I couldn't go to the movies, or a concert, or a play by myself. I hung out after dark in my Rambler, with no radio, and afraid to use a flashlight for fear of being caught and asked to move on. Worse, I could be attacked. They'd break my windshield and then what would I do? My mind spun like a top. I imagined pulling my own string so hard I'd jump the curb into traffic, get hit, and all this would finally be over. A sweet release.

Going to sleep took forever. I'd be startled awake, having dreamed of spiders. Being alone in my hometown hurt my gut. I wanted to leave.

I went to my "second chance" meetings and soon after, started going to the Alcoholics Anonymous meetings. In my very first meeting I recognized Barbara, an acquaintance of my mother's, sitting at the table. I felt my way through the cigarette smoke to the least likely place Barbara would look, behind her, in back of a large man, and hoped I hadn't been caught. Smoke hung above the single long table where most everyone sat, but loners, like myself, and the big man, occupied the chairs near the walls. At the table, people visited in low voices, and an occasional burst of laughter erupted from a few clusters.

Most of the thirty people shared during the meeting, and after the hour, I walked out the door absolutely stunned. They talked about stuff I had never imagined people would openly share. Seven people (I counted) mentioned thoughts of suicide. But the weird part, suicide just got funnier. Even I laughed a little.

One man had actually pointed a shotgun at his head. He was afraid of missing, and having to live with his face shot off. He couldn't manage a sure-fire aim unless he pulled the trigger using his toe, and he couldn't get his toe just right without tipping the barrel off to the side. He gave up and tried AA instead. The group howled at his story. The next person said he wouldn't even try to top that.

My meager attempt at suicide seemed so tame, but swallowing those pills in that hotel room didn't strike me as the least bit funny, and I couldn't imagine telling a room full of people what I'd done.

I didn't see a single person staring at the floor, trying to disappear. They were looking at each other, even smiling. Then a woman mentioned the gravity of the subject, the dark depression that lead to attempting suicide, how many of us don't make it into these rooms, but succeed, and are no longer walking around on the planet. I could feel the energy in the room shift from light to dark. My energy dropped too, as I remembered the pain I'd felt, the hope that I would die.

I didn't drink near as much as Bobby or my mother or Ben. I'd never passed out in the gutter. I owned a house, was saving money, kept my promises. Fear didn't run my life. I wasn't a flake. Mostly, I had already recovered from this supposed "bottom" everyone in AA talked about. I knew I didn't belong in AA. I wasn't an alcoholic.

And these people thought they'd been insane! How could I possibly relate to people who considered being hung over, puking, and throwing up as insanity?

But I liked going to meetings and listening to people talk. Women spoke about waking up in strange beds, not knowing the name of who was beside them. At least I'd always known the man's name. I felt such relief hearing what I'd done come out of other women's mouths, but all the laughing jarred me completely, threw me off balance. I'd leave the meetings emotionally confused.

My longing to befriend these people grew. They appeared so connected to each other. I imagined them having barbeques too, and I wanted to be invited. I wanted a friend to go with me on walks. I wanted to talk about my truck driving and how I was writing a book.

I didn't dare tell them I'd gone crazy. If they knew how little I used to drink, they'd know I wasn't an alcoholic. They'd send me to a group for crazies, like at Beverly Manor.

I couldn't talk about much, because my family, especially my mother, didn't need anyone to know how much she drank. Her elephants and skeletons had to remain secrets. If I talked, my behavior would reflect on her mothering, like I was saying it was her fault I was so fucked up. I never volunteered to share, and if the chair called on me, I'd pass.

Hey, I don't drink that much, but my mother's a drunk. By the way, no one likes me and I don't know why. And I went crazy too.

I'd heard volumes on the absurdity of adults blaming their parents for their own poor choices. Being raised by an alcoholic might be an interesting aside, but I could hardly blame my mother for my predicament. Besides, for being drunk every night of her life, she sure had plenty of people who loved her. She held a good job and never missed work. Who was I to cut her down in an AA meeting? And really, why would I blow the whistle on her when my mother was the one friend I had?

The Sapphire
AA

October 1980
Eureka, California

The AA chairperson picked self pity as the evening's topic. This one lady said, "I was going to have a big pity party and invite all my friends, but *she* couldn't come!" The whole place busted up. I hollered too. I'd never laughed about not having a friend before. It certainly hadn't occurred to me that having no friends might be funny. But here we all were laughing our heads off. And I hadn't thought of self pity as something I had any choice about, either.

That lady was one of those kind my mother called *goodie goodie two shoes*. While she actually wore a sweatshirt, I pictured her wearing a huge round white collar with a lavish satin bow flopping down to her waist. At every meeting she'd start off by telling the newcomer, "We're going to love you till you can love yourself." Gag me with a spoon.

All different kinds of people showed up at meetings. A few men wore white shirts and ties under dark suits, or they hung tailored herringbone jackets on their chair backs. But most men wore t-shirts and some of those shirts had holes and were filthy. The older men arrived clean, wearing cardigan sweaters and pants that sagged in the behind. Shoes ranged from dress to biker to cowboy to tennis shoes, some without socks. Lots of ball caps, long hair and beards.

Women wore short skirts and spike heels or thrift store pants and work boots like mine. Painted faces or no make-up. Beautician smocks, nursing scrubs, polyester from J.C. Penny's, or dry-clean only.

I guessed most everyone at meetings had at least ten years on me. At each meeting, I'd see two or three women and maybe one man
174

under thirty. I'd wind myself up holding my breath, thinking, what can I possibly say? I wanted to tell them to make lemonade out of their lemons, for God's sake. They seemed so stuck. I figured I had it easier than all of them because I had the intelligence to problem solve. *Try going off on an adventure. Take a risk.*

One night, Bob, a real self-appointed AA preacher, threw out, "You can't be too dumb for AA, but you can be too smart." Seemed like everyone mumbled in agreement. I felt he was directing his words at me. My face tingled and felt hot while all the heads nodded, like they didn't care or didn't even recognize that Bob was a know-it-all.

At my eighth meeting, I finally spoke.

"I'm Margot. I'm an alcoholic, but..." I stammered. "Oh, I don't really think I'm an alcoholic. Compared to my family, I don't drink that much. I'm here because I got a DUI."

The whole room busted up laughing.

I had to laugh too when I thought about what I'd just said.

After that meeting Barbara, my mother's friend, approached me in the parking lot, practically racing me to my car.

"Margot, how are you? I'm glad you shared tonight."

"I'm fine Barbara, a little nervous. I had no idea people were going to laugh."

"We related to what you said. None of us wants to think we're alcoholic. AA is the largest club that no one ever wanted to join."

I fake laughed.

"What did you think about the meeting?" The topic had been *worry*.

I put my hand on my chin. "My Mom drinks way more than I do. I worry someone will find out if I talk. I really can't share anything about my family or my problems. It's such a small town."

She nodded. "You don't have to talk about your family."

"Barbara, saying anything at all feels like I'm telling on my mother."

Barbara took a step back and crossed her arms against the cool breeze. "What about when Mary said 'worry is faith in a negative outcome?' What'd you think of that?"

"I'll have to think about that one." I shifted my weight to the other hip. "If I talk about my past, there could be quite a negative outcome."

I wondered if Barbara knew about me being crazy. I wondered if she realized the degree to which people I knew had avoided eye contact with me in parking lots and grocery stores.

"Here's one more that nobody said." Barbara stepped forward again and put her hand gently on my shoulder. "I've lived a long hard life, most of which has never come to pass." She paused a beat, took her hand off my shoulder, crossed her arms again. "Mark Twain said that."

"That's true too." Actually, I thought my hard life *had* come to pass, that maybe if I'd worried a little more, I might not have slept with Donald. I smiled back at Barbara as if she'd turned on the light bulb in my head. "Thank you, Barbara." I wanted this conversation to end.

"Try not to worry about all that might happen, Margot. Try to give this a shot."

"Okay. Thanks, Barbara." Back in my Rambler, I could smell my perspiration.

Hey all, I went crazy and took my clothes off at the Red Lion. I got locked up in an insane asylum for three months a couple years ago. It was a hoot. And I agreed to marry the coke head of Humboldt County three weeks after I met him. I was going to go through with it, because I said I would, rather than tell anyone that I'd fucked up. I would have too, except, at his bachelor party, he fractured his skull and I looked up at the stars and thanked God.

Great! Come on over after the meeting. We're having a barbeque!

At the very next meeting, this other guy, Ed, said somewhere in his endless diatribe "Denial: It means, Don't Even Notice I Am Lying."

I wasn't in denial. If anything, I battled a hyper-awareness of what my life was like, of every decision I made and why I made my choices. And I didn't lie.

The topic had been "honesty." Laughter abounded when a man covered in dirt said, "You can tell an alcoholic but you can't tell 'em much." He'd just talked about his "cash register" honesty, how he'd spent days in the gutter being proud about refusing to steal even though he was hungry, and all the time grinning from ear to ear saying "everything is just fine, couldn't be better."

I was attending meetings, staying for the whole sixty minutes and getting my Lucky Deuce card signed. At Lucky Deuce, a few guys were in the corner blatantly signing each other's cards. They treated this program like a farce. I was doing the deal, showing up, staying sober, being responsible, and fulfilling my obligation.

I'd bang around in my head after the meetings. Letting AA people have their beliefs, knowing I didn't have the same situation, but truly enjoying their stories. I started going to a fourth meeting each week. Partly because I didn't have much else to do, and partly because of all these cool quotes being tossed around.

Always remember you are absolutely unique. Just like everyone else. I loved when the whole room laughed. Margaret Mead said that.

If you really do put a small value on yourself, rest assured, the world will not raise your price. That one bothered me as I settled in for the night on a dark street over behind the Eureka Mall. I was smart, capable. I'd kept my price high. But in my sleeping bag on the back seat of my car, with my high price, I started to cry. Confusion I couldn't anesthetize roiled around in my head. Did I have a high price or a low price? Did sleeping around mean I had a low price? Was this just another quote somebody tossed into the room or was this an official AA recovery slogan?

Louise talked me into attending a women's meeting she was responsible for leading. A man-bashing meeting. God, they complained. I'd never understood why women blamed men for holding them back. Afterward, I helped Louise clean up the coffee stuff and wipe the tables down, even though I didn't drink coffee. And I didn't leave my ashes all over the table either, like the woman who dramatically leaned back and exhaled her smoke the whole meeting.

"So have you done the steps?" I asked her.

"Yeah. You?"

"I've read them. What else do you do?"

"You're supposed to tell someone everything you've done wrong."

"I don't know if I've done anything wrong."

"You start by telling the person everything that makes you mad, everyone you resent."

"I don't resent anyone." I wrung out my dishtowel and hung it on the

177

rack. "And I don't owe anyone an apology."

"I didn't have too much to do either." Louise emptied the last wastebasket. "Some people have more work to do. Lower bottoms, you know. They've done worse things. Some of *those* people, they make their whole lives about AA. I think it's like AA becomes their crutch, just like alcohol."

"Yeah, I think so too." I started down the steps ahead of Louise and as she was locking the door, I waved. "See you."

She went off to meet Matt. I slept in the little alcove off her kitchen, got up early and left before her roommates would find me.

My story was nothing compared to those folks in AA meetings. Homeless by the highway, prison, kids taken away, winding up in the hospital's ICU. And nobody talked about a family like mine either. Not even the suits.

Who amongst them had a father who owned a V-tailed plane — a Bonanza — and flew his family to Mexico? With maybe five mansions in Eureka, did anyone sitting in these chairs grow up in one of the other four? Or at least the biggest house in their hometown? What would Mr. Ditch Digger think if I talked about my bedroom being on the third floor, not the fourth, in a house with six bathrooms, a walk-in freezer, a wine cellar and a swimming pool? What if I told this crowd I grew up with a live-in maid and that we had negro butlers serve hors d'oeuvres at our Christmas parties?

My family. I pictured an image of my three brothers and me in a circle. A hug, a kiss, an award, maybe a compliment placed in the middle. The gun would go off, and we'd scrabble and fight to get to the goods. Could that count as hard knocks?

In my third week home, a small miracle happened. The woman who had rented my house wanted out of her six-month lease. Suzanne apologized profusely, but having lived in Southern California her whole life, she couldn't handle the weather, the small town, and being away from her family and friends. I assured her that I understood, gratefully returned her deposit, and moved home the week before Halloween.

I mowed the lawn, washed the windows, vacuumed, dusted, and slept in clean sheets. What a gift. A bed.

My bedroom had built-in drawers that I'd reserved for my own stuff. Unpacking my dishes, working down to the old sweatshirts, I hung up the few nice shirts I hadn't taken with me, and unpacked my towels. One drawer, packed to the brim, held my yellow writing pads and journals, and wrapped in Kleenex I found the little figurines I'd had since ... well, one was given to me when I was born. An angel. Three angels altogether, an old man, a little black elephant, and eight milk white horses, brought home from a trip to China Town in San Francisco when I was maybe eight or nine.

I had yearbooks from high school, a big cheerleading letter with a megaphone running through it, athletic patches from junior high, and record albums. Maybe twenty albums. All of Peter, Paul and Mary, most of Donavan, some Dylan, The Beatles, Joni Mitchell, Carole King.

My record player was packed in the fourth drawer, under all the underwear, socks, slips, bras, and tank tops I'd left behind. I'd wanted desperately to play my music again, and wondered if I shouldn't just toss these ratty looking underthings as I dug down to my turntable. I held a handful of mismatched socks and was pushing myself up off the floor when I noticed something sparkle, or flash, from the right edge of the drawer, from where I'd just grabbed the socks.

I looked closer. Nothing. Did the sun hit a button? I threw the socks in the trash, got back down on my knees and pulled out my record player. As the cords trailed out of the drawer, upturning my tank tops, I saw the flash again. I picked up the little round blue object, held it to the light, and marveled at the perfect star in the very same sapphire I'd lost three and a half years ago.

Stunned, my memories flowered out in all directions. The hospital, the suicide, sleeping in my car. New Mexico's sky. Robbery in a Chicago ghetto, Albert in Indianapolis, Monte in L.A. Across the room, little angels from childhood, high school memorabilia. What had I been doing for the last ten years? College. Marriage. I couldn't see one fucking clue in this pile of my life that suggested someone precious had lived here. Someone loved. Just achievements and store-bought stuff I'd saved for and bought myself. No scrapbook of memories. No birthday cards, gifts, or thank-you notes.

I stared at the stone, closed my fingers around it, and determined at that moment to live fully, for the rest of my life, whoever I would become.

Inebriated Merriment

Twice a year

November, 1980
Eureka, California

The world breaks everyone and, afterword, some are stronger in the broken places. Ernest Hemingway. I walked out of that AA meeting feeling an aura around my head. After Miriam quoted Hemingway, I smiled at people in the meeting, looked them in the eye. I'd gone crazy and survived. Wanting to marry Jeff seemed more like a foolish girl's solution to relieve loneliness. Leaving town on an adventure, driving eighteen-wheelers, writing a book, I was stronger in my broken places. And I had my sapphire back.

November sailed by. I watched my six-inch TV, read mysteries from the library, participated in my "second chance" and AA meetings.

I started talking in meetings about my loneliness. I told those people about my night on the top of Fickle Hill, the poem I wrote. I could now see the poem for what it was. Self-pity. Now, I had a way out of that hole I'd dug for myself, thanks to AA. I had the way out they talked about, and I could protect myself from falling again.

I didn't want to walk down to the Vista, slap my quarter on the bar for a draft beer, and shoot the shit. I wanted to hear the stories at AA meetings.

If you won't risk anything, you risk even more. Erica Jong. I'd offer up that quote anytime someone mentioned risk. "What have you got to lose? How will you feel if you don't try it? What's the worst that can happen?"

During the week, I ate lunch with the workers at Mom's office. We'd talk about my trucking adventures, but I'd also throw out the euphuisms

I kept hearing. *The most you can do is also the least you can do.* Sam and John and Charlene would engage me with questions about AA. I'd ask about Charlene's daughters, admire John's hothouse tomatoes and offer to help weed his garden.

Peacefulness washed over me. I felt calm.

Since I'd turned nineteen, I'd never contacted Mom after five o'clock, except for Thanksgiving and Christmas. Friend though she was during daylight, after five, vodka took her away. Repetitive, slurred sentences, and her blackouts had been my memory for years, and when I married Aaron I never called or visited her in the evening. She never complained.

But social convention required the family to celebrate Thanksgiving, and we did. We all joined for dinner in the beautiful Trinidad home. Ben barbequed turkey. Mom cooked frozen lima beans. Cranberry sauce came out of the can.

Bobbie brought Ellie. He hardly left the liquor cabinet and practically guzzled the free booze. Ellie only visited a few times each year, and she and my mother started the evening on the deck, catching up on all things wise and wonderful. Terry sipped wine and kept Ben company out on the back porch. Terry and Ben's laughter met with Mom's exclamations over Ellie's junior college successes.

I joined Mom and Ellie, watched Bobby refill his glass, and sipped my Diet Coke. The sun sent a beam across the water. The air chilled. Ben's laughter came in spurts. Ellie loved her history class. Bobby interrupted Ellie to announce the sun was setting. More laughter from Terry and Ben. Ellie and I talked about her writing class, my poetry, my trucking, and how she loved being back in school. Mom went in to water her stuffing.

The stuffing had spread into a kind of mush with nuts. Mom had added water, for hours, while we waited for the turkey's temperature to come up. Just another half hour for the turkey to cool on the counter, and Mom boiled water for her beans.

Nine p.m. rolled by before Ben finally lit the traditional thirty-inch candles, and Mom needed help spooning stuffing and beans onto plates. "Go sit down, Mom, I'll do this." Terry rescued our dinner.

She sat with her thirtieth vodka, head nodding a bit, asking Ben to start the Harry Bellefonte record over again before he sat down. Bobby, at her side, his hand on hers, "Ellie is the smartes' wom'n there is ... and she knocks that junr college flat." His head drops some, and he doesn't hear Mom or see her nod. "All her 'fessrs love 'er." Bobby didn't eat but a bite or two.

White wine with dry turkey, lima beans, cranberry sauce, and a ball of brown goo. I loaded up on the cranberries, skipped the beans and stuffing, poured out my wine and filled the glass with water. No one noticed. Cheers around. All glasses clinked.

More watching and less participating, I went home early. I hadn't even wanted a drink. My Mom looked obnoxious.

On December 1st, I turned twenty-nine. No friends, phone calls, or presents. Well, Mom called me and wished me a happy birthday. I watched TV.

Besides "don't drink," AA kept another message constantly running through the meetings: be kind, do something for someone else, try giving instead of taking. I shopped for, and found, the best Christmas presents. Wrapped each one in multiple colors of tissue paper. Decorated a tree. Made cookies. Watched with pleasure when Bobby opened his huge colored pencil set, when Terry opened his wind instrument from Peru.

Mom gave me a long flannel nightgown. She'd never slept in a sleeping bag. Terry gave me a Heart Beats tape. I got a cartoon woman driving a truck to tape up in the sleeper from Bobby. I got one of his good hugs too, because of the eggnog. I loved the cartoon woman in her truck, arm out the window, hair flying. I didn't take it with me, but kept it safe, tucked away in my bottom drawer for when this stage of my life became a precious memory.

On New Year's Eve, I went to bed early. The following week I completed the paperwork for my DUI, saw the judge and closed that chapter, believing I wouldn't drink again. I rented my house to Louise and Matt. Dispatch welcomed me back to work, asking if I had any requests regarding a partner.

"Someone clean," came off the top of my head, which seemed like a safe bet, but turned out to be the exact opposite.

Mike, Partner #4

Los Banos, California

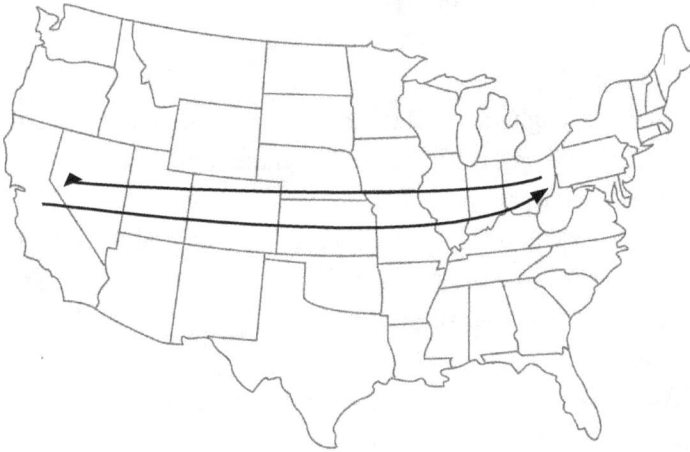

January 28, 1981
I-80 to Cincinnati

At 5'4, I stood two inches taller than Mike, except when he had his hat on, which was all the time. A big 10-gallon John Wayne cowboy hat. The huge belt buckle, high-heeled cowboy boots, jeans, red, white, and blue plaid, the caricature I'd seen in movies, and now I got to ride with him.

Orderly, spotless, manicured, stocky, chiseled. I'd call him handsome, in a cherub kind of way, but his loud, demanding, voice trumped all appearances. He talked non-stop.

I got the clean partner I had requested. But Mike went beyond clean. Two kinds of spray cleaner, one for the seats and one for the inside of the windows. After use, I had to leverage my body weight in order to jam the spray cans between the doghouse and the jump seat. Bracing them with a towel on the floor, no way. That would make Mike's face screw into a bunch of lines, like parenthesis, with a pound sign on his forehead.

After loading bell peppers and tomatoes, even before we docked for our third pick up in Central California —lettuce—I'd sucked up more than I thought possible.

We headed for Cincinnati.

"Clean that." He yelled over the engine noise and pointed to the middle of the windshield.

I squinted to find the spot.

"Now!"

"I can't see it."

"Right there. Right there." He stood up from the driver's seat, no easy feat, and put his finger up to the middle of the windshield.

I sprayed and cleaned.

When we left the truck, we put everything in its place. We wiped the truck sterile when we returned. Before, during, and after, Mike talked.

"How do you like your steak cooked?

"Medium."

"I like mine rare with the blood dripping off and if the meat was slaughtered just the day before, that's when it's the best. Ever seen a steer slaughtered? I have. They do it real humane these days. Steer never feels a thing, but it sure smells in that slaughterhouse. I'd never work in a slaughterhouse, but I've worked on a ranch and branded steer before. I held the front legs. You pull the front legs out straight and hold the rope. The steer squeals but it doesn't hurt, and then you have to let the ropes go at the same time as the back legs and that takes timing. What'd you do in, how do you say it? U-re..."

"U-ree-ka. I worked at an answering service."

"I branded those steers in Wyoming too. Worked in Colorado, but there's not much work after it starts snowing. Arizona gets cold too. So does New Mexico. I like Wyoming the best. I'm going to buy a ranch there. Have cattle. Get a four-wheeler and ride the fences.

"Colorado is great for hunting. Got me a 30-30. I want a 30-06. Didn't get one this year. A deer I mean. Come fall though, I'm going out till I get me a three pointer. Ever eat deer meat? It's kinda' tough, but if you pound it good it cuts nice. Blood rare doesn't taste as good, too strong. You gotta cook it longer. Give me beef steak any day. But

184

I'd cut up that deer meat, freeze it. You like deer meat? Margot! You like deer meat?

"No, not really."

Mike finally talked back to the CB. "Radio check."

"Good to go." A male voice answered.

"What's your 10-20?" Mike asked.

"The 101 yardstick."

"Handle?"

"I be Just Right. What do they call you?"

"Sweet Meat," Mike answers. "You be in that Portable Parking Lot up ahead?" I wondered if anyone else ever worried about that last car on a car carrier, like any moment the straps would break and the brand new Ford (in this case) would fly off in my face.

"I'm in The Big R. Going to the left coast. You in that Shirley Temple going east?" Which Big R, I thought. Orange Roadway trucks clotted the freeway. They ought to pay extra highway taxes. I saw "Big R's" even more than I saw us, "Shirley Temples."

"10-4. Got me a pretty little filly now."

Mike was a real stallion. I wondered if he might still be a virgin. God help me.

The voice in the CB started to crackle and fade. "Backin' out. See you on the flip flop."

"10-4. Copy that."

Less than a minute later. "Sweet Meat!" A new voice. "Still got those ears on?"

"You be comin' in loud and proud," Mike hollers over our engine.

"Shirley Temple, going east a mile back of you. Tell me about that little filly of yours."

The new voice was going east, worked for Tanksley. We'd see him at the terminal.

I got out my boom box and headphones. Hadn't used them much with Kent, and never bothered with Donald. The tape player ate tapes. The radio crackled too much. I put on my head phones, nodded my head in four-four time, and pretended to be absorbed in music that wasn't there.

West of Albuquerque, the cab heat went out. January is damn cold in New Mexico. In fifteen minutes my fingers and toes stiffened up. I tucked my hands in my armpits and bounced my feet. Mike called to the other Tanksley driver, "gettin' off the big slab."

"10-4."

"Copy that." Mike turned south, heading for the Tanksley terminal in Moriarity, New Mexico, to deal with our heater.

We warmed up in the truckers' lounge for two hours while the mechanic dealt with the problem. The water temperature was high, above 200 degrees. Finally, he dumped water in the radiator and the cab heat came back on.

Before we left, I got my coat and mittens out of second-seat's compartment. Mike didn't allow a loose coat in the cab, or in the sleeper, so I wore it and stuffed the mittens in my pocket.

Back on the highway, Mike had been driving upwards of twelve hours, albeit with the two-hour break in Moriarty. Grateful for the CB, I blotted out Mike's drone again with the headphones, and waited for my favorite view, always a surprise on I-40 going east.

Impressive during daylight but jaw dropping at night, at the top of a rise, the entire city of Albuquerque comes into view all at once, like looking down on the city from outer space. A purple sky at twilight, the city lights twinkled like a spray of sequins across the hips of a silky lavender gown. I tried to imagine breasts somewhere over the gulf, feet in Colorado. I loved New Mexico.

"We're eating now." Mike pulled into the ever-popular 76 station on I-40. "Put that boom box back in your compartment."

Thankful for my coat and mittens, I headed out to the bathroom. Mike ran to catch up, turned to face me and blocked my path. "What are you doing?"

"I'm going to the bathroom."

"You wait for me." Mike stuck his hands in his arm pits. "That's totally rude to not wait for me." He turned, blew into his hands, grasped the metal handle, and opened the restaurant door. We walked into the truck stop together, the warmth ... heaven. "Wait right here. We'll get a table together."

"I'm not eating here." Not stopping to talk, I turned toward the
186

restroom. He followed. I saw him push on the Mens' door.

I thought I was fast, but he was waiting outside the restroom.

"What do you mean, you're not eating here?"

"I've got food in the truck. I'm saving money. I'll eat my food in the truck."

"You can't do that. You'll get food everywhere. You have to eat in here, I locked the truck and I'm not going back out there."

"Give me the key, then."

"You can't go out there alone." I stood there and stared at him till he grunted a big displeasure and shouldered me out the door, like I was his girlfriend and we were having a bit of a tiff. He walked me to the truck, planted his feet, crossed his arms, and waited while I got out my granola and apple.

Back to the restaurant, his hand crept from my shoulder to the middle of my neck. I managed a twist and a shrug, so instead, he used his deserted hand to open the door for me, all smooth, like it was his idea.

The restaurant had no hot tea. I ordered milk, and poured it on top of my granola. Crunched my apple.

"Miss!" The waitress had her back to us. "Miss!" Mike said again. "We'd like to order our dinner now."

She arrived with the coffee pot. "We need more sugar, and I want cream for my coffee, not this caramel flavored stuff." He sifted the flavored cups through his fingers onto the table. She turned without saying a word.

"Miss!" Mike called again to her back. "We need to order now."

I spooned granola into my dry mouth.

"She shouldn't have left. She should have taken our order."

"But you wanted regular cream." I offered.

The waitress brought regular cream cups. Mike ordered a hamburger.

"These are the best hamburgers on I-40. The French fries are too greasy, but they're the only option ... Once I tried the potato salad, made 'em take it back so I wouldn't get that poisoning —

The waitress delivered Mike's hamburger and fries and left.

Trying to sell rotten stuff so they don't lose money. Lose customers, that's what'll happen, except they know they've got the best hamburgers, don't have to do anything else." He barely swallowed before he took another bite. "They had to make a bigger parking lot a few years back ... Everyone eats here ... At least the hamburger is fresh. Buns are too soggy. I tried to make them toast mine, but you just can't get good service anymore. Miss! More coffee!"

I finished my apple. Put the lid back on my Tupperware.

"Miss! We need our checks. Gotta get out there and make some money."

When she brought the checks, he said, "You married?" She waved a ring in front of his face. "That's too bad." He leered up at her. She turned her back. She looked so tired.

"Didn't even thank us, tell us to be safe." Mike didn't leave a tip. I left two dollars under my milk carton, as an apology.

Finally, Mike relinquished the driver's seat. First, though, he wiped everything down, leaving the cab doors open. Our breath came out in white clouds. I'd never been in temperatures that cold. The gauge in the truck stop had said -3 degrees. Inhaling actually hurt my throat.

Being taller, I had to let a little air out of the driver's seat. So satisfying.

"Hold the steering wheel firm. Put your thumbs around it, Margot. There. Yes. Like that. You have to hold on with your arms. If a rabbit runs out and hits the front tire, it'll knock you right into the other lane."

Bullshit.

"And if you hit a deer, and you're not holding on, we're dead. If you see a deer, don't swerve, you'll tip the trailer. Turn your high beams on. If someone's coming up fast behind you, blink your lights. Wake 'em up. They could crash into the back of us. Don't let it get too hot in here. You could fall asleep. Plenty a truckers done that. I seen it happen. You think we're safe cause we're in a big truck. But crashing into a car 'll kill us just the same. Don't be fooled by an empty road. When it's cold like this, there's black ice and you can't see it."

I listened for when he would inhale, a break in his monologue, which sounded like a kid's model airplane. His words buzzed around me, like a monster fly, or an incessant mosquito. Trapped in the driver's seat I was being slowly impaled through my right ear.

Finally, he got in the sleeper and snapped the curtain closed.

No Heat

10 degrees outside. -17 chill factor.

January 31, 1981
I-40 New Mexico

Midnight. Black sky. Stars. Oncoming headlights. Little red taillights. CB voices discussing the temperature.

"How cold is it out there?" I asked.

"It's so cold I couldn't even get into a heated argument with my wife."

"It's so cold, New Jersey politicians have their hands in their own pockets."

"Copy that. It's so cold, someone spilled hot coffee on me and I thanked them."

I'd asked the wrong question. "Seriously, how cold is it?" I tried again.

"10 degrees outside with a -17 chill factor, darlin'."

"Any black ice?"

Nobody reported any black ice. With Mike finally in the sleeper, I'd dropped my shoulders, inhaled deep breaths, but my gut still hadn't relaxed. By remembering the goodness in Monte, I shook off Mike somewhat. Mike wouldn't be the last person I'd meet.

Fuck Mike and the horse he rode in on. Just try to push me, asshole.

An hour later, the cab heat went out again. I looked at the water temperature —180 degrees— and thought maybe the radiator needed more water, like in Moriarty. I pulled into a funky truck stop and used a wastebasket to get water from the faucet to the radiator.

Only one mitten came out of my coat pocket. My teeth started chattering. Engine running, with one mitten, I balanced on the bumper and poured freezing cold water into the radiator that was above my head. Ice water streamed down my arms, soaked my coat and shirtsleeves. My hands ached. Breathing hurt my nostrils and throat. I watched my white breath waft away like cigarette smoke.

But the heat didn't come back on. I drove another half hour, bouncing my left foot and squeezing my bare hands on the wheel, before coming to the next truck stop, another lonely little thing, but with lights on and a mechanics' bay. I pulled in, parked, and woke Mike.

"Mike, the cab heat went out." I called through the plastic sleeper curtain.

Mike roared out of the sleeper. "Damn it! Why didn't you put water in the radiator?"

"I did." His eyebrows screwed into his nose. "While you were asleep." *You stupid fuck of a human.* Just looking at him sent me into rage. I felt fear too, that crazy would trump rage the longer I held this bomb inside.

"Get in the lounge. It's freezing out here."

I ran to the tiny truckers' lounge. As soon as the door shut behind him, Mike, under his 10-gallon hat, chin jutting forward, moved toward me even as I backed away. "I don't know what I'm going to do with you."

What had I done wrong this time?

Hit with the smell of cigarette smoke, we both gagged and Mike coughed. The poorly heated, barren lounge offered no candy or sodas, one white plastic chair, dirty linoleum, and a shelf with a few cans of motor oil. Greasy yellowed white walls. The two big windows, colored with dust and smoke, looked more like cardboard. And, of course, the ever-popular florescent lighting. My hands slowly thawed in my armpits. My breath, even inside this room, dissipated slowly, like a wet mist. We both stomped. Left, right, hop hop.

The mechanic came in from the bay. He and Mike talked man-to-man, and then Mike stalked back out the way we came in. I followed the mechanic, who opened the door to the truck bay. Mike pulled the cab inside after disconnecting the trailer, and the mechanic closed the huge door. The mechanics bay, even with the high ceiling, was warmer than the lounge. I noticed a TV and armchair in the mechanics corner, and a space heater blasted bright red heat at the chair. But since I wasn't allowed in Miguel's mechanics' corner, I walked back to the lounge to wait, which turned out to be a big mistake.

I watched the black mold grow in the corners and along the baseboard. No coffee table or magazine. A crack in the back of the chair yawned when I leaned into it. The wall clock said 3 a.m. I watched the second hand move around in little clicks.

At 4 a.m., Mike stormed in. "The fan was broke. It wasn't blowing air from the heater into the cab." He stood directly in front of me, both feet planted, arms crossed."

"Oh." I took a moment to marvel at Mike's huge hat.

"The heat's back on. I've already hooked her to the trailer. Let's go." He turned on a dime, and hoofed it to the passenger side, so I followed suit, and climbed in behind the wheel.

"I'm sorry I swore back there, but you can hardly blame me."

I don't blame you. I hate your guts.

"Margot, I know you're a beginner, but you were irresponsible in there." Big sigh, "You're my job, Missy. You want to learn, I'll teach ya. But you gotta pay attention or I'm quittin' you."

Well, ain't I the lucky one.

"The short form," Mike's voice raised an octave on the word *form.* "The problem was e-LECT-rical." His face fully over the doghouse, he leaned on his elbow to hold himself in position.

Mocking him, I leaned in on my elbow, and put my face twelve inches away from his, "So, you think it's my fault the heat went out?" My voice sweet as apple pie.

"It *is* your fault!" Mike screamed. I jerked back, practically banged my head on the window. Sitting up again, he yelled. "The driver handles any problems. Off duty means *off duty.*"

I stared. "Was I supposed to let you keep sleeping?"

"I had to handle this problem on your shift."

"I thought you'd freeze." *What the fuck did you do, oh God-of-the-road, to handle this problem?*

191

Mike squinted and screwed up his forehead. I made my eyes big, rocked my head back, tucked my chin. "Even if I had known what was wrong, Mike, we still needed a mechanic to fix it." Even sweeter than apple pie.

"How in the hell, I'm sorry, but how in the hell are you going to learn what to say to a mechanic if you're sitting in the lounge?"

"Ohhhh." My sarcasm popped out like an escape artist. "You wanted me to come with you into the mechanics' bay." I nodded my head, and watched the last little bit of frost evaporate off the windshield.

"Don't you sass me, you little tart. Get back in that lounge."

He's going to leave me here.

"The company wouldn't blame me if..."

"I'm sorry," I interrupted, and got out of the cab.

"... We're going to straighten this out once and for all —

I slammed the door hard, and trotted back into the sorry-ass pretense of a truck stop lounge.

The frigid air jolted my senses. I knew he would leave me here.

"If the electrical shorts out the fan won't turn on. There's plenty of heat but it doesn't get into the cab because the fan isn't working. Understand?"

While he talked, I mumbled apologizes, looked at my shoes, shifted my weight from one foot to the other.

"You need to see if a fuse has blown. Do you know where to find the fuses?"

I shook my head no.

"I didn't either when I first started, but that didn't stop me from finding out. But Margot, you should have disconnected the trailer. That was your job. I had to go out in that cold, on your shift..."

I would have needed help to disconnect the trailer. I'd only done that once, last spring in the class. I didn't realize he expected me to follow him out to the cab, I hadn't even heard what he and the mechanic had talked about.

"I'm sorry." I actually meant it ... a little.

Mike calmed down. He even made a joke about when he first started driving.

"The first time I crossed the scales, I got outta the truck before they weighed me. They thought I was tryin' to cheat! Like I was overweight." He laughed. "Get it?"

Forty minutes later (His back was to the wall clock. I timed him.), he turned abruptly. With his back to me said, "Let's get this show on the road."

I imagined shoving cotton down his throat, him choking, and dying on the spot.

We got back in the truck, and as I pulled out of the parking lot and up onto the freeway, he continued talking.

"Back when I first started, both right rear tires went flat. I noticed the trailer was leanin' but drove a hundred miles with that crooked trailer. If your trailer leans, stop, Margot. Check those tires. We stopped at the 76 and had her fixed. I took complete responsibility for that error. My first seat driver slept the whole time. Never even told him what happened."

I shifted into tenth. Set the cruise control. Almost 5:00 a.m.

"One time, when I was new, I went to hose the bugs off the windshield and that nozzle sprayed me, leaked like crazy. Got soaked. Cost me a full hour changin' clothes. Had to pay for the shower. My partner never heard a word about it.

"I knew the first time I heard an air leak in the break pot, Margot. It whistled like a balloon. You know that sound? Margot! Do you know the sound of air leaving a balloon?"

I thought he'd asked a rhetorical question. "Oh yes, Mike. We used to squeak the air out when we were kids."

"Not that sound. The sound when you let the balloon go and it flies around letting air out. That sound. Do you know that sound?"

"Yes, Mike."

"That's the sound of an air leak. Remember it."

Last summer, when Big Red put the penny and dime in our air line, to block the air leak, the leak sounded like air hissing out of an air line. *Maybe the hiss of a leak in my Coke can after I'd dropped it, Mike, but not a balloon flying, fuck head.*

"I reported it right away." Mike continued. "Checked all the lines, made sure they were good, had Oklahoma City fix that pot. Never bothered my first driver. It's not by accident they made me first seat as soon as they did. So I'm telling you, always listen to all your air lines, listen for that balloon.

If I have to listen much longer, I might have to buy a gun. No! The tire thumper! I could hit him over the head when he listens for air leaks.

"If you would quit being so stubborn, so obstinate..."

I'd have to knock his hat off first.

"... you might make first seat one day, but you got to change your attitude, or it'll never happen on my watch."

Maybe a hit-and run, wash the truck after. It'd have to be at night...

"I'm going to get some shut-eye now." He hopped into the sleeper and snapped the curtain shut.

I can't kill him. I can't leave him. I can't even hit him.

Suddenly, I thought of having a beer, and that thought grew to sitting in a warm establishment. Music. Laughing. Friends. I saw myself dancing. The guy would be tall, have blonde hair.

There was that guy in the AA meetings...

Sunrise turned the horizon a bright red, and the landscape became a one-dimensional silhouette of black trees. Ten minutes later, the trees took shape. I saw smooth rolling land ahead, and the gray turned green all around me. The sun. A new day. I would outlast Mike, so help me.

I-70 Out of Eaton, Ohio
The coincidence worth remembering

February 3, 1981

For the rest of the trip, I shut my ears. I imagined myself flying above the cab, looking down at Mike, watching him yak away in that fucking hat. I'm gliding along barefoot, in a long flowing skirt, the scene in that Shirley Temple truck below me, just a figment. Effortless, no wind, at 55 mph, arms spread like wings, the sun warm, my hair flowing...

I hated Mike's constant meaningless monologue, much of it, thank God, into the CB. Riding with Mike, I went into fits of despair. *Oh boy, sure am turning my life around. Sure am having an adventure. What a fraud. I'm a mental patient who left town, who ran away. The little girl who ran away. An embarrassment to my own name.*

And now I'll go deaf for sure. Terry was right.

We delivered our load to Kroger's in Cincinnati, dropped our trailer, deadheaded to pick up an empty one, took that one through a trailer wash, and then moved the clean trailer across town, where we picked up a loaded trailer full of conveyor belt parts in Eaton, Ohio. Around noon we headed out for Reno, Nevada, where the belt parts were expected in four days.

I thought the time moving trailers about equaled the time we would have spent loading, but Mike didn't see it that way.

"Darn it, Miss Avenue. They use me for every extra job they have. You know we don't get paid for this wash job."

"I know."

"They take advantage of me. Not just a new driver to train, but now they make me switch trailers and wash one out."

It's not like they made you get in there with a sponge, asshole. We could have relaxed with a piece of pie at the truck wash.

"That trailer's gonna grow mold now. I couldn't make the guy air it out. He just walked away. I've a mind to get him fired."

You supervised him to death, you pig, you fake cowboy, you little man. Mike had made me witness him berating the attendant because I "needed to learn how."

"Did you see what I had to do to get the sun to shine through the back door?"

"That was an awesome park job, Mike."

"A complete jackknife. A car couldn't even have done what I did. And un-hooking the trailer like that, inching the cab out at that angle, they're lucky to have me. Because of me, that trailer will dry out. They won't ruin their next load."

Mike had pulled forward into the lot, almost up to the fence line. He'd disconnected the cab from the trailer at a 90-degree angle, an absolute no-no according to Dick Dart. He'd left the trailer doors open thinking the sun would dry it out. The next driver would need to have the trailer towed away from the fence before he could hook up to it.

"I might just make a formal complaint about how they use me." Mike stood in the driver's seat, adjusting his air. "All that writing you do, maybe you could write the letter. What do you say?"

I'd say we work in the lowest of the low entry-level coast-to-coast trucking jobs. Do your own work, move up the ladder. "I don't know Mike. I think you'd need more than one trucker to complain."

"Yeah. Maybe I'll talk to a few guys, feel 'em out. Ya can't be too careful though, ya never know who's gonna rat on you. But you're right, Margot. I'm proud of you! Maybe, if you make first seat, you'll write me a letter too. What do ya say?"

"That's a possibility."

"You mean you would?"

"I think I would, Mike." *Never happen.*

Out of the Indianapolis fueling terminal, onward into Illinois, I tried to ignore Mike's constant stream of words. I watched the endless urban panorama roll by my window. Run down houses behind the freeway's concrete wall, shitty little backyards with crap covering dead lawns. The view from a truck, great for seeing over cars to anticipate danger, but invasive, seeing those sickly backyards, like seeing the family's dirty laundry.

"I found the Windex, Margot. You didn't forget to put it away, you just threw it on the floor."

"I'm sorry, Mike. I can't get it to stick between my seat and the doghouse. It keeps popping out. "

"If you leave it on the floor, it rolls around and ... "

"I blocked it with my foot. I didn't let it roll."

"Don't you interrupt me! On its side, it rolls around and loses its carbonation. It's worthless."

Chlorofluorocarbons, asshole. I wanted to scream. I wanted to hit him. I hated him with all my might. I couldn't hold it in much longer. Mike would have no warning. They'd lock me up again.

I thought of having a beer. Getting good and drunk.

"You need to change lanes faster. You turn your signal on, and wait too long to pull out to pass."

Oh please shut the fuck up. Maybe when we get to Reno, I will get drunk.

"And your attitude. It's pitiful. You need to acknowledge me when I'm talking. I'm the instructor. Show some respect."

I gave all my respect to the windshield.

"Answer me!"

What's the question?

Mike jerked the wheel, pulled into the fast lane, and passed a car carrier. "You'll never make first seat."

I took the bait. "What do you want me to do?"

"Well for starters, you could try being a little kinder."

"What does kindness look like to you, Mike?"

"See what I mean? Ya go off on this crap, pardon my language but..."

"I'm serious. What could I do that would look kind?"

He stopped for a moment. "How 'bout dressing a little nicer."

"What's wrong with my clothes?"

"Well, look at you!"

I looked down at my mid-section. Navy blue T-shirt, my favorite faded green corduroy pants, man's plaid shirt, waterproof hiking boots. I'm clean.

I'm interested now. "What should I look like?" He didn't like the baggy, comfortable, second-hand look.

"Try something that fits! Do you even have any make-up?"

I looked out the passenger window. Did those poor people in house after house, living with the constant freeway noise, have to wear make-up?

"You could at least comb your hair, put it up or something when we go in the restaurant. And I have to get your hair out of the sleeper every time I get back there. It's gross. If you wore a cap in the sleeper, that would *look like kindness*." Mike imitated my words with a high-pitched squeak. "Ya know what, your sleeping bag is not rolled up tight enough. I have to roll it up every time so it'll fit in your bin."

I looked back in the sleeper. My sleeping bag was tucked securely in my storage bin, puffed out above the edge by maybe five inches. "I've never had anyone complain about my sleeping bag," I lied.

"I'm not them, Margot." Mike's voice escalated into his fucking hat. He looked at me too long, and had to swerve back into our lane. "I don't have to put up with a slob." He yelled at the windshield, approaching the tail end of a Ford pickup. "We live together, and if you can't even get your sleeping bag put away... "

Right then, right in the middle of his sentence, our engine blew up. I cracked the tiniest smile while Mike shouted into CB.

"Break. Got a 10-33," Mike hollered.

"10-4."

"Shirley Temple down at the 15 yardstick, going to the left coast. Engine down. Need a Shirley Temple headed east to send a tow truck from the Indy 500."

"10-4. Copy that." And then we heard. "Any Shirley Temples going east got your ears on?"

Silence.

"Big R going east. Come again on that Shirley Temple being down?"

"At the 15 yardstick. Needs a tow from his terminal in the Indy 500."

"10-4" And we heard the message repeated. And repeated again and again until it faded completely out.

Not fifteen minutes later, we got word back.

"Shirley Temple, at the 15 yardstick. Tow truck's on the way."

"10-4," Mike responded. "Much obliged."

The tow truck arrived. Side by side, we watched the driver hitch the truck and wench it up, cigarette dangling from his lips. Mike put his arm around my shoulders. "We'd like a smoke." He addressed the mechanic. "Can we borrow one?"

The driver didn't respond.

I rotated my shoulder, pulled my elbow back, and glared a big "fuck you" in Mike's face. "You don't smoke. What are you doing?"

"Doesn't hurt to be friendly." Mike turned and walked to the end of the trailer. With his back to me, I saw him fiddling, like reaching in his shirt pocket, or unbuttoning his shirt. He put his hand to his mouth, knocked his head back, like he was eating a handful of peanuts. He did his about face and marched back.

"What were you doing back there?"

"None a your damn business." He turned and doubled up on his attention to the driver.

In the cab, the driver delivered two Marlboros. I shook my head, and he passed them over me to Mike. Mike didn't light up. The driver never said a word.

Mike pushed himself against me from shoulder to knee, even though I'd scooted toward the driver as close as I could. Snuggled in, Mike started talking. "We're comin' from Eaton. Got conveyor belt parts. Had to switch trailers and we're pissed about that."

The driver didn't speak.

"We're so tired. I'm Sweet Meat. This here's my partner, Sunny Avenue. We're gonna be mighty hungry, when we get to town. Where ya think we should chow down?"

Yeah, we want some grub. Ride out on the range and sleep with our hats on.

"Sunny Avenue likes good food, don't ya Miss Avenue." Mike nudged me with his elbow.

"Company will take you to the Motel. Restaurants all around it."

"Free motel. Can't make any money, though. Got a good truck waitin' for us?"

"Wouldn't know about that."

"Hope it doesn't take long. We need to be making the do-re-mi, if you know what I mean."

Mr. OCD continued to talk. I couldn't wait to get to my motel room and shut the door.

The driver turned on the radio. Mike talked over the music, about how the company wanted him to teach me to drive and how I was coming along, making progress, and he was thinking "steady as she goes" if you know what I mean, heh heh.

Maybe I'd skip dinner, just take a cold six-pack to the room. Watch TV.

The driver turned up the volume.

Mike finally shut his mouth.

We arrived at the terminal. They'd booked separate rooms for us, and the manager pulled up next to our truck in an old Ford 150. Mike reached for my suitcase, but I beat him to it. I loaded all my stuff into the bed of the manager's pickup, which would be parked inside the terminal for the night.

"You're making a mistake, Margot." The manager could hear Mike. "You don't know these mechanics. They'll rip you off. Is your suitcase locked? They'll go through it. It's happened to me."

The manager walked past Mike without looking at him. "My mechanics won't touch your stuff." He sounded tired, like he'd heard all this before. He got in the pickup, shut the door.

Mike turned and blocked me from continuing to the passenger door. "He doesn't know what those mechanics will do, Margot. Trust me. Take all your stuff to the motel. One time in Rawlins this guy tried to..."

I sidestepped him.

"Margot!"

He reached to stop me but I dodged him and opened the passenger door.

The manager delivered us to the motel, me with an overnight case, and Mike with sheets and blankets, suitcase, hanging clothes, cleaning products, toiletries kit, and I don't know what all.

I shut the door of my motel room. Quiet. A warm room. I knew the mini-mart across the street would sell beer and headed over there. I stood in front of the refrigerated drinks and stared.

I have no idea why, but I turned my back on the beer, bought potato chips, a Diet Coke, two Baby Ruths, and a chocolate covered doughnut.

Back in my room, I stood in the shower. I laid on the soft, still bed. I didn't turn on the TV, didn't try to read. I could hear myself breathing. Thought about the irony of fifteen hours of freedom in a locked room. Slept deeply. Dreamed about angels flying around barefoot and laughing.

The next morning, back at the terminal, I did laundry and waited around while Mike sterilized our new truck. We were so late with our load we had no opportunity to argue. One of us slept while the other drove.

Stark landscape on I-80 across Iowa. The Platte River in Nebraska looked hard, with cracks in it, and next to that Nebraska rest stop Bob liked, where the corn grew last July, a frozen pond reflected sunlight making it look like a mirror. Clean, cold air. Bright sun. Leafless trees sparkled, the wet branches reflecting light, creating halos. The trees looked elfin to me. No wonder our redwoods staggered the tourists.

From about 1 a.m. to 6:00, my driving shift provided the most serenity. With Mike in the sleeper, I listened to CB conversations. In Wyoming, I opened the mic and sang "Old Stewball was a race horse, and I wish he were mine..." They all chattered about me for the next fifteen minutes.

"Sure wish that pretty little voice would finish her song ..."

"Probably off in some mountain range, singing the cows to sleep."

"Ain't no mountain range that I can see."

"Maybe she's gettin' a bite to eat."

I didn't say another word.

Reno, Nevada
The Hallmark Poem

February 4, 1981

We finally delivered the conveyor belt parts to Reno, and dispatch told us we didn't have to be in Ontario, Oregon, until Monday morning. Mike decided we'd hang in Reno for the weekend. He came out of the truck stop store with a card for me, an affectionate Hallmark poem about his special friend.

"Thanks, Mike." I evaded his hug by rotating ninety degrees. "I called a friend. I'm meeting him in the coffee shop." Mike's face reddened. "We're having dinner and I'll catch up with you later. What time do you want to meet?"

Mike stomped to the passenger door and opened it. "Get in. We have to do logs."

Getting my logbook from my purse took more time than recording the last five-hour driving stretch. Mike snorted, "Who is this guy?"

"A friend."

Mike threw his logbook at the windshield. "You're a witch, you know that?"

My jaw dropped. A fly could have flown in my mouth. I slammed the door in his face and went to the coffee shop to meet my friend, Larry.

Larry and I came back to the truck. I introduced Larry but Mike turned his back on us like he was way too busy in his luggage compartment.

"Larry's putting me up at his house." I said to Mike's back. "I need to get my stuff."

Mike didn't say a word, but walked to my side of the cab, where he opened my compartment. I grabbed my overnight case.

"Shall we meet back here at noon tomorrow?"

Mike grunted, which I figured amounted to consent.

I had met Larry at an AA meeting in Eureka. He was visiting from Reno and heard me share a story about truck driving. Afterward, he'd given me his card, told me if I was ever in the neighborhood, he'd take me to a meeting. At the time, I only accepted his card to be polite.

Larry wore overalls and a navy t-shirt. The knees were worn almost white. Balding with a gray ponytail, approaching sixty, his large paunch reminded me of Dick Dart. His false teeth were the obvious pearly whites, all in a perfect row. Larry's demeanor felt as relaxed and honest as his clothes looked.

"Glad you called. Meeting starts at 7:30. It's a good one."

"Thank you so much for picking me up. You really got me out of a jam."

"That guy was steamed!" Larry drove slowly, keeping his eyes on the road.

"You don't know the half of it."

We parked in the driveway of a little box-like stucco house, cream colored like all the other houses on Larry's block.

I followed Larry into a small, dark living room. His wife and son walked around an upright vacuum cleaner, blocking the kitchen door. "Meet my wife Marge, and this is our son, Lawrence the third."

The room smelled like some kind of vegetable soup, which steamed up the windows. Larry stepped behind me, opened the curtain, and cracked the window.

Marge took my hand, for just a moment, in both of hers. "Are you hungry? We're just about to sit down to dinner." Her cold hands, the blue veins visible, felt so small, and soft, like she'd used a lifetime of lotion.

I shifted my weight to the other foot. "I was hoping to take you all to dinner."

"Nonsense. I made a pot of chicken soup this afternoon. We've got more than we can eat."

"Lawrence, put the vacuum away." Larry herded us all to the table and Lawrence III sat down beside me. He could have starred in a high school boy-meets-girl-for-the-first-time movie. Pimples, skinny, shy, but no glasses. His body arched over the table like a question mark.

Marge looked the picture of a nurturing hostess, complete with a checked apron. The conversation bounced from Lawrence's school to AA to Marge's grocery shopping. I kept thinking how a glass of red wine, or a cold beer would help me relax. If I moved my shoulders, I thought my neck would crack. I pictured my head, stuck on my neck, and how I probably looked like a lollipop with hair.

The carrots were overcooked and the chicken had bones. I ate half a bowl, remembering how Bobby snuck lima beans into his pocket, but forgot about them and Mom found them in the wash. I remembered how Dad would snip Daniel or Bobby's head at the dinner table and they said how much it hurt. Thoughts jumped out like some kind of centrifuge spitting them into my consciousness at high speed. All through dinner I pretended to listen to Larry, Lawrence III and Marge, hoping I looked normal, even though I couldn't talk.

Larry and I headed off to the AA meeting, a ten-minute drive to the back of a Methodist church nowhere near all the casinos. About fifty people, seated in rows, were listening to the Serenity Prayer when we walked in and sat in the back. Anyone who spoke walked to the front and talked from the podium. One lady — fortyish, thin, dressed in a pantsuit and heels — rambled on about her husband and how her church kicked her out for divorcing him. Her story matched her tired face, too many lines dragging her smile down.

Her five kids were no longer allowed to speak to her either. She didn't know how she'd survive without us, her tribe, and she thanked all of us for helping her get through the loss of her church friends and her kids. Her last comment struck me. "I'm an alcoholic," she said. "I can't handle anger. I know I have to cease fighting anyone or anything."

The next day, Larry dropped me off before noon, but Mike didn't show up until after 3:30. When he finally arrived, I watched him park, jump down from the truck, and head for the building. I got up, grabbed my overnight case, and walked out to meet him.

We faced off by the fuel pumps. Mike crossed his arms over the American flag: stars across his shoulders, pearl snaps down the red and white stripes. "You are an unsuitable partner." His signature hat shaded his face. "Margot, a whore is better than you. You're a major whacko and I hope you get help, 'cause you need it."

With an about face, he stomped back to the truck and I followed. He unlocked the passenger door, unlocked my second-seat compartment and watched me as I loaded my overnight case. I pulled on the chicken bar, stepped into the cab, and he slammed my door. I watched that big white hat bounce around the front windows and pop-up in the driver's seat.

"Despicable, that's what you are! Despicable!" A full-forced yell.

I didn't respond. I *'ceased fighting anyone or anything'*.

"Don't you have anything to say for yourself? Are you just a hooker, going off with that guy?"

I stabbed him with my eyes and didn't say a word.

"Answer me, bitch."

My laser beams bored into his chest but I kept my mouth shut. He squirmed like a trapped rabbit. *Maybe he'll have a stroke and I'll be done with him.*

"I've never sworn at a woman before, but you're no woman, you're a slut. Don't try to tell me you did it for free, cause you're a liar. Tell me, how much did he pay you? At least a prostitute is honest about what she's doing."

How long can he keep yelling? Odd, I felt remarkably calm.

"I better not see any Certs wrappers on the floor, do you hear me? I'm sick of it. And no trash bags on the driver's side. Forget using the CB. Forget having a key to the truck."

You never gave me a key in the first place, jerk.

"You're not allowed to sleep on the doghouse, and you can't use the heat or the air conditioning."

You going to jump out of the sleeper and turn off the heat?

His voice pounded my eardrums. "You hereby forfeit all privileges. Is that clear?"

Fuck you, pig.

I watched his blood boil over and marveled that mine only simmered.

"I will leave any truck stop, anywhere, anytime, whenever I feel like it. I won't wait for you. If you leave the truck, I'll assume you quit."

I started getting a headache. My gut knotted.

Then he said, "You can sit up and listen to me, or you can take your stuff off the truck."

"I'll get off the truck." I got into the sleeper, threw my stuff on the jump seat, and when I started back out of the sleeper, Mike grabbed my shoulder. I flung my arm out, pushing him off me and I back handed his face. I hadn't pre-meditated it, but the back of my hand stung. I'd hit his cheek pretty hard.

"Fuck you, Mike." I enunciated all three syllables. "I'm tired of being ordered around like a dog." Silence. "You talk non-stop, Mike. Do you realize that?"

"But..."

"*Shut-up!*" They might have heard me in California. His head blew back in surprise at my volume. "Not one more word." I shouted, and pointed my finger at his face and then curled it back into my fist. I crawled around my stuff on the jump seat.

"You miserable little slut." His words hung in the cab.

I threw my sleeping bag down to the pavement. Followed it.

With both feet planted on the ground, I ordered Mike, "Unlock my compartment."

He did.

In five minutes, I had all my stuff sitting in a pile, soaking up the smell of asphalt.

"Do you want to put this on hold till tomorrow?"

"No." I walked toward the building, turned, and got the last shot. "I hate your hat."

In the terminal, I called Larry. When I returned to the parking lot, to collect the rest of my stuff, the truck was gone. I felt humiliated, and wanted to explain to the fuel jockeys what had happened as they watched me carry my stuff —four trips—back inside.

My voice hurt, hoarse from shouting. My jaw hurt like I'd been grinding my teeth for months.

"Put your stuff there." The attendant hardly batted an eye, like this happened every day. We stored my granola, sleeping bag, tennis racket, ice chest, suitcase and laundry bag behind the counter.

206

Larry arrived around 4:30 and ten silent minutes later, we walked in the front door of Larry's house.

"You can sleep out here again." Larry's arm waved at the couch, where folded blankets and a pillow sat at one end.

"I'm so sorry." I desperately wished I'd called a taxi, stayed in a motel. I didn't want to be in his house.

Bent on saving money to fix-up my own house, I had pinched every penny out of my minimum-wage job. I had no intention of coming home empty-handed. But I really didn't want to talk to Larry either, much less eat more of Marge's chicken soup. I could feel my back seizing into a brick. The thoughts started coming on.

I want a beer. That tub-o-lard raped me in Hawaii. Opium was the best. I wonder what Gary is doing now?

"So what's your part in all of this?" Larry asked.

Gary rhymes with Larry. I wonder how long Larry's had those teeth? Oh, Larry is waiting. It must be my turn to talk.

Larry asked the go-to Alcoholics Anonymous question again. "What's your part?" Larry had attended meetings for some thirty years.

"Larry, I have no idea." I paused. "He wanted to sleep with me. I wouldn't. That's my part."

"What were you doing on the truck with him?" Larry stood there looking at me, lips sealed, arms at his sides.

"I didn't ask for this. I'm not dressed like sex. I didn't lead him on."

"One more time. What are *you* doing on *his* truck?"

"I'm having an adventure."

"Did you ever ask the company what they expected of you?"

He had me there. "I didn't want to complain."

"Let me ask you this. What are you doing *here*?"

I froze.

He waited a beat. "I'm going to take a shower. Think about it." He stopped in the hallway and called to me. "You hungry?"

"No, I'm good."

"We'll get dinner and go to a meeting."

Marge and Lawrence III were nowhere to be seen.

What the fuck was my part?

Donner Pass

Ed and Penny

February 5, 1981

"Get a bus ticket to Los Banos. We'll pay for it." The dispatcher cut me off in mid-sentence, hung-up, said nothing about keeping me employed.

I couldn't face coming home if I got fired.

Moving five gallons of granola, sleeping bag, pillow, and full ice chest to the bus stop looked difficult enough. I also had luggage, hanging clothes, a dirty laundry bag, boom box, headphones, toiletries, tennis racket and a cardboard box of dry food. *Greyhound* would never accept all that.

I decided to hitchhike. In Sacramento, I'd find another Tanskley truck, bum a ride to the Los Banos terminal, and with a little luck, talk my way on to another truck.

I surveyed the truckers coming in from the parking lot, and after about an hour, a couple approached the restaurant. I met them outside the door. "Yes, we're headed to Sacramento," the man answered. The woman said nothing, but the man said, "Can do." We fumbled over who would hold the restaurant door for the other one. I lost.

"I don't know ..." Ed rubbed his chin, looking at my belongings. "Can you combine some of that stuff?"

I threw away my ice chest, all my food, and dumped the granola out of the five-gallon bucket. I tossed the broken boom box. The granola gone, I stuffed my pillow in the bucket and crammed the hanging clothes and dirty clothes in the suitcase.

Ed and Penny drove an old hay truck. No sleeper, with stick-out headlights. It used to be green. I couldn't see any tread on the tires.

Donner Pass on bald tires.

I piled all my stuff onto the passenger's floorboard, and after they ate, I climbed in next to Penny. Because my boots and her black flats rested on top of my luggage, our thighs looked like tuck and roll jeans, and our knees like a miniature mountain range. With my purse on my lap, I thanked Penny for putting up with all this.

Penny shrugged her shoulder. "Humph."

If Penny was a working girl, her career had to be long over. Wrinkles, shoulder length brown straw, stained red t-shirt, big hips, no bra. Ed was tall and round, wore pointed cowboy boots, baggy gray pants and a thin, tan jacket. He looked at least as old as my Mom.

"Boy, you gotta lot of stuff! ... Where you from? ... What happened back there? ..."

I inhaled the truck's farm smells and answered Ed's questions. A loud hiss spewed from the tandem axles.

"Ed, did you hear that?"

"No. What?"

"Sounds like we just popped an air leak."

"You could hear that?"

"Well, something popped. Want to check?"

So before driving down Donner Pass, Ed borrowed my knife and we all looked through the junk behind the seats for a piece of wire to fix the air line. Ed sprayed water along the line till some bubbled at the rip he'd found. He cut out the part with the leak, whittled down one end of the air hose, shoved the other end over it and wrapped the wire around it.

Good God.

I started talking, I suppose to cover my fear. For the next half hour, I told them every detail I could remember about riding with Mike, omitting any mention of sex in case Penny was a prostitute.

Going down Donner with bald tires and a leak in the brake line.

"Let's cool off those brakes and get some coffee." Ed slowed to a stop at a roadside diner just off the I-80.

The brakes were smoking.

To settle my stomach, I ordered a chocolate milkshake with my hamburger and fries.

Back on the road, I watched the passenger mirror for sparks behind our rear wheels.

My side of I-80 dropped off a cliff. I could smell the brakes, like hot oil or burning tar.

If we get to Sacramento, I'll quit.

My thoughts spun, and I talked, filling the silence with everything I could remember about Bob, Kent, and Donald. I even mentioned Donald's false teeth and then regretted it because maybe Ed or Penny had false teeth.

If the air line held, and the brake pads didn't catch on fire, and the tires didn't fall off...

"Penny, are you comfortable? Sorry, about all this." I waved at my luggage.

"Don't worry about it." She got a cigarette out of her purse, lit it with a match and then leaned across Ed and threw the match out the window.

Terry was right. I'm really stupid.

"You ever drive back east? It's way different back there. Did you know they shrink wrap all the fruit in grocery stores? I had no idea!"

My fucking part, Larry, is I have no business being on this truck.

"Did you know that green tomatoes get gassed to turn red and then get sold?

"No, I never knew that." Ed kept the truck in seventh gear. The engine screamed. I prayed he wouldn't try shifting to eighth.

"If iceberg lettuce has cracked ribs, don't buy it. It'll be white on the inside."

Ed didn't respond.

Maybe he wants me to shut up.

Penny inhaled her cigarette smoke and blew it out at the windshield. Ed finally said he didn't know about cracked ribs, and he didn't like tomatoes anyway.

My part, Larry, is I don't belong.

We passed the second Runaway Truck sign. Ed stayed in seventh gear. I couldn't see sparks, but the brakes smelled to holy high hell.

210

Didn't belong in my marriage or AA. Didn't belong in my family. Or even in Eureka for that matter.

Finally, we got off the mountain. Downhill flattened into something manageable, but my head reeled.

Would have married a total jerk ...

When we finally rolled into Sacramento after sunset, I smelled ripe from worry. Penny was off like a shot. Maybe she had to pee.

"Penny's uncle needs ..." Ed's lips kept moving but I couldn't hear him for all the screaming inside my head. *You're a fraud. You'll never get a life. You'll never be happy.*

"... and her aunt's friends all chipped in. So that's why Penny is riding with me."

Ed helped me haul my belongings into the truck stop. The attendant didn't flinch. "Put your stuff there." He pointed to the empty square footage behind the counter, earmarked for lost souls. Like the guy in Reno, he'd seen too many of us to care.

I nodded. Thanked him. Thanked Ed. Said goodbye, turned my stiff body around and walked, I hoped, toward the bathroom. I never saw Penny again.

Dave, Partner #5
Sacramento

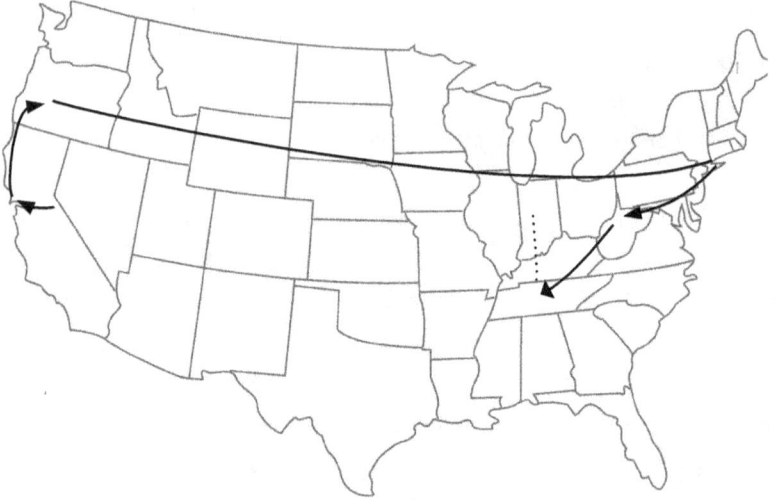

February 5, 1981

I perused the parking lot and found a Tanksley truck. I had the attendant page its driver. Dave showed up.

"I'm Margot. I need to get to Los Banos. Can you give me a ride?"

"I'm going to the Bay Area. I can take you to Los Banos after I deliver. I don't got a partner."

"I don't know." My stomach hurt. I felt like throwing up. I couldn't get a bead on this guy, and his greasy hair bothered me. He wasn't a cowboy, but I could smell cigarette smoke on him. His shirt looked like he'd knotted it up and just untied it.

"I'm leavin' when I finish my laundry, so you'll have to decide by then."

I looked right at him. "I won't sleep with you."

Dave laughed, an easy relaxed chuckle. He smiled. "I won't lay a hand on you. You got my word on that."

I opened his truck's door and the smell of Dave's sweat and cigarette smoke hit my face. I hauled up my sleeping bag first. Tobacco stains coated the sleeper walls with dirty yellow grime. The mattress had no sheets. I couldn't see bedding anywhere. Dave brushed an armful of Coke cups, straws, and fast food bags off the jump seat, adding to the garbage on the floor. I held my breath and loaded my stuff in the sleeper compartment. Off we went, to deliver his light bulbs to Emeryville, just outside of Oakland.

Forty-three. Married twenty years. Divorced three. Been on his own since he was twelve, when he left his grandparents house and picked up any work he could to support himself. Went to fourteen different schools and got his high school diploma. Spent time in the Navy as a seaman. Worked on Chrysler's assembly line. Drove a milk truck.

Dave cracked the window to let out his cigarette smoke. "Knock knock."

"Who's there?"

"Little old lady."

"Little old lady who?"

"I didn't know you could yodel!" Dave slapped the steering wheel with the palm of his hand and laughed. "Knock knock."

"Who's there."

"Boo hoo."

I knew what was coming. "Boo hoo who?"

"Aw girl, you don't have to cry." And Dave rocked back in his seat and hollered again.

More knock-knock jokes, nothing R rated, and somewhere around Vallejo, my stomach stopped hurting.

We delivered the light bulbs in Emeryville and parked at a 76 truck stop off I-80. We ate greasy hamburgers and fries. Dave had coffee and I bought a Coke.

"Do you think they're going to fire me?"

"All depends on if they need drivers at the moment."

"I know. And if they keep me, no telling whose truck I'd have to get on." I nursed my Coke, gave up on the fries and wiped my mouth. Dave put down his coffee cup.

"You want to ride with me?"

"You want a partner?"

"They'll give me one whether I want one or not. Gotta get my logs legal."

"I would ..." *How should I say this?* "It's just that, well, I don't smoke. And it smells pretty raw in there. How would you feel if I cleaned the cab?"

"You'd do me right proud." Dave answered sincerely. "No problem, girl. Let's go get the cleanin' stuff. Whaddaya need, bleach?"

"I want some air freshener too." Dave started laughing.

The grime was hopeless, but when I finished, the truck smelled like bleach and jasmine. Dispatch said I could stay on his truck. They gave us a load to pick up in Medford, Oregon, on Monday morning, with thirty-six hours to make the 15-hour drive.

"Dave!" I practically shouted. "I live on the way to Medford! We can go up US-101. I can see my family!"

"I never been up 101 before. You sure we can go up that way?"

"It's beautiful. You'll love it. Wait till you see!"

Dave talked about wanting to fish after we passed Santa Rosa and 101 started following the Russian River.

"That's Squaw Rock," I pointed and explained. "Some say it was named after a woman who committed suicide off it."

A few hours later, we hit the two-lane road through Leggett at dusk. Dave slowed the truck to a crawl. "Girl, you didn't tell me it was a narrow mountain road on a cliff!"

"Everything gets trucked into Humboldt County. It's got to be okay."

"We're 52 feet, plus the cab. We're not even licensed for a road like this. How long does it last?"

"Not very long. And this is the worst."

In order for the trailer to miss the cliff, Dave had to pull into the middle of the southbound lane to round the blind stretch. Our horn bellowed loud and long.

"Awk!" Dave hollered. "Look at that drop-off!"

"I'm sorry. I didn't realize."

214

At night, the redwoods looked monstrous going through Richardson's Grove, another narrow two-lane road. Navigating through them at a snail's space, Dave worried out loud, "I hope we make it around these trees." Crawling along, honking, the high beams sending streams of light into the forest, I breathed in the scent of redwood through my open window, loving the cool night air. Happy to be home, I kept a lookout for on-coming headlights.

I didn't tell him about US-199 out of Crescent City, the only way north to Medford, Oregon.

We parked at Denny's in Eureka. Since Dave didn't get in the sleeper, ever, I unrolled my sleeping bag in there without touching the pegboard walls. Dave slept sitting up in the driver's seat. Didn't even use a pillow.

I called Mom before we ordered breakfast.

"You're here? In Eureka?"

"Yes! Come see!"

"I'll be there by ten."

A crisp Sunday morning, I watched Mom pull in and park next to the truck. I bear-hugged her. "This is Dave. Dave, this is my Mom."

"Pleased to meet you ma'am." Dave stuck out his hand. Mom shook it and managed a smile. I boosted her up into the jump seat. She looked around, hesitated at first, then put her head back in the sleeper. I saw her scrutinize the living arrangements. She came right back out and I held her tiny hips as she came back down to the ground.

"What time do you want me back here?" I asked Dave.

"How about three?"

"Great. See you then. And thanks." Smiling from head to toe, I walked around the cab and climbed into Mom's Nissan.

"Oh, Margot." Mom's faced screwed into a knot. She looked at the steering wheel, her hand on her face, shielding me from seeing her eyes.

"I know," I interrupted. "This truck's the dirtiest one I've been on."

"It looks so small." She looked at me. "Do you both sleep in there?"

"Dave sleeps in the driver's seat. But with the others, when we're both in the truck, I sleep on the doghouse."

"The doghouse?" Mom looked so fragile all of a sudden. Her face went slack with big sad puppy eyes.

"But he's the nicest guy. Honest."

She faced the windshield while I explained the comfortable doghouse, looking out the windows, how perfectly I fit because I was short. She started the engine, and I thought of a walnut when I saw the lines in her face go pinching back into her nose. She was trying so hard to be supportive.

Having the truck right there in front of my mother caused a rush of adrenaline to surge up from my gut. I felt so independent. Mom was seeing the real me. Her distress didn't daunt my pride. Her walnut face didn't trigger my shame.

"Where shall we go?" She asked.

"Let's see if Bobby's home." Off we went.

We found Bobby in his studio above the Art Center. He and Mom hadn't seen each other in a while. Bobby must have been in a productive cycle because he looked healthy and happy. We toured his studio getting the lowdown on all his latest projects. Wedding invitations. A business logo. Ten sandblasted glass windows for a restaurant.

"But that's enough out of me," Bobby patted my shoulder. "Your turn!"

I told them about Ed and Penny and the junker hay truck. Mike, and all my stuff stacked there in the truck stop. Dave's knock-knock jokes. I talked about all the rabbits in New Mexico, that awful spider at the drinking fountain, the urban blight in Philadelphia compared to the fresh air we lived in. "You know what gets me?" I paused. "The sunset is red back east. You can look right at it and it doesn't even hurt!"

I took a big breath. "We are so lucky to live in all this clean beauty." Mom and Bobby nodded, perhaps thinking *Margot is lucky to be living.*

Bobby came along with Mom to drop me off at the truck, and to meet Dave. "Wow! That's huge, Margot!"

The truck did look huge, standing all by itself instead of parked at the 76 with a hundred other rigs all the same size. Maybe our trailer really was longer than anything I'd seen up here in Humboldt County. Maybe our truck really wasn't legal.

216

Highway 199

Oops

February 9, 1981

Mom hugged me too tight and too long. I tensed my muscles to meet her grip. Bobby wrapped me in his spirit. So happy for him, wanting his good cycle to last, I hoped he felt my love in return.

With a big smile, I waved a final goodbye out the window. Dave and I took off for Medford, Oregon with two hours of daylight left. Dave gaped at Humboldt Bay and the ocean views. I swelled up like I owned the place. When the highway twisted through the lagoons, I talked about Yurok oral history, the big bear that stomped through and made the lagoons in one single event.

"They've found whole Sitka spruce trees under the water in the Mad River Slough." I waited a beat. "They think it must have been a huge earthquake." [4]

The road narrowed after Big Lagoon. Mountain on our right, drop off into the ocean on our left. Dave turned on our high beams and started sounding the horn.

"I wish we could stop so you could really see a redwood forest."

"I'm seein' it. It's big all right." He shifted down, honked. We came around the corner and begin climbing uphill. Big Lagoon behind us, the sun brilliant over the ocean at dusk, the sky looked clear all the way to Japan, nothing red about it at all.

"Do you know what a *Moses Hole* is?" I asked.

"A Moses Hole?"

"Sunlight shoots through a redwood canopy and shines a beam of light down through the trees. The water in that sunlight looks like dust. You've probably seen pictures. It's the most beautiful."

"Oh, I seen pictures of those. They're real pretty."

"The air feels heavy in a redwood forest. It's so quiet." Later, "You know what trilliums are?" I described the three-petal blooms, wild white beauties covering swaths of the forest floor in spring.

All the way to Crescent City, whole sentences tumbled out of me. "The wild rhododendrons are the best ... Maybe we'll get to see the elk when we get to Prairie Creek ... Look! A deer! ... That's Freshwater Lagoon. In the summer, this whole flat stretch is filled with campers. You can't even see the ocean ... Skunk Cabbage trail, my favorite ..."

We sped through Prairie Creek state park. "This road is murder in the summer. All the Runamuckas creep along at ten miles an hour. But it's straight all the way through. You can go sixty if you want."

"Runamuckas!" Dave bellowed.

"That's what we call 'em. ... Wait till you see the golden bears guarding the Klamath River Bridge ... otters live in a pond right back there ..."

We managed the forest road in fifth gear. Dave took advantage of every passing lane to navigate around the curves. He wiped sweat from his forehead with a leftover napkin, leaving a trace of mustard on his hairline.

In the rear-view mirror, I saw the line of cars stacked up behind us. One time I counted eight because the straight part lasted long enough. I couldn't see the end of the line.

Not a single paved turnout. No pull-off remotely long enough for us. Dave shifted down, tried to wave people around us, but twilight, and the winding road, made his arm impossible to see.

"Damn, girl!"

"I'm sorry."

"Sweat's getting in my eyes. Hand me that napkin again."

I picked up the napkin from right where he'd thrown it, at my feet. I watched. He left grit from the floor stuck to his face. I couldn't see the mustard splotch after that.

Dave shifted into tenth to manage the final drop into Crescent City. Along the flat stretch into town, Dave leaned back and gulped a lung-full of air. "So that's it?"

"There's a big right turn up ahead. I don't know how we're going to make it." I fully realized now that US-101 was not built for our truck. "It's got a median. We can't use the south lanes."

We started in our left lane. Cars on the right backed up. Our trailer wheels went up on the sidewalk. We missed a telephone pole by inches.

"The road gets skinny, now." I said, nervous, when we exited 101. I didn't know how we would climb that first ten miles of tight curves on 199. The redwood canopy blotted out the sky, making night black. Our headlights beamed into the trees downhill on the left or into the cliff on the right, but never on the road. For ten miles, we took up both lanes and squeaked around each turn, running our trailer wheels off the pavement, into carpets of redwood needles. No shoulder on either side.

Edging fully into the opposite lane to start, we barely made it around the curves. I offered to walk ahead and act as a signal, but Dave declined. He laid on the horn. Waited. Inched. Thank God no one was driving drunk into Crescent City that night.

We pulled off at Hiouchi Hamlet, a roadside RV park with a restaurant and a grocery store. "What's next?" Dave said.

"It gets really narrow now, Dave. I'm sorry. Can I buy you dinner?" The restaurant was closed. "Something in the market?"

"Get me a Coke and some chips."

We inched our way from Hiouchi to Gasquet along the Smith River. At night, in the mountains, traffic was slight. Our headlights beamed over the river, possibly warning any on-coming cars. The guardrail, a knee-high steel rail on wood posts, wouldn't have helped if we'd followed our headlights. One foot too far and we'd plunge fifty feet, taking the guardrail with us into the gorgeous Smith River, which Dave never got to see.

We reached Patrick's Creek. "Only one more bad stretch." I said, as much to myself as to Dave. "When we come down into Oregon, the road straightens out."

Dave was quiet. I could smell him.

"Totally my fault we're in this pickle, Dave. I'm really sorry."

"You didn't know any better. Jus' wanted to see your Mom is all."

When we finally hit I-5 at Grants Pass, Dave sighed. "That was some drive, girl!"

Galesburg, Illinois
Poetry

February 10, 1981

We made the quick jaunt to Medford, talking about frightening curves and close calls, and the pickup that stopped for us at that first curve right after Patrick's Creek.

"Lucky for us he didn't barrel around the curve. He would have rammed head-on into our trailer."

"He must have heard the horn, seen our headlights."

I crawled into the sleeper. Dave slept in the driver's seat.

The next morning we picked up our 840 boxes of pears before breakfast. In the Pilot truck stop, having skipped his shower, Dave already had his food when I arrived at the table, clean, with wet hair and a fresh change of clothes.

I scooted into my side of the booth. Dave's face matched his shirt, like camouflage. The dirt, streaked with sweat, had dried. One wrinkle, caked with mud, looked like a dirty fingernail. He needed a shave. Had I just met him, I would have guessed he dug ditches for a living, and came to this restaurant on his lunch hour.

"We weren't legal on 199." Dave announced. "We were legal on 101 up till Benbow, but not after that." The waitress came by with a pot of coffee and he held up his mug. She poured.

"How'd you find out?"

"I looked it up. There's a STAA chart behind the counter. You just have to ask for it."

"STAA?"

Dave didn't know what it stood for either. While waiting for my scrambled eggs and toast, I took a look for myself. Surface Transportation Assistance Act. We were okay on our overall length, but our king pin-to-rear axle was too long. Our turning radius was too wide.

220

Stomachs full, Dave still at the wheel, we headed south down I-5 over the Cascade Range back to I-80.

Truck stop to truck stop. At one, after refueling at the terminal outside Rawlins, Wyoming, Dave carefully pulled two yellowed pieces of paper from his wallet. The old paper had tears in the creases. He pointed to the teacher's red 'A' on each of them. "Wrote these in high school. What d'ya think?" He offered them across the table.

Poems. I pushed his hand back. "Read them to me."

One was about girls in their swinging skirts.

"Cool, Dave. It rhymes perfectly. Read me the other one."

"I ain't never shared these with anyone before." He read the next one, another rhyming poem about being on the move. Iambic Pentameter. Full page poems, both of them.

"I love 'em Dave." I put down my hamburger and dug out my journal. "Listen to this."

Sense of Place
There is oil everywhere. And mud.
Lots of water on the floor. Dirty.
Very dirty.

I had to pay $2.50 to shower.
Believe it or not,
I paid $2.50 to get clean in this slime pit
of a tiled bathroom in some 76 truck stop
on I-40 outside of Oklahoma.

It smelled like raw sewer.
Walls papered with graffiti.
Wet tissue strewn everywhere.

I had flip-flops to wear
but nowhere to hang my towel.

Dave's laugh was more like a holler. I couldn't help but see his black teeth. He hadn't showered since Sacramento. I'd never known anyone so filthy, so smelly before, much less liked them, as I liked Dave.

Dave didn't do log books, so I did them for both of us.

Back in the truck, I finally got in the driver's seat. Dave offered me a stick of *Doublemint*, then threw his wrapper on the floor. I did the same.

I let the engine warm-up, adjusted the air in my seat, and moved out of the lot.

"Been married?" He asked.

"Once. Right out of high school. You?"

"Yeah. Not no more. How long have you been truckin'?"

"Let me see," I counted. "Almost seven months now. How 'bout you?"

"Off and on, maybe ten years."

"What else did you do?"

"I worked trap. Had fourteen miles once up on the Indiana Wild Cat."

"What's trap?"

"Trapping. Catch mink, fox, muskrat, beaver. Bring 'em in and sell the skins."

"You skin 'em?"

"Not gonna carry the whole animal back with me." He smiled.

"You do anything with the meat?"

"Use some as bait, leave the rest."

I shifted my weight, checked the rear-view mirror, my speed. Traffic was light. "Look!" I pointed up ahead, "On the right."

"Antelope!" Dave said. "Don't see too many of those."

No snow or ice, but barely twenty degrees outside. Clear and cold.

Dave combed the greasy strands of hair from his forehead with his fingers. "I homesteaded in Alaska once. I want to get back out in the wilderness. If I can get the money together, I want to quit by next month, get back up there."

"What about children? Ever have any kids?"

"I got seven kids. All boys."

"Seven sons! Are you a seventh son too by any chance?"

"Don't know. Could be I suppose."

"Tell me about your kids."

"One is in jail for murdering a 70-year-old woman. She was found dead with a pencil and a knife stuck in her neck. Brian is fifteen but the State of Indiana is waiving his juvenile rights and trying him as an adult. They could hang him." He kept right on talking. "I got another son in jail for burglary."

About five minutes later he said "I shot my oldest son through the leg when I was drunk. Don't drink no more."

"I don't drink either. You go to AA?"

"Naw. I just quit."

Suddenly, Dave climbed into the sleeper and snapped the curtain shut.

Is he mad?

Why did I like this guy? And Donald too, with his eighth-grade education and false teeth. I thoroughly hated Mr. Clean, and Kent, the poor sad sack. And, of course, I hated Bob. Two out of five ain't bad, I decided.

A few hours later, Dave emerged from the sleeper, excited to recite a new poem. Full of playful rhymes about "Margot the motor mouth, carrying her crates of fruit, her pallets of pears, in the wilds of Wyoming," he read the perfect rhyme over the engine noise. "... wheels rollin' along, singin' a song, she's a trucker and a talker, she's a worker and a walker ..."

In Galesburg, Illinois, Dave agreed to have dinner in town. We endured a tough steak and canned string beans. Even I would have preferred truck stop food to our meal. Home of Carl Sandburg. I pooh-poohed his poem about fog creeping on little cat's feet. "Sandburg never saw fog roll in over Humboldt Bay."

"I spose yur right."

"But, I'd give him a high five on Chicago being the city of big shoulders. Great image. Want to walk around town a bit?"

Galesburg's old brick churches stood on corners as a testament to Christianity. I gaped at the huge multi-colored stained glass windows. I

223

could have walked for hours, but Dave wanted to get back on the road.

Whole frozen rivers. The Mississippi looked frozen. In Pennsylvania, a whole frozen fountain shot up like an abstract ice cube.

After four tries, I backed into the Finast loading dock in Windsor Locks, Connecticut, where we delivered our pears. Immediately, dispatch sent us to pick up more fluorescent light bulbs in Fairmont, West Virginia.

A ten-hour deadhead. Dave didn't complain, wasn't even grouchy. Truck stop to truck stop, rest breaks and pit stops, he'd driven the last twenty hours. I wished he'd let me drive.

I came out of a much-needed shower at the Nashville terminal and started moving my laundry into the dryer, when the office guy told me I had a phone call.

In the Nashville terminal? Who knew I was there?

"Margot, we're pulling you off Dave's truck."

Tom, Partner #6

Indianapolis

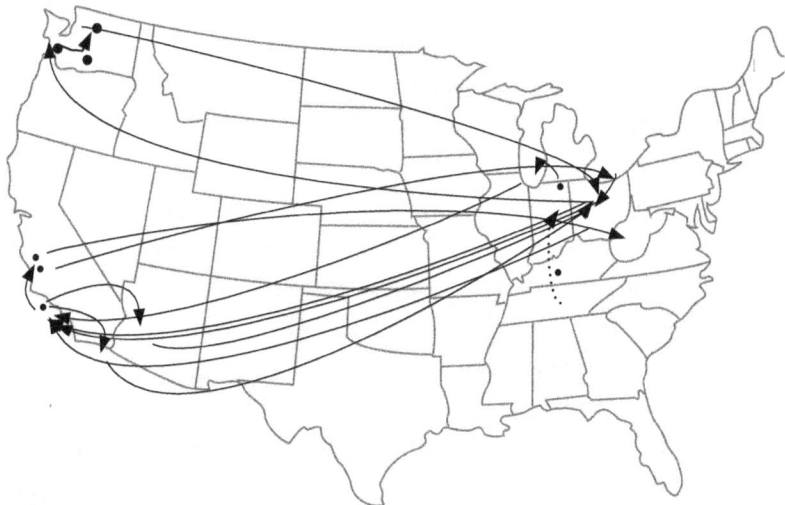

February 17, 1981

The crisp formal voice on the phone continued, "Dave called in, says you're a nice girl and a good driver but he can't ride with you anymore."

"Why?"

"Men and women usually don't last long together. It's no reflection on you."

But it did reflect on me. I thought I was making the partnership work.

"We're sending you up to Indianapolis to get on a nice gentleman's truck. He's been with us a while. His name is Tom. He's made himself clear that he's only taking a woman partner as a favor to the company. He's got a great truck, real clean, and we think you'll be a good partner for him."

"How will I get there?"

"We've booked a flight for you. The mechanic will take you to the airport this afternoon. Someone will pick you up in Indianapolis. Tom will be coming down from North Manchester. You'll like him. Don't worry."

I hung up the phone, went to look for Dave, but the truck was gone. "He fueled up and pulled out," the attendant said without looking up. "I put your stuff in the office."

My jaw dropped. He must have called dispatch back on I-65.

I didn't feel hurt, exactly. Dumbfounded was more like it. I thought I could read people.

What was my part in this one, Larry?

I boarded a small commercial plane and flew from Nashville to Indianapolis. The fuel jockey was waiting to transport me to Tanksley's terminal. At the terminal, I sat down on a greasy orange plastic chair in the florescent lighting of the drivers' lounge to wait for Tom. At 6:00, the office manager locked his door, barely acknowledging me on his way out.

Surrounded by my luggage, with no one else around, and nothing to read, I perused the candy and Coke machines, bought a Butterfinger. The night mechanic came in twice, first for a Snickers and later for a 7-Up. I walked outside once, got as far as the truck entrance, but the cold air zapped me, so I returned to the warmth, and endured the speckled linoleum reflecting glaring light into my eyes.

Tom finally showed up at midnight. He wore a white pin-striped, collared shirt, khakis, and brown leather shoes. Blonde, receding hairline, fair complexion, mid-twenties. Husky.

Cold shoulder didn't describe his greeting. Freezing was more like it.

"I have no idea what happened," I told Tom as I loaded my stuff onto his truck and climbed in.

"He put you off the truck because you wouldn't sleep with him." Tom didn't look at me.

"What? Really?"

Tom didn't acknowledge my surprise. He drove us out of the parking lot and turned toward the freeway.

"Where are we headed?" I asked.

"Krogers. Cincinnati." I figured Tom wouldn't appreciate having a conversation, so I kept my mouth shut. We drove two hours southeast to Kroger's loading dock in silence. Tom promptly climbed into the sleeper, handed me my sleeping bag, and snapped the curtain shut.

Dispatch had only said Tom's truck was new and clean. They didn't mention his stereo system that boomed through four speakers. A booster took the distortion out of the CB. A Whistler radar detector was mounted top-center of our windshield. A small TV was affixed to the ceiling in the sleeper.

At 6:00 a.m., fourth in line to unload, we waited in the truck and ate without talking. With both of us carrying food in our storage compartments, we wouldn't be eating at truck stops. We left Kroger's by 8 a.m. and immediately dispatch gave us a rush load of Time magazine inserts from Chicago to Los Angeles.

Tom's icy mood permeated the truck.

This partner thing was the shits.

From Cincinnati, we drove north on I-69 to North Manchester, Indiana, where Tom's grandparents lived. Tom gave his grandmother a sack of dirty clothes and put the clean ones in his storage compartment.

His grandparents' double-wide trailer sat in the middle of about a half-acre of perfectly flat and freshly mown green grass. Plastic lawn ornaments. A squirrel, Bunny. A deer and two fawns. Tom's grandmother, I never learned her name, showed me her home, every room. She talked about how much they loved Tom, how he was a hard worker and a good boy. I wondered if she hoped Tom and I would become a couple.

After our twenty-minute visit, we drove northwest to Chicago. Northern Indiana is pretty flat and squared-off, like Ohio. We arrived without a hitch, loaded, signed, and drove south on I-55 to St. Louis, then southwest on I-44 to I-40 in Oklahoma City. We each drove five-hour shifts. Tom didn't ride in the jump seat. He snapped himself in the sleeper when I was driving.

Barely civil and only necessary communications. "It's your turn to drive ... I'll be back in a half hour ..." He never looked at me when he talked.

I puzzled over his behavior. I'd showered. My clean clothes didn't smell like Dave's truck. I'd packed the smelly ones in my outside compartment. Maybe Tom got jilted by a female partner, and his silence had nothing to do with me, or maybe he's one of those gay men who doesn't like women. Or maybe I'm an awful defective person. He knows I'm a fraud.

I thought gay men mostly liked women.

He knows I'm an intellectual snob.

Once, as we were changing shifts, I asked him, "How many tapes do you have?" A huge box of tapes filled his sleeper compartment.

"Over ninety."

"Your stereo sound's great."

"$850 dollars. Not including the tapes."

Eight words. No eye contact. Would it have hurt to look at me? Illinois, Missouri, Arkansas, Oklahoma, New Mexico, Arizona, California. We didn't eat together. He'd pull into someplace after I'd moved into the sleeper, tell me he'd be right back, and leave for an hour. When I needed to eat, he'd already eaten. "Stop wherever you want." And he'd snap the curtain shut.

In Los Angeles, Tom let me back into the loading dock. Afterward, he drove up I-10, put me up in a *Motel 6* saying he would spend his layover with a friend. He would leave a message each morning at the front desk with dispatch's instructions. "Expect long layovers on the west coast this time of year." Tom didn't say goodbye. Just walked off.

For each of the four trips we made into Los Angeles, he dropped me off at the *Motel 6*. All together, I spent about thirteen days over the next month, sleeping in that *Motel 6*.

Once, Tom didn't leave a message for me. He arrived late in the afternoon with a horrible black eye and a swollen, strawberry-red cheek. His hair was greasy and his clothes looked like he'd slept in dirt.

"What happened?"

"Got blocked in."

"What?"

"Truck in front of me. Truck in back. Couldn't get out."

"Couldn't you have called?"

"No. I couldn't have."

"Well, what happened to you?"

"Never mind. I'm just hung over."

"Oh, come on, Tom."

"I got in a fight, all right? I don't want to talk about it."

Los Angeles
Motel 6

February/March 1981

The motel had a dirty pool surrounded by a chain-link fence. Weeds pushed up through the cracks in the cement. Five of the seven pool recliners were broken. I spent my first day by the pool listening to the freeway, still with nothing to read. I watched TV that night. In the morning, I checked for Tom's message. We'd be staying another day. I started walking around the seemingly endless strip malls, all painted gray. I bought detective novels.

Finally, I thought to look up Alcoholics Anonymous.

"Where are you?"

"On Wilshire Blvd off I-10."

"Hang on a minute." It wasn't even a minute. "There's a meeting at 8:00 about a mile from you. It's on Commonwealth. You gotta map?"

I had the front-desk's map.

"It's at the First Congregational Church. Just walk down 6th toward the freeway. You can't miss it. The meeting is in the back. You'll find it."

I walked the mile plus and found AA's triangle-within-a-circle sign a good ten minutes before the meeting started. Maybe a hundred people had already arrived. In the huge room, clouded with cigarette smoke, men and women stood in little clumps around the chairs blabbering to each other and laughing. Invisible, I sat on the edge near an exit sign.

A woman spoke for fifteen minutes about her resentments and how these people had done her wrong and how they all lived in her head for years until she got into this 12-step program. "The topic for tonight is *You spot it - you got it.*" I'd heard that slogan mentioned in a meeting before. Evidently, if you resented a behavior in someone else, then you had that behavior yourself. I'd resented the hell out of Kent and Bob and Mike. So did that mean I behaved just like them?

I got a meeting schedule and walked back to the motel with a boat-load of thoughts. So, what did Tom spot in me that he hated? My gender? Dave was easy. I spotted his kindness so that meant I was kind. Jeff, my cokehead fiancé. Two lonely hearts? What about Mike the bully, Kent the victim, and Bob the slime wad? Angry. Clean. Stupid. Unreasonable. Am I those things?

That night I dreamed I wanted this guy, real bad. I walked out naked in front of him and tried to hug him but he wasn't having it. Then it was Aaron and he didn't want me. Then it was Mike! I felt repulsed but at the same time I kept trying to get him in bed. Then I was in this dirty bathroom and I had to pee but everything was so dirty and poop was everywhere.

I woke up with a full bladder, the dream vivid. After I did my business, I walked next door to the House of Pancakes, ordered bacon and eggs with my cakes, and mulled over what the dream could have meant. I knew Mike and Bob had no clue how I felt on the inside, didn't know what I thought about, or hoped for. I resented their selfish, inconsiderate need for my attention.

I slathered butter and poured syrup. Ate my scrambled eggs.

I'd never considered who was inside all those bodies I'd chased for the last five years. I'd just wanted a man. Never asked what any of them wanted, or hoped for.

That card Mike brought me from the truck stop store. He had assumed I wanted to read a hallmark apology. Never asked me what I wanted.

I felt the sadness wash over me.

Bob would have paid for all my meals, bought me beer and slept in a twin bed next to me for the rest of eternity if only I would have kept him company.

I stared at my empty plate. No charcoal gray fog in my eyes. No confusion. No need to decorate people with reasons. No insane spinning over the why of myself. Mike, Bob, Kent, and I were lonely, and we hadn't a clue what to do about it.

Los Angeles
Lessons

February to March 1981

When I lay over in Los Angeles, I went to Alcoholics Anonymous meetings. I journaled about them as actively as I wrote about my driving adventure. I'd get in my shitty *Motel 6* bed, write down what I remembered, and then sleep. I'd wake, sit up, and record what I'd dreamed.

When you identify instead of compare, your heart is open. The lady said to stop judging people, bring them into a circle. Take 'em off the ladder. Huh. I had a ladder all right. Terry hung out at the top. I'd put Darrel - Terry's best friend - on rung two. I'd move Bobby up or down a few rungs, depending. Goodie-goodie-two-shoes never got above rung one. Everyone was either way up at the top till I kicked 'em off or below me, so if they left me, who cared anyway?

When I was crazy though, running an education revolution and preventing WWIII, I ranked at least ten rungs higher than Terry. Of course, when I came out of the hospital, the abyss didn't even have a bottom rung I could grab.

Either better than or worse than but never a part of. AA called this *terminal uniqueness.*

I dreamed I screamed at Terry. Told him to get out of my house. And I kept finding new rooms, or my house would be over on O Street, just half finished with a swimming pool and expansive lawns. One time I found a "jewel" in a new room. Bobby had left a small sparkly diamond.

I kept dreaming about poop. The absolute worst dreams. I'd wake up feeling so embarrassed. I always had to poop real bad. One time I pooped in a toilet out in the intersection of Del Norte and J Streets. Several times I'd go outside my house trying to find a place to poop in some trees, but there'd be so much poop I couldn't find a place to step. I'd poop in strange people's houses. I'd walk out holding poop in my hand to show somebody. Most of the time, though, I'd find a public rest room. The stalls would be tiny and poop would be smeared on everything. The floors would be wet. No toilet paper. I couldn't poop.

Clearly, my dreams were telling me I needed to get rid of something.

I didn't meet anyone at AA. Nobody introduced themselves to me or shook my hand. I didn't care, but I always hoped this guy Mark would be at the meeting and he never disappointed. People called him *Keychain Mark*, because a chain of colored plastic key rings dangled from his belt to his knee. He reminded me of a walrus, or Santa Claus with no beard, and usually, he'd get the whole group laughing. *I stopped arguing with idiots when I noticed that bystanders couldn't tell us apart.* Fifty people belly laughed and I cracked-up right along with everyone else. Right after the meetings, I'd slip out and walk back to the motel.

I started seeing how I covered my fear with bravado.

I still didn't ask Tom why he didn't like me, but I tried to let go of my anger toward the fuel jockey when he put grease on my steering wheel. When the truck stop waitress brought me mashed potatoes instead of French fries and never came back with the fries, I tipped her anyways. I tried to show idiots a smile instead of a scowl. I tried to be patient with slow people. I even left the shower cleaner than I received it. Mostly though, I boiled inside while I was doing all these good deeds. At least the self-pity abated. Anger felt so much better.

North Manchester, Indiana
East Coast Deliveries

February to April, 1981

We were going east in New Mexico, in February. At the truck stop, I'd taken a shower. My hair was wet. I carried my purse over my shoulder and I'd stuffed my dirty socks and underwear in the pockets of my baggy green corduroys. I started back to the truck, noticing how crisp the air felt on my wet head.

Suddenly, a policeman barreled straight at me. He didn't stop in time, and he drove his vehicle right over the cement parking bumper. "Where are you going, miss?" He called through his window.

Me? "To my truck."

"Is that right. Your truck, huh?"

"Yes." I dug in my purse. "Here's my log book." I didn't offer to hand it to him.

"What's in your pockets?"

I dug. Out came my underwear. Cotton. No lace.

"Okay." I heard his back tires thump over the divider. His engine idled along behind me. I walked the length of my trailer and glanced back before I stuck my key in the passenger side compartment. He was still there, watching me load my under things into my dirty clothes bag. Finally, he drove away.

Did prostitutes wear waterproof work boots? Was it my earrings that gave me away? Jeez! Down the road a piece, I realized he probably thought I had drugs for sale. A whole baggy full in both pockets.

Although out west we suffered long lay overs, back east we loaded right out. Tom got off the truck in North Manchester and I'd deliver the east coast loads alone. I'd get back to North Manchester, and while he spent his last hours relaxing at home, I'd walk all over town. A population of 1200, every one of them greeted me with a smile.

Right on Main Street, I came upon a retail headstone store. A sign in the window advertised, "Custom Engraving." I couldn't just walk past.

Inside, maybe thirty styles to choose from. Three rows, like grocery aisles displaying the selection. The older gentleman behind the counter, smiling, called out, "May I help you?"

"Just looking!"

Since I delivered the east coast loads alone, I learned to drop and hitch trailers without getting covered in grease. I backed-up in tight quarters, sometimes with the sun in my face and shade hiding the dock. I could tell if a tire was flat after one thump. I didn't need directions to Cincinnati's Kroger's. And one day, after three tries, I backed into that loading dock.

I knew the freeways, hated deadheading long distances, and ate in truck stops. My job wasn't new anymore. I was planning to quit come September, and I needed to make first seat before then. First seat would be proof. I could claim success, and my book would have a great ending.

On the way back west, I was dozing in the sleeper when suddenly the whole left side of the truck tilted, putting my feet above my head. I shot out of the sleeper, "What's happening?"

"The steering tire blew. I got it. Don't worry." On straight, level, dry freeway, Tom let the truck coast to a stop on the shoulder. I hated to think about a front tire blow-out in the mountains. Rolling to a stop wouldn't have been an option. Braking would cause more instability. Keeping the truck going straight meant having enough arm strength to steer the truck against the truck's inclination to veer.

Tom assured me I'd have the strength to hold the truck steady. Through the CB relay, we got a tow almost immediately to a nearby tiny truck stop. Two hours later, we were driving across the state again on I-40. For the tow, the use of their truck bay, the tire patched till we could get to Oklahoma City, the bill was $19.00.

Around the first of March, I learned why truckers nicknamed the state of Missouri, *Misery.* Not only did it have a plethora of highway patrol, but its weight limits were more strict than the rest of the states and all our gross weights had to comply with Missouri's weight limits.

Driving through *Misery*, the weigh master accused us of being over the weight limit.

Tom was livid. He dug into his logbook. "Look!" He jerked the weight receipt out the window, held it above the weigh master's head.

The weigh master had to stretch to take the receipt. "Park over there." He pointed. Come into the office."

Past twilight and getting cold. Tom yanked the truck off to the side, let it cool, and turned off the engine. I started out of the truck, intending to follow Tom into the office.

"Stay here." An order.

Tom stalked off and I waited twenty minutes.

"He fined me $183.00. That cocksucker." Tom slammed the door. Fired up the engine. Turned on the heat.

"But you had the weight receipt."

"He said it looked forged. I asked him how could I even get a receipt to forge in the first place? He said 'Not my problem'." Tom used the weigh master's snotty tone. "We're grounded. He says we're 2100 pounds overweight."

"What's that mean?"

"It means we can't move until we get rid of 2100 pounds. What an asshole."

We waited for the next Tanskley truck to come through the scales. Three Tanksley's later, one came through that could take our 2100 pounds. We backed our ass ends together with the other company truck and heaved 2,100 pounds of lettuce into their trailer, agreeing to meet in Indianapolis and collect our produce that evening. To pay the fine, Tom had to get a com-check from dispatch.

"Happens all the time." *Lightfoot* appeased Tom. "Happened to me once. They pocket the money. Nothing the company can do."

More driving. More loads. More deliveries.

So tired of riding alongside Tom's cold shoulder, what a relief when he started talking.

"My dad's a millionaire. Self-made."

"Wow! What'd he do?"

"He's got 350,000 chickens. They all lay an egg every day but never get out of their cages. Wanted me to go into business with him. I couldn't do it."

"I couldn't either."

236

"You ever smelled a chicken house?" Tom asked.

"Never have. Never even owned a chicken."

"Makes me gag to go in one of those houses. My Dad thinks I should just get over it."

"My parents would like me to get over a few things too."

"My sister wants to be a hog farmer more than anything else."

"Really? Why?" *Conversation finally.*

"Hogs have individual personalities and are quite loveable."

"You're kidding."

"No. They're really smart. And hogs aren't dirty. That's just a wives' tale."

We drove. I told Tom how my parents wanted me to eat food that was good for me, no matter how bad it tasted. I told him my Dad was a doctor. In our small town he was quite well known.

"I won a Corvette contest once." Tom started another story. "Beat sixty-three other Corvettes."

"What? You mean a race?"

"No. A show. You don't ever drive a show car. My Dad bought me the Corvette. I painted it up, had it shipped to Chicago, and I won. I'll show you pictures when we get to my grandmother's."

His grandmother pulled out the scrapbook. A pearly white 1969 Stingray with a flaming woman painted on the hood. Deep purple covered the pop-up headlights and front fenders. Orange flames came out of the purple and ended behind the doors. The lady, long blonde hair, huge bosoms (of course), wore a wonder woman type costume, except it was orange and purple. White leather tuck-and-roll upholstery. But, hard to fathom, Tom insisted he installed white carpeting *under* the hood and covered the spare tire *under* the car. After the contest, Tom gave the car to his mother.

How much easier to ride with a partner who talked. I'd enjoyed the quiet with Donald and Dave, but they hadn't been angry. I remembered my refusal even to talk to Bob much less befriend him. I hadn't offered even an inkling of companionship. I'd been a complete bitch.

West to east. East to west. The engine vibrated the steering wheel. The jump seat jarred over every pothole, and the rhythm of every shift, which increased the noise before quieting it down, accentuated the monotony.

At least the skies changed. Gray, stark Wyoming would get colored for five minutes at sunrise or sunset. Once, in Utah, clouds morphed from a muddy gray to a precise reflection of purple.

Even Nevada, that monochrome nothingness, got artistic once. The sun, hidden by a depressing charcoal layer of clouds, broke through. I could see a rainstorm and a rainbow miles away, but we never got wet.

Dispatch called me to ask about whether Dave had ever filched fuel while I was with him. No, I thought Dave was an upstanding guy. Did I see him getting money from another truck driver? No. They told me Mike got fired. He had a fender bender. Did I think he took whites?

"I saw him taking something that time our engine blew up. He talked non-stop, that's for sure." I relished learning that Mike got his due.

Tom and I started sharing meals with truck drivers we met through the CB. *Snowdragon, Sourmash, Polygrip, Ugly. Snowdragon* was my fault. Good conversationalist through the mic, but what a slob. *Sourmash* was a trucker Tom had met before and his partner was *Polygrip. Ugly* was gorgeous. He hauled band equipment around the country, talked about history and music. We'd read the same books. He ordered a salad. I fantasized about a roll in the hay.

Tom took me through Tehachapi Pass on US 78 from Escondido to Brawley, California, instead of taking the freeways. We passed orange groves, strawberry fields, fruit and almonds stands, horses, and handwritten signs advertising oak firewood for sale. Bees for sale in the town of Julian. General stores, creeks with wooden bridges crossing them headed up to farm homes. Antique stores, health food stores, wood storefronts and not much traffic. We drove through Escondido's finest neighborhood too, homes all landscaped and blooming, before coming upon the San Diego Wildlife Zoo Park Reserve. I caught the animal smells, earthy and pungent, through my open window. Away from freeways. Food for the eyes. Just a few hours driving through small town life. My mood soared.

Ellensburg, Washington
The Outrageous Taco

March-April, 1981

For six months I'd driven I-80 and I-40. I knew which shifts and when to make them over Donner Pass. I knew the freeway exchanges through St. Louis, which rest stops to avoid, and which truck stops had the best food. Finally, we got a load headed for someplace different, Tacoma, Washington. Babies needed their Gerber's in the Pacific Northwest. I got to drive I-84 through Utah. Lost Creek roared through a narrow gorge. The infamous *Cabbage*, a steep hill in Oregon, looked more ominous than it actually was, because from top to bottom, the view was wide and clear. *Cabbage* didn't hold a candle to Donner Pass.

We delivered our baby food, and drove through a watery landscape up I-5 to Seattle, then cut east to Ellensburg on I-90. Tom hoped we'd get a load of apples instead of potatoes. Apples paid more.

We laid over in Ellensburg, a small town surrounding Central Washington State College. The cool, fresh air and high overcast reminded me of home.

A no-nukes demonstration blared through a loud speaker in the parking lot right off Main Street. The college was on spring break, but a small, enthusiastic audience stood in front of the makeshift stage. Two bearded guys took turns being the emcee, passing the megaphone back and forth, urging about thirty folks to get active. A girl got up on stage, played a guitar and sang, but without a microphone, I could barely hear her.

Radioactive waste got buried in Hanford, Washington, just sixty-five miles from Ellensburg. I crossed my arms and stood with both feet planted. A hot snarl boiled up in my cheeks.

Warning flags popped. No one had been rude to me, or disrespected me, yet my hands balled into fists. My muscles knotted. I wanted to hit someone.

Little Iodine piped up. *Do something about it. Stand up and be someone for once.*

Me: *You're just too emotional, Margot. Give it a rest.*

Iodine: *Come on. Make a difference. You're such a wuss.*

Me: *They bury radioactive waste all over the country. Why so angry now?*

I dug out my journal, sat down and fumed in words. Nuclear waste in this gorgeous landscape? Jesus! The whole environment losing to a massive human ego trip. News reports flooded my thoughts. I couldn't get the words out fast enough.

> You are the gluttonous, red-assed ape
> of the eighties, oh John Q Public.

Little Iodine in my left ear: "Yeah, get on that megaphone. Let 'em have it.

> sporting those tits and that red ass for
> every macho penis walking by ...

that's it ... let 'em have it.

> like on TV wagging with a blue butt
> shooting out little white stars and
> stripes for Reagan's neutron bomb.

I let Little Iodine wail.

> Good Luck, Utah. It's the long, pointed,
> and red-tipped cock-missile practicing
> rape on your mountain until you lay all
> your bodies down like sandbags holding
> off a tidal wave.

Me: *I'm sick of being kind.*

Iodine agreed: *Who ever righted a wrong because they were*

*kind? This is good shit, Margot. Get up there on that megaphone.
Get 'em motivated.*

Then I remembered how my plans for a teaching revolution got me
incarcerated.

So many people in power ruining what I cared about. I let Iodine rage
on the page. She spit out her frustration in marathon sentences.

> Washington deserves a monument.
> Of tears. Some great big good Joe
> Veteran Monument with a teardrop
> steeple to commemorate being your
> nuclear toilet.

> ... Yesterday you moved eight hundred
> nerve gas bombs from Colorado to
> Utah. You shot down two Libyan
> Planes. You murdered an old lady in
> Detroit for seventeen dollars. You
> raped your granddaughter, spilled oil
> on Idaho and leaked contaminated gas
> all over San Francisco.

> On and on ...

Three pages later, my hand hurt. Ink colored my baby finger. But
Iodine was finally quiet.

Because I gave my mailing address as Oklahoma City on the petition,
the taller bearded guy announced me as being the furthest from home and
thanked me for my donation ($5.00) publicly.

"Come to dinner with us." A short red-headed man called. I looked
up. *Me?* I pointed to myself. "Yes. Come on." I closed my journal and
went to dinner with the group.

Twelve of us ate Mexican food at *The Outrageous Taco* and talked
angrily about nuclear waste. Later, we discussed everything from babies
to books to truck driving and the loneliness of spring break.

I wanted to drink with them. Maybe just one beer. I probably would have, but I was wedged deep in the booth and the waitress never came back. Plus I'd told everyone at the table that alcohol made me sick. I sat with my Coke, talked as if I belonged, and waited, thinking I'd pick up a six-pack later to drink in the cab.

The redhead dropped me off back at the truck. No stores anywhere. Tom was watching TV in the sleeper. He snapped the curtain shut. I didn't drink.

The next day, March 30, 1981, Tom and I drove up to Chelan and loaded apples. Lake Chelan reflected the surrounding mountains like a huge mirror. A sign actually read *Hitch Hiking Permitted* along alternate Route 97.

Tom loaned me $15 to buy an antique radio back in Ellensburg, where we headed to hook up with Interstate 90. I spun the dial and got some just breaking news. "President Reagan has been shot!" The assassin, Hinckley, had been caught immediately.

I mailed the radio home to my mother, and we headed out. Eleven months earlier, on May 18th 1980, Mt. St. Helen's dumped ash all over those same freeways. Closed them for over a week. Fifty-seven people killed, two hundred houses destroyed, 185 miles of road wrecked, forty-seven bridges failed. The biggest volcano eruption in the U.S. since we started keeping records.

Concentrating on the road, looking straight ahead, Tom announced. "I got another job. I'm getting off the truck in Cedar Rapids."

"I didn't know you were looking for another job!"

"Benefits. Better pay. Guaranteed time-off in North Manchester."

"Oh. Guess you'll take your stereo."

"Yeah."

"Can I buy your TV?"

"No. I'm taking that too."

He drove. I stared out my window.

"I'm gay. Sorry I didn't talk more."

"Yeah. That's okay. I kind of figured it."

"I've never talked about it to a straight person before." He shifted down and I watched Lost Creek roar through the gorge. "I had a friend

242

in Los Angeles."

"Had?"

"Yeah, that ended last month. That time I didn't show up at the motel to get you."

"What happened? You looked awful."

"We walked out of a bar together. Big mistake. Someone must have seen us get into the truck. Two truckers blocked us in. When I got out of the truck to take a leak, this guy grabbed me, beat me up pretty bad. Another guy pulled Bill out of the truck and beat him up too. After they finally left, I crawled over to Bill. He was doubled over and spitting up blood. I had to wait in the truck while he limped across the parking lot to call his Dad."

"Why didn't you help him?"

"Their trucks were still blocking us in. If they saw us together again I was afraid they'd kill us. Anyway, Bill wouldn't let me help him. I watched his Dad pick him up at the phone booth in front of the bar. That's the last I time I saw him."

I heard Tom's voice catch. He looked out his window, lost his power and had to down-shift to pick it up again.

"I wish you could have told me. I would have understood."

"I couldn't take that chance. This isn't exactly a gay-friendly job."

"I'm sorry that happened to you."

More silence. I thought the conversation was over, but maybe ten minutes later Tom said, "The next trip out, I called him. His Dad answered. He told me to never call again and hung up on me. I never even found out if Bill was okay."

"That's awful."

"My dad disowned me a year ago. Told me I was an abomination."

"And I thought I had it tough." I sighed. As an afterthought, I added "I thought your grandmother wanted us to be a couple."

"Yeah. She doesn't know. She's a Baptist. It would kill her."

In Cedar Rapids, Tom gave me a glowing recommendation over the phone. I inherited his perfectly running truck. With his last armload of belongings, Tom looked off to the side, half-swallowed his goodbye and walked away.

Morehead, Kentucky

Promoted

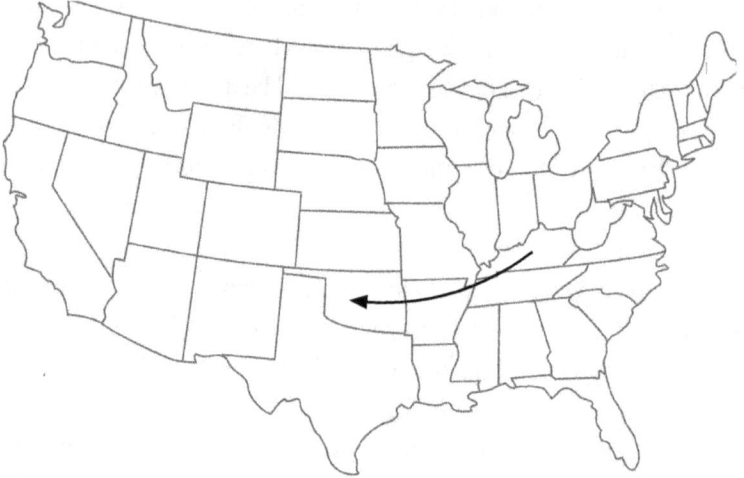

Spring 1981

Tom gone, I delivered our apples to Pic and Pay in Circleville, Ohio. From there, I took DuPont chemicals to Los Angeles, and immediately loaded broccoli bound for Charleston, West Virginia. 6,500 miles driving alone. I made 18 percent wages, kept my driving hours legal, and slept much deeper in a still, private truck. On April 16th, dispatch promoted me to first seat. I wrote them a thank you card. They sent me three hours north on I-77 to Payden City, West Virginia, to pick up a load of Corningware.

After loading the Corningware, I celebrated my promotion outside of Charleston, West Virginia. The *Good Times Lounge* looked decent, advertised live country music, and seventy feet of parking was conveniently located right on the street. The Laurel Mountain Boys played hard core Appalachian bluegrass and sang in three-part harmony to an all-white audience. The banjo player was the guitar player's son.

Fingers blurred across the strings but produced incredible clarity during *Cripple Creek* and *Foggy Mountain Breakdown.* I didn't drink or dance. Just watched and listened.

Back in the truck, I thought about junior high school, listening to Dylan music for hours after school, with as many as ten white friends at my house. I wondered if the black people I'd met treated me special *because* I was the white person in their neighborhood. In the Appalachian bar, as another white person, I was not special. Just alone.

Southbound on I-77, from Charleston to Roanoke, Virginia, I bounced over the worst potholes but enjoyed jaw-dropping scenery. Purple blooms and lush green foliage started at the road's shoulder. The houses looked like they were painted last week.

Morehead, Kentucky. I explored Morehead State College. Restricted visiting hours posted on the women's dorms. Telephone poles advertised Christian religious activities. Muddy-yellow brick houses with small windows. Everyone in Morehead smiled, same as North Manchester.

I found the college's recreation room, lost a game of pool and won a game of ping pong. With about fifteen college students, I watched an old *James Bond* film, *Goldfinger.* A couple whispered and giggled, three boys did homework, and I wondered really, whose life was less complicated. Maybe all of us were just trying to work out who we were.

A truck driver hanging out in a college's recreation room.

While watching Sean Connery save Fort Knox's gold, the temperature outside dropped to below freezing. I hadn't worn a heavy jacket and I'd parked the truck a good mile from the college. When I finally climbed into my sleeping bag, shivering, the warmth was heaven and I fell asleep immediately.

First-seat drivers used bedding instead of a sleeping bag. I bought pillows, sheets, and blanket. I tacked a huge cotton tapestry bedspread to the ceiling and walls. My hanging clothes hid behind the spread, protected from a partner's all-saturating cigarette smoke. I'd never have to look at that depressing pegboard again.

Half way to the Nashville terminal, I stopped at a rest area in Kentucky to dig into my granola. Weather appropriate, no partner to consider, I changed into cut-offs and put on my flip-flops.

The green field next door was so inviting, I decided 'to hell with the bugs'. If there weren't ants, I'd sit under that gorgeous maple tree, a huge cauliflower shape totally filled out with new leaves. Eating lunch with my back against a tree, all I needed was a creek and a fishing pole and I'd be in a Mark Twain novel.

I got about twenty yards into the grass when my ankles caught on fire! I looked down, nothing! Jesus! I ran out of there. I sat down on the curb. Red splotches multiplied all over my ankles, climbed up my shins. My feet were on fire. The blotches started bubbling into lumps. Just touching them stung.

A U.P.S. guy walked past me on the way back to his truck. I asked him if he knew what had happened.

"Looks like chiggers. Where you been?"

I pointed. "Out there. What can I do?"

"Nothing. Maybe get some cream or something, but they'll go away in a few hours." And then he said, "Unless you're allergic."

All I had was *Tinactin*. I tried a little on my ankle. No help. So I drove to Nashville through all that idyllic green, with stinging welts from my shins to my toes.

How could I have known about chiggers?

I should have asked someone. It could have been hornets, or black widows.   Lighten up, Margot. If you can walk off a cliff following the lure of a man, you can certainly be excused for walking into chiggers. By the time I reached Nashville, the welts were gone.

Robert, Partner #7
Oklahoma City

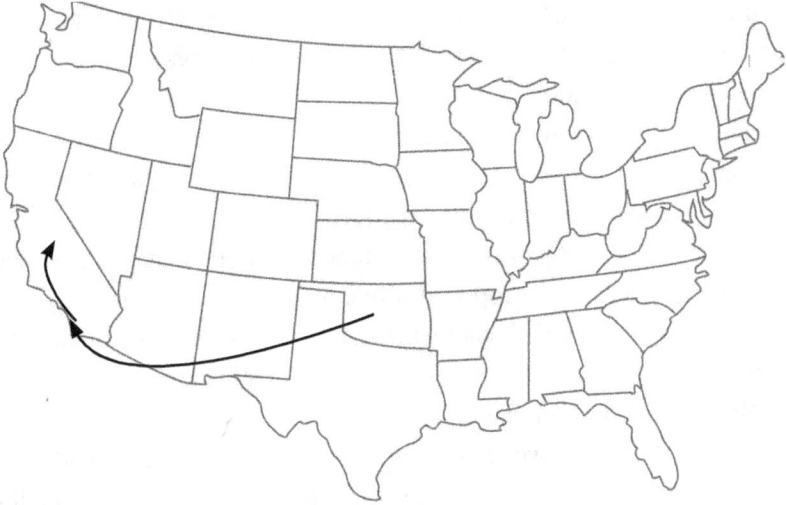

April 18, 1981

In Oklahoma, I picked up my new driving partner, Robert. Right off, I noticed the large growth pushing Robert's eyebrow down into his eye. Maybe that was genetic, but nobody gets born with a nose that made a right turn and stopped just above the sores at the corner of his mouth. Scrappy looking, skinny, but with little baseball-sized muscles under his shirt sleeves, which were rolled up holding cigarettes, both sides.

"Only been with Tanksley a couple of months. Haven't been driving that long." I had him take the first shift, to watch his driving. "I'm from Missouri. Got me a wife back home. She's pregnant. We're going to have a kid come July or August."

"What'd you do before you started driving?"

"I worked on the river. Worked on the river all my life."

"You get down to New Orleans?"

"Nah. I worked the dock. Running messages and stuff. Sometimes they let me load cargo."

I didn't ask why he left "the river" to start a long-haul job that would almost never get him back to his pregnant wife in Missouri.

He drove safe enough. I napped across Oklahoma and through the Texas panhandle into Albuquerque. The most boring stretch of smooth, white freeway — with the exception of I-5 in Central California — I didn't have to tuck my hands under me to keep them from flopping. I took my shift, and seven hours later, lay over in Flagstaff, agreeing to leave early in the morning.

Robert split right away. I stopped in *The Museum Club*, but without beer, my courage went south. I opted for a good night's sleep and left. Robert got back to the truck around 3:00 a.m.

Hung over the next morning, he wretched out his door and then without asking, crawled in the sleeper. I drove to Barstow. In Barstow, I saw him sneaking around with another trucker while we were doing laundry. Back on the road, he broke out in a sweat something awful.

"What'd you do back there?"

"Nothing." His answer came out in a rush. He fidgeted around in the jump seat, crawled in the sleeper for ten minutes, came back out smelling like whiskey. Whiskey wafted all over the cab.

"You buy liquor from that guy?"

"Sorry. I spilled a little. I'll be good to go in a minute."

"Good to go where?" Half question, half invitation to a castration, but he didn't answer.

I jackknifed the truck into the loading dock, and Robert took off. Two hours later, my trailer empty, I wanted to leave but Robert was nowhere. Dispatch instructed me to wait till three, and that's when he showed, so drunk his drunk buddies had to shove him up in the jump seat, where he passed out. His head bounced on the passenger window and his neck whip-lashed back and forth until I dropped him off at the old *Motel 6*. Three days later, when I picked him up, he opened the motel door on his knees, turned and crawled back to his bed, groaning.

I put him in the jump seat, drove to Los Banos, and got rid of him.

248

James, Partner #8

Council Bluffs, Iowa

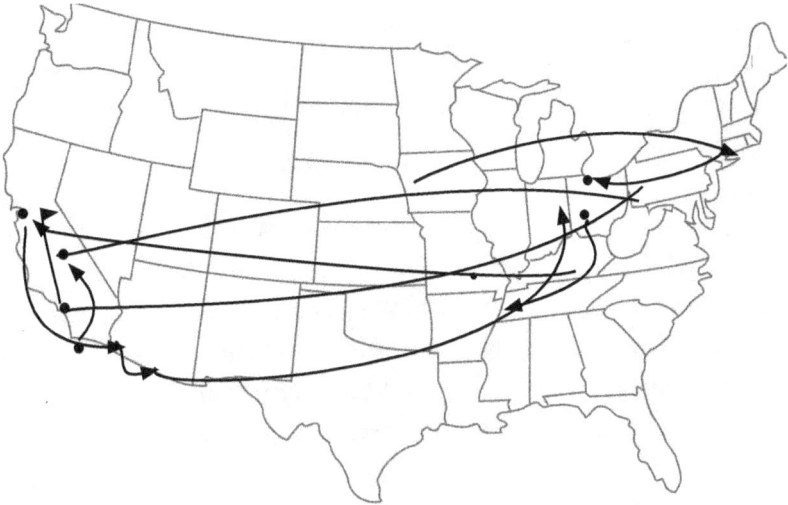

April 22, 1981

"I heard you got first seat! Congratulations." Miguel came into the lounge, bought a Coke out of the machine, and sat down beside me.

"Thanks. How'd you know?"

"Office manager told us." Miguel smiled

I got all warm inside. "I have some time. What are you doing after work?"

"I pick the kids up at my Mom's. I could call her ..."

"Oh, don't. I put my hand on his forearm. "I'd love to meet Mateo and Sophie. We could have dinner. Celebrate. My treat."

We ate at a local Mexican diner. Miguel called the waitresses by name. The cook came to our table. Miguel introduced me to everyone, and they all seemed to give him knowing smiles as if to say, "We're rootin' for you, Miguel."

I watched Miguel put the napkin in Mateo's lap. Sophie and I talked about our hair, and how we like to have it styled. Miguel wiped Mateo's chin twice and afterword, picked the burrito parts up off the floor. And Miguel wouldn't let me pay. "Your promotion present. You deserve it. Will you be here tomorrow?"

"I'd love to stay, but I need to get going tonight."

He dropped me off at the terminal. "Here's my phone number. Let me know when you will be coming through Los Banos again. I'll try to get a day off."

Sophie, in the back seat said, "Yeah. I'll comb your hair if you want."

Mateo said, "Yeah."

Miguel's entire world was pulling for him. A woman to replace the wife who'd left him for another man.

Loaded with lettuce on my way to Windsor Locks, Connecticut, spring bloomed on I-80. In Utah, huge flocks of inland gulls flashed their light and dark sides back and forth. In Nebraska, magpies squawked like crows. I'd heard farmers paid ten cents for every dead magpie, because they ate crop seeds.

From Iowa to Pennsylvania, wild flowers. Pink, purple, blue, orange, yellow, and green. Even Wyoming had yellow patches of flowers blooming in that dusty gray-green scrub brush. Soon, new colts, lambs and calves would be following their mothers around. I-80 would be something to look forward to again.

James boarded at the terminal in Council Bluffs, Iowa. His determined stride measured just short of a stomp. James wore a straw cowboy hat, the kind with the brim all bent up and curved down over his forehead. Denim legs walked on cowboy boots. His plaid belly strode to the truck, silver belt buckle leading, and he stuffed his single suitcase into second-seat's compartment. James had dark hair, looked freshly shaven, and greeted me with a smile.

"Want to take the first shift?" I asked.

He looked pleased. "Sure do." He threw his sleeping bag and daypack on my bedding, pulled himself into the driver's seat, and before we'd even climbed to fifty-five, James pushed "talk" on the CB. "Radio
250

check."

"Affirmative," came the answer. James put the mic back in its handle.

Ten seconds later, the CB called to us, "Big R here, you got your ears on, Shirley?"

James had the mic in his hand before he'd shifted into tenth gear. "You be comin' in loud and proud." His hand came down for the shift, didn't miss a beat.

The voice cut in and out. "They checkin' comic books in the coop?"

"Can't say. Just pulled on the boulevard."

"10-4." Static garbled the voice.

"Radio check." Jim held the mic to his mouth.

Did he really think our CB just broke?

"You be fine, Shirley. I be Tommy comin' up your back door."

"Southern Comfort back at you, Tommy. Got a handle?"

"I be Proud Papa."

"10-4. Your better half in the cab?

"Naw. Home takin' care of the new ankle biter."

James' voice boomed over our engine. "Got me a new beaver today."

Oh Jesus Christ, I frowned, and looked out the window.

The Tommy England truck passed us. The driver gaped, trying to see me —Jim's beaver.

"Gettin' back home soon?" Southern Comfort continued.

"Not till I flip flop."

"My home 20 be the Gateway." James continued. St. Louis was James' hometown.

So fucking what. Was James going to talk the whole time?

"Shirley Temple." A new voice. Older. Clear reception. "Smooth Move on your back door. You got some bumper sticker." (A car following close behind us.)

"Must be savin' fuel." James' thumb popped the mic's button —on off on off— moving the mic to his mouth to talk, resting his hand on the gearshift when listening — a seasoned pro.

"Four pretty young beavers."

"Proud Papa backin' out."

"See you on the flip side, Proud Papa."

Old man again. "Sweethearts. All of 'em."

"I'd back off, get 'em in the hammer lane, but I'd hate to see their greasy side up."

"Copy that."

I considered ripping the mic out of the dash. But James was cheerful, clean, sober, a good driver, and at least he wasn't talking to me. I watched the scenery before sliding back into the sleeper.

I didn't want to be so mad all the time. After Robert, drinking turned me off. Maybe I'd try to get to one of those meetings.

We took five-hour driving shifts. I ate from my stash in the truck and let James stop where he wanted. With the curtain snapped shut, I couldn't hear his conversations; but when I rode in the jump seat, his voice dominated the cab. I couldn't order him to shut-up. I missed driving alone. All the noise and vibration made me cranky and instead of resting, I grew even more tired and frustrated.

Twice, once in Illinois and another time in Pennsylvania, a huge pheasant flew right past the windshield while I was driving. But even their brilliant plumage, so close up and personal, didn't lighten my mood.

Our lettuce had cracked ribs. We waited twelve hours, without pay, for Finast and Tanksley to settle on a price. James napped in the sleeper. I didn't want to walk or read. Couldn't sleep. Totally irritated. What the hell was I doing *living* with James? He didn't read and he certainly didn't walk anywhere. He wanted to eat greasy food, go from truck stop to truck stop, and talk on the CB. I didn't think he could have come up with a higher level thinking skill had he been tortured. Had he ever even appreciated a sunset? I hated his cowboy image. How phony. And the worst, of my own free will, I was living with him 24/7.

I thought of Charles Bukowski, the drunk poet, who kept searching in the bars, hoping for a woman good enough to love. With a miniscule of relief, I finally put pen to paper.

Oh, Charles Bukowski

I thought you'd be at the
loading dock by now
loaded and ...ok
leering at me and quick
figuring out something to say
to this
Unique Woman Truck Driver
that you've never seen before
who maybe has a brain
and a free will
and what the hell,
might as well give her
a fair chance, right?
...

And then I would say
after introductions and small talk
that you shouldn't throw-up on your poems.
I could read them.
You could watch.
You could direct.
You could really have a good time
and I wouldn't charge you anything
for it.

I thought for sure I'd have
found you by now

instead of all these shipping clerks.

San Francisco

Lettin' The Air Out

April 24, 1981

"We're hauling dispatcher brains." James announced to every passing truck. We'd loaded glassware in Brockway, Pa., due in Pomona in six days.

"You ever haul plastic?" I interrupted his CB conversation. "Glass is heavy compared to plastic."

"Couldn't hear you. My beaver was talking," he called back to his talking buddy.

The truth? Truck driving culture consistently displayed courteous, chivalrous words and actions in front of women. Truckers didn't swear. Being a beaver wasn't an insult. Sexist, yes, but meant as a compliment. *Southern Comfort* thought I was pretty.

"*Southern Comfort* here, on the flip flop. You got a handle?"

"I be *Alley Cat, Southern* ... What's your 10-20?"

James talked and drove. I bounced and scowled, my upper lip stuck in a snarl on James's shift. Illinois still had the worst pavement. Iowa the worst traffic jams.

James and I made two more round-trips together. Glassware to Pomona, produce to Cincinnati. Down to Kentucky for the load of Levi's and finally, to San Francisco to deliver them.

"*The Gay Bay*" had hills that defied standard transmissions, a bay filled with sailboats, and skyscrapers clumped together downtown. I parked the truck along the Embarcadero, walked the length of it and window-shopped through Fisherman's Wharf. Next, up the hill on a streetcar to walk the length of Chinatown's main street. From there, I hopped a bus to the Haight, where flower children and hippies reigned ten years earlier.

I didn't know what James did and I didn't care.

In the Haight, I searched the Salvation Army thrift store. Then, next door, I purchased a punk greeting card. I guessed the store clerk to be eighteen, and she looked desperate. She reminded me of those college students in Morehead Kentucky. Totally the opposite in appearance and circumstance, but still, she looked like she was suffering, with not knowing the why of herself. The idea struck home again. This time, I found a coffee shop, ordered a Diet Coke, and wrote.

Red Lipstick

Red Lipstick. Huge breasts. Obese.
White white whale like skin. Freckled.
Her blonde hair, butched and waxed,
nearly bald on the sides, and maybe
an inch and a half straight up on top.
Low cut, sleeveless, ruffly
polka-dot dress above the knees.
Maybe she's eighteen.

I worked for Bank of America when I was eighteen.
And I was a drunk, in a football stadium,
cheering, finally gettin' some air out.

I was a good woman gettin' off on my man's stuff.
I could get next to that man, get under his arm,
walk so close you'd almost think I had good stuff.
And a lotta people did think I had it good.
And I just let 'em think it.
Thinkin' Margot had good stuff.

Ten years later my memory is still raw.

Not rotten like eggs or raw like meat,
but raw like a loss of innocence.
It feels ok to me now.
Like when the sun burns me a little.
It feels kind of good.

So yesterday, when the red-lipped sales clerk
sold me a greeting card from the Haight-Ashbury
in San Francisco, I wondered about her stuff.
Whether she's got it good or bad,
or whether she's just gettin' a little air out right now
and feelin' a bit raw.

All that walking pushed my mood back to the positive side. James was James. A respectful, cheerful, competent, clean cowboy. I was in his world, he wasn't in mine. I knew he wanted to spend time in St. Louis. Next time around, I'd try to be kind.

Los Banos
Miguel

May 8, 1981

As first seat, I had the luxury of determining where we lay over, and I drove the two hours over to Los Banos from San Francisco, because Miguel lived there.

I bit my lip and apologized to James. "Next load, I'll stop in St. Louis, James. Sorry I didn't give you any time off there."

"Never mind. I already asked for a new partner. I don't want to be stuck in Los Banos and we could be here for days."

"Okay. I'll recommend you for first seat." I gave him Miguel's number in case he needed to reach me and told him I'd call each morning with dispatch's instructions.

Miguel's ex-sister-in-law invited us to a plush estate that housed three hundred race-horses. She worked there as a stable hand. The estate, all a Texas brown — a swept-clean brown — had an expansive view of the Central Valley. We shared a dinner of hot dogs and beans but couldn't tour the stables. Strict safety precautions kept anyone without credentials from seeing the horses, which were shipped in and out on a daily basis.

More brown the next day at the Los Banos Creek reservoir. Dust, like dried cinnamon, rose up into my nose. Zero humidity. The kids and I didn't throw rocks in the reservoir because Miguel said we shouldn't. Just concrete and dust, blonde grass on its way to a crackly brown, and a gravel parking lot.

Later, Old Spice announced Miguel's presence when he opened the back door for me. He introduced me to his family, offered me a chair and a Coke, and even though the ice chest sat in the shade across the yard, his aftershave never left my side.

A cool eighty in the shade, the family had gathered outside, sitting on plastic lawn chairs. Not concerned about the gnats, they swished them away between sips of ice-cold drinks. Constant chatter among the relatives floated around the yard. Some of the kids sat with us, on dying patches of grass. I imagined the bare dirt, packed down like concrete, came from plenty of kid play.

Miguel's dad barbequed beside a table spread with two kinds of Jello salad, tamales, rellenos, enchiladas, refried beans, and some homemade very hot sauce. White bread and butter just out of the fridge sat next to the disposable forks and knives.

I ate dinner with his extended family. Aunts and uncles, cousins, sisters, brothers, parents. The children —about ten of them— ran in and out of the house and yelling. Adults laughed, half of them drinking Coors, the other half sipping Cokes, shushed the kids.

In the living room, half full cans left rings on every surface. A fluorescent, neon, velvet bullfighter dominated one wall. Pictures of soccer teams, honor roll certificates, Miguel's softball team, and his ex-wife's hair-styling license surrounded the bullfighter. Framed pictures of family rested on every tabletop, even beside the huge TV. I noticed two Bibles, one by the sofa and another with the magazines under the coffee table. The couch wore lace doilies. Extension cords led from the outlets up to Sears-Roebuck wall sconces. Painted white with gold flecks, their clear light bulbs shown through like tear drops.

Sophie combed and brushed my hair and put pins in it. When Miguel's sister, Angelia, learned that having my hair played with pleased me as much as it entertained Sophie, she offered to braid my hair. The next day I closed my eyes and practically swooned while she put my hair into thirty braids. Turns out that even though my hair looks thick, it produces very thin braids. My scalp, a lily white between each dark braid, made quite a contrast. I took the braids out shortly after I left, but the hour it took to accomplish that feat sent me to heaven.

Later, though I tried, I couldn't ever remember being given that much attention ... with no strings attached. Extended family like that. I'd never seen that before either, except on TV. I'd loved *Walton's Mountain*.

Miguel and I took Sophie and Mateo to Hagerman's park. Green because they water the grass, shade under huge old maple trees. A policeman, in full uniform, blew his whistle if the kids ventured beyond their knees into the swift Merced River. I watched him blow his whistle, sweep his arm across his chest, and the kids obediently moved back to shore. I turned. He'd parked his cop car in the shade.

"I can't believe that." I was shaking my head.

"What?"

"A policeman playing lifeguard. Is he actually paid to do that?"

"I don't know. Maybe." Miguel opened the ice chest. His Mom had made ice-tea for us. "I think he's just here for a couple of hours."

I sighed, looked up through the Maples, and shook my head one last time. Miguel smiled, amused with my astonishment, and gently passed me a plastic cup of cold, sweet Lipton's.

I took a sip. "No one will ever believe me, Miguel. A policeman, directing children at the river."

We both watched Mateo and Sophie splashing water with three other children. Mateo in water to his ankles, Sophie sitting beside him.

"Miguel, I like you so much."

"I like you too. So do my kids."

"I want us to keep being friends, but I know I'll never settle here."

"I know."

"I could never live in this heat."

"I can't believe you watered the roses in the middle of the day. Who doesn't know that about roses?"

"I live in the fog. We water roses anytime we want. I hope I didn't kill 'em."

"They won't die. They'll just get brown spots. I'll water them tonight."

"Miguel," I looked at him. "I don't want to have a break-up down the road. I want to stay friends."

He put his arm around my shoulder and squeezed. "Gotcha."

Douglas, Arizona
Dad

May 11, 1981

Our fourth pick-up of produce put us in Yuma, Arizona. Since I'd be driving east on I-8, I received permission to drive a hundred miles off-route to visit my father, in Douglas, Arizona.

I hadn't seen my dad since his visit to Napa State Mental Hospital, when he'd taken me for that long awful drive. We never talked on the phone, or wrote letters. For years, my only contact with my father was the May Day bouquet he sent me every year, and the perfunctory thank you note I returned.

I'd show my father I was a *somebody* now. A first-seat long haul truck driver.

From Tucson, down to Douglas — on the Mexican border — I drove through the night. James wasn't having any of the hundred extra miles. I let him sleep. Didn't ask him to drive.

In the middle of nowhere, in pitch dark with no warning, I charged into a small roundabout, screeched on the brakes, made it around the turn but threw James in a panic thinking we were going to flip, become one of those huge sow bugs on the side of the road. He roared out of the sleeper, stared in a daze, while I explained what had happened.

"I thought we were going over," he said. "I thought you were swerving to miss a deer."

"There were no lights. I didn't see it coming."

"You know you don't swerve for an animal, don't you."

"I know."

He crawled back in the sleeper.

After midnight I reached my father's house. I jumped out of the truck and James got behind the wheel. While Dad carried my overnight case inside, James and I agreed to meet me at noon the next day. I didn't introduce them.

Dad came back out his front door and we admired a night cereus plant, a cactus that blooms only once a year, at night, and only for twelve hours. I'd hit the jackpot. A white flower on a dusty gray plant, lit by my Dad's flashlight. I feigned enthusiasm. We didn't hug. I went to bed. Then I slept through breakfast and Anne, Dad's wife, got me up in time to meet James at noon. I'd spent my entire layover in their guestroom.

Driving all that extra way just to sleep. Dad must think I'm an idiot.

While I slept, Dad went to his office at Phelps-Dodge, the mining company that pretty much supported the town. He'd retired from his general practice in Eureka and moved to Douglas two years before I'd gone crazy. He gave physicals and referred worker injuries to other doctors. Dad spoke fluent Spanish, a second language I'd never mastered at our dinner table lectures all those years ago.

Dad skipped two grades and graduated from high school at fifteen. He graduated from college a year early and started medical school at 18-years-old. At the ripe old age of twenty-four, my father was on a Marine hospital ship, serving at the pleasure of the Navy, at Guadalcanal.

Dad was a stickler for taking the high road. *If you're smart enough to do it illegally and get away with it, then you're smart enough to do it legally. Might as well be legal. You'll never have to watch your back.*

I'd never displayed any intellect, and this stupid layover added to the string of poor choices my Dad had watched me make. My father had never spanked me, or yelled at me, although he demanded much from my brothers —competitive swimming, grades, respect— but it seemed to me that all I needed to do was wear a dress and find a husband. Since he had already left for work that morning, I didn't have to see his half-smile, which meant either *you're a sweet little air-head,* or *I forgive you for being a dumb ass.*

On the way out of town, I saw a shock of bright red topped by a black cap as a hooded oriole flew across the highway in front of our windshield.

Kathy, Partner #9

Mapleton, Illinois

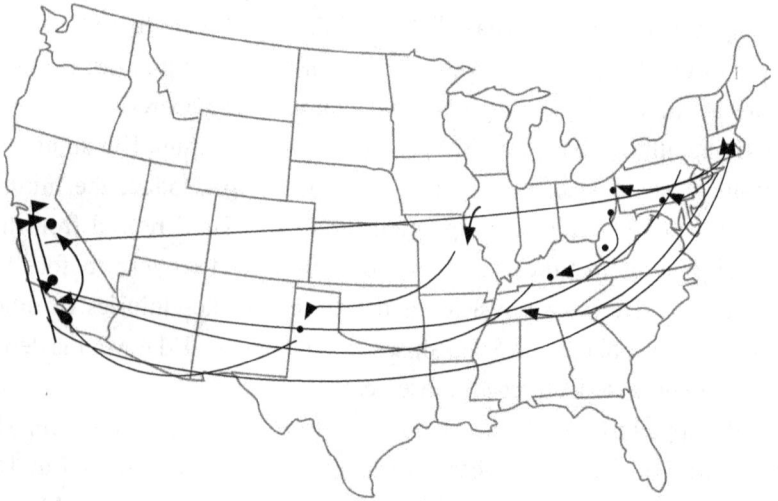

May 18, 1981

We dropped half our load in Indianapolis. James got off the truck. I recommended him for first seat and delivered the remaining produce in Fort Wayne, Indiana. Dispatch asked me what I thought about riding with a woman.

"That would be fine."

"She's overweight. How are you with that?"

"Huh? Can she get in the truck by herself?"

"That wouldn't be a problem. "

"Okay."

"Tell you what, we'll send you both to Mapleton, Illinois. Meet Kathy, see what you think, and if you want to take her on as a second seat, let me know. We'll bring you both into the Cape (Cape Girardeau, Missouri). She can get on your truck here."

"Okay."

He gave me the directions and hung-up.

Interesting. It didn't matter if someone smoked, smelled bad, or talked non-stop, but if she were fat, that was justifiable grounds for refusal? How fat was she? I imagined jiggling arms, a belly hanging out under her t-shirt, pants ripping at the seams. I remembered that guy waiting for a second seat driver last year, after I'd been put off Bob's truck. Rolls of fat laying on his thighs, so fat he couldn't scoot himself up to the table. I thought Kathy's hair would be strands of grease, that she'd stuff gobs of cookies in her mouth while she talked, and have food stains down her blouse. Of course she'd smell bad too.

I arrived at the plant ready to be repulsed, so when Kathy introduced herself, she caught me off guard. "You're Kathy?" I lowered my eyebrows and covered my high-pitched reaction with a smile. I stuck out my hand. "Hi, I'm Margot."

Sure, she was over-weight. Even bigger than a "roundy-round," my mother's enduring words. But solid. Nothing jiggly about her. Clean. Straight, brown, shoulder-length hair curled under in a pageboy. Clear skin, an infectious laugh, and she didn't smoke. Shorter than me, she hopped on her truck, into the sleeper and out again. She wanted to catch up her logbook. How cool was that.

Kathy met me in Cape Girardeau. She loaded her stuff onto my truck, and we headed off to Lubbock, Texas, with my load of anti-freeze.

The red-winged black birds were out in vast numbers, competing with my windshield to catch the bugs. Splotches of yellow, directly in my line of sight, I didn't dare turn on the wipers. I had the truck washed in Oklahoma City.

"Dispatch told me they offered you first seat and you turned it down," I reported to Kathy, who sat in the jump seat. "They said you can't back-up."

"Yeah. I gotta learn."

"Okay. You never have to hit anything if you don't want to. You can always get out and look."

Kathy didn't look convinced, but when I explained the hands-on-the-bottom-of-the-steering-wheel trick, she waved her fist in a rah rah football cheer and said, "Let's do it!"

A woman in the cab with me.   Suddenly, there was so much to talk about.

"Who was your worst partner?" I asked.

"This little short guy. Wore a huge cowboy hat. Name was Mike."

"Really!" I screamed. "Did he talk constantly?"

"Never shut up. Always mad at me too. Everything was my fault."

"I rode with Mike too!" I told her about pulling my stuff off his truck at Sierra Sid's in Sparks, Nevada.

"Mike left me at a truck stop in Alabama. He took off with all my belongings. All I had was my purse."

"Oh my God, what'd you do?"

"The Indianapolis terminal manager detained him. Searched his truck and got my stuff. I didn't get it back for two weeks."

"Did you know he got fired?"

"No! Why?"

"They caught him taking whites."   We high-fived across the doghouse.

Kathy had ridden with five partners. She was my ninth. She'd worked a full year for Tanksley, five months longer than me.

"I've never been to Alabama. Mostly, I end up in Cincinnati," I complained.

"I been all over the south. Alabama, Georgia, Louisiana, Texas..."

"How many flat tires have you had?"

"I don't know. First seat always did all that."

"I see." I made her thump all the tires from then on.

"Diesel Kitty comin' back at ya." Kathy joined the CB conversation as soon as she took the wheel.

"You in that Shirley Temple?"

"10-4. Just out of the yard. Where you be?"

"Just passed the 132 yardstick. *Portable Parking Lot* going west."

"Any east bound got their ears on?"

"10-4, Kitty. I be "*Movin' Smooth*"

"*Movin'*, your bird dog be workin'?"

"Double nickel it, sweetheart. Trap at 100. I heard they's checkin' comic books."

264

Kathy milked the CB entertainment clear past Amarillo. Like a romance novel, the plot thickened with every invitation to stop and get acquainted. I took my time climbing into the sleeper, not wanting to miss out on the good parts. Finally, we turned south on 27 for the last leg of our drive into Lubbock.

Lubbock, Texas, smelled like fertilizer, even with the windows rolled-up. Miles and miles of shit smell on flat-brown land, all the way into town. Not as bad as California's I-5 slaughterhouse, but I ate mints till my throat hurt.

For the twenty minutes it took the dock workers to empty our trailer, both of us lay out flat in the truck, engine vibrating to keep the air conditioner running, me in the sleeper, Kathy on the doghouse. We had driven straight through from *The Cape* in Missouri.

Immediately after signing off on the load, we deadheaded 500 miles back the way we came to pick up baby food in Springfield, Missouri. The busy season underway, we would make more money.

Birds in spring. Colorful wing. Can't hear them sing. The engine's king. I rhymed away, vibrating on I-44, spotting yellow birds, gray-yellow birds, yellow-black ones, redwing black birds. All on a green background. *I'm a truck driver*, I marveled. Kathy got off the truck in Tulsa to stay with friends. I made the round trip from Tulsa to Springfield and back, and she took over from there.

Headed to San Diego with our load of Gerber's, we got as far as Barstow. We left our load for the fuel jockey to deliver, hitched to an empty trailer and drove north to the Central Valley for a load of oranges due in Windsor Locks, Connecticut seven days later.

I spent two days off in Los Banos with Miguel. Kathy stayed in the truck. I cooked breakfasts and dinners, baked cookies with Sophie. On day two Sophie combed my hair, we hunted for frogs at the reservoir, played hide and seek, ate popcorn in front of the TV. Miguel invited me camping in the mountains south of Yosemite. I agreed to take a week off in June.

Kathy and I paid for my visit with continuous driving to make our delivery on time.

Fort Smith, Arkansas
Grandmother

May 28, 1981

We had needed that rest in Los Banos, but pushing straight through to make our scheduled delivery sucked. And from Windsor Locks, Connecticut, they dispatched us immediately to Bristol, Pennsylvania, for books and magazines, which we delivered five days later in Los Angeles. We were beat.

Kathy still hadn't backed up.

"I'm sorry I lay over so long in Los Banos. We should have left a day earlier."

"How about we take I-40 and layover in Nashville next time around?"

"Perfect." Kathy, ever the cheerful problem solver. She played on the CB just like James did, but I enjoyed listening, even laughed along. God, I was a bitch to James. No wonder I had ten partners to Kathy's five.

Nevada, Utah, Wyoming, Nebraska, Iowa, Illinois, Indiana, Ohio, Pennsylvania, New York, and finally Windsor Locks, Connecticut. At the Finast warehouse, I used the pallet jack and unloaded our oranges by myself. Kathy slept.

Los Angeles ordered more books and magazines from Bristol, Pennsylvania, so we set off immediately again, but this time, with a layover in Kathy's hometown, Nashville.

Kathy shared an apartment with a single mom who had two children, Mandy (6) and Jennifer (6 months). Kathy owned every single Elvis Presley album. While Mandy "helped" me clean the truck, Elvis crooned "Love Me Tender" through the open front door. Mandy, who combed my hair for hours, wanted to be a truck driver when she grew up. Funny, how kids touched my heart now, made me feel like I was home. Sure did hate babysitting them back in high school.

Showered, rested, we drove five hundred miles to stop for the night in Fort Smith, Arkansas, so I could visit my grandmother, Hermonsé Lamoreaux. Unfortunately, I'd driven the afternoon shift, wearing my contact lenses. With the sun in my eyes, I'd squinted at that white road for six solid hours. My eyes felt like I'd walked through a sand storm.

I wanted to talk to my grandmother about Mom's drinking. My grandfather had passed away years ago, and I wanted to hear her take on grandfather's drinking also, which had been a hush-hush subject in my house. When inebriated, Mom would mention how cruel grandmother was to grandfather because he *drank for a few years after the war*. Sober, mom would clip my question off at the socks. "He drank three years at the most, Margot. Your grandmother never let him forget it."

Grandfather, a career army man, earned his reputation in our family as a big wig in the building of the Panama Canal. Mom was born in Bordeaux, France, and spent two years of her early childhood in the Philippines. What I learned from my cousin, Carol, however, was that grandfather, a colonel, got sent home from the Philippines, released early from the military. A couple of enlisted men found grandfather laying in a ditch, passed out drunk on the side of the road, and hauled him back to the base. The military gave my grandfather an honorable discharge and a pension, but he never worked again.

According to Carol, her father — my Uncle Tom — spent his childhood pulling grandfather out of bars. Grandmother cleaned up grandfather's messes and kept the family secret. Uncle Tom didn't drink at all. Didn't want Carol to drink either. I wondered if my uncle had shielded his sister from the misery same as my brother kept me from seeing Mom's suicide attempts. Maybe Mom really didn't know the truth about her father.

Grandfather finally did sober up, dry as a bone, after his kids were grown. But in 1960, when grandmother broke her hip, he went on a spree. Apparently, my uncle reamed grandfather a new asshole, saying he'd better not let his wife down the one time she really needed him. Did my Mom actually not know about this?

To his credit, grandfather stepped up, and he died sober a few years after that.

I pulled off I-40 and drove through a stately neighborhood of tree-lined streets with blocks of old, beautifully maintained, two and three-story colonial houses.

"Ooh, look at that one!" Kathy pointed to a three-storey home with columns and plenty of wide steps up to the front entry. Neither of us mentioned its lawn jockey, the statue of a happy black man, arm outstretched waiting to hold your horse. Seemed like every third house had a lawn jockey.

On Grandmother's street, the oak tree branches stretched out, touching each other at the centerline. I pulled up in front of her two-storey home, eager to show off my exciting, creative life in this huge truck. Grandmother came down her front steps. She was looking up and pointing.

I couldn't shut the engine off till it had cooled down, so I jumped out to hug my grandmother and over the noise, she yelled "Look!"

I'd hit the tree. I'd crunched the right top corner of the trailer box and opened up a ten-inch smile. The tree came out unscathed.

Kathy took the truck. I followed my grandmother into her home, and my eyes started burning. I'd stared at that white road too long with contacts lenses in my eyes. Uncle Tom took me to the eye doctor, who gave me pain medicine, and assured me I'd feel better in the morning. Instead of visiting with my grandmother, I had to shove my poor eyes into a pillow and sleep it off.

Blind, I smelled her cooking downstairs. The odor scared me. I was going to have to eat beans or okra, surely some vegetable cooked into mush with stringy green stems or brown lumps. Instead of sleeping, I worried, practically gagging the smell was so heavy.

Grandmother's cooking made the air in her house wet. The dark green goo turned out to be something she was canning and I exhaled my relief. I had to inhale the smell again, but felt grateful I wouldn't be expected to eat what she stirred with her wooden spoon.

I waited till I was out the door before I asked.

"Okra," Grandmother smiled, hugging me goodbye.

Thankfully, the dry air wouldn't threaten our books and magazines. Oaklahoma City repaired our trailer, which came off without a hitch.

The Pacific Ocean
Volleyball

May 30, 1981
Huntington Beach, California

I bought a nightgown in Flagstaff. I didn't have to shut the sleeper curtain. I propped my pillows, and managed to slump comfortably. I brushed my hair, stretched my legs, or lay on my stomach and visited with Kathy while she drove. I listened to her talk on the CB. Time off in the sleeper expanded from a flashlight in the dark, to include the entire cab, shared with a friend. And while my living arrangements grew in comfort, Kathy learned more first seat tasks.

"That's it, isn't it? It's flat!" Kathy dimpled up her cheeks. Thirty million times thumping tires and we finally got one.

"It is. Which tire is it?"

"Uh." She looked at the ground, then at the tire. "Driver's side inside rear tandem axle."

"Yes. You can report this one in Barstow."

Tire changed, laundry clean, we headed into L.A. Kathy took her first turn over the grapevine.

"You've never seen the Pacific Ocean? Really?" Incredulous, to be that close and not visit even once.

"Nope. Haven't seen the Atlantic either." She took three tries to back into the L.A. warehouse. After unloading, they put a few pallets of *Hustler Magazine* on our tail end, instructing us to make a quick (two hour) jaunt to San Diego before heading back east. With rush hour lasting at least two more hours, I drove to Huntington Beach instead. Kathy rolled up her pants, marched right out there and stepped in the water.

"What's that?" she gasped. Kathy had never felt an undertow.

We sat in the sand with our fast food and soft drinks, toes digging in. I inhaled the salt air like it was candy. Then, to my surprise, she marched up to a volleyball game and asked if she could play. I followed her like a little kid, scared to death. Yes! We stepped into the game. Feet in warm sand, sun in our eyes, soft ocean breezes and the scent of salt water. I listened to the grunts, groans and laughter of my teammates. I set up a spike for this guy and I made a great spike too. Kathy struck up conversations and laughed with the guys as easily as breathing. The game over, we climbed into our cab all sandy and headed for San Diego. Both of us had grins plastered on our faces the whole way.

San Diego provided only one adequate loading dock for our 52-foot trailer. From a two-lane busy street, back through two cyclone-fence gates and around a parking lot full of magazine delivery trucks, the one available slot was at a ninety-degree angle from the street. Forty-five-footers were backed in on either side. The dock-worker actually shook my hand, said most times they have to bring a fork lift out on the lot to unload the big trucks.

Kathy trembled watching me back into that San Diego loading dock. I didn't want to give up my fearless talent for backing-up, but I envied the ease with which Kathy engaged with other people. Without Kathy, I'd have had to knock back a six-pack before asking to join a volleyball game. Kathy's first time on the beach, she had said, "What have we got to lose?"

I didn't want to drive to Connecticut at all, much less in five days. Kathy was tired too. No time for a layover this trip. We focused on the money. Kathy, ever cheerful, brought up our favorite conversation.

"We took this wrong turn once ... " she explained "... drove miles and miles down this narrow country road. My partner finally decided to back into a private driveway, uphill. He worked for hours to avoid a ditch, fell into it anyways, and we had to be towed out.

I told her about the drive-through bank lane.

"One time I cut this corner too wide in Phoenix ..."

"I cut that same corner!" We laughed. "Six hundred lanes of traffic and I blocked every one!"

"I was in this huge parking lot," she told me. "A big mall and it was closed. I was backing around, practicing, and I backed right into a street lamp. I didn't even see it. I don't know if I'll ever be able to back up."

"You will. Hang in there. And really, you can always get someone to back in for you."

Two flat tires and refrigeration problems took all the extra time we didn't have. With only two hours to lay still in Nashville, at least we got showered. Mandy combed my hair just enough to make my neck tingle.

In Virginia, Kathy blabbered away on the CB, and hardly noticed me coming out of the sleeper.

"10-4 copy that," and she hung the mic back on its hook.

I stared at the emerald and lime colors. God, I loved green. I'd never appreciated the evergreen trees when I lived in them.

"So I got acquainted and was wondering ..." Kathy hemmed. "what'd you think ..."

"What, Kathy?" She usually didn't hesitate like this. "Spit it out. Is anything wrong?"

"No. It's just, well, this guy is going to Bean Town, and ... uh ... what would you think if I rode with him till Connecticut?"

"You're going to get laid!" I screamed, laughing, and put my hand up to give her a high-five. "Who is it?" I worried that she hadn't met him yet.

"Oh, it's *Smokin' Moses*. That sweetheart we had lunch with."

"Oh. Good choice!" I gave her a mischievous smile.

About a half hour before I reached the Finast loading dock in Windsr Locks, Kathy climbed back in the truck. She laughed and giggled and blushed. I laughed and quizzed and kidded her. We both felt real good.

Why did I hate *myself* after getting laid? Oh yeah, I got laid a hundred times, nothing like "Oh boy! I finally scored!" And Kathy was stone cold sober. Amazing.

On our way back west, with magazines, I forgave Indiana and Illinois for boring me in March, since every living lush green thing attached to the ground looked full of water. I drove the late afternoon and graveyard shifts, watched sunsets and sunrises. That eerie red on the east coast, the brilliance of God across the plains, a staggering huge midnight blue universe becoming cobalt turning sapphire working its way to powder blue by 9:00 a.m. New Mexico wins the gold medal for her skies. Best of show goes to Arizona, for the art of changing colors.

Then came the thrill of Southern California, the skill required maneuvering in traffic, four-leaf clovers, merging cars, exits, and finding our destination. I loved looking down on cars. And finally, backing in at 6:00 a.m., because I knew how.

Kathy dropped me in Los Banos, and went on without me in this perfectly running truck. I swept up armfuls of emotion, like winning the whole poker pot, and began my two-week vacation.

Miguel
Mateo and Sophie

June 1981
Sierra Nevada, California

Miguel had already packed. Even the ice chest had ice.

"We're going to sleep in a tent!" Mateo tugged at my T-shirt, jumping up and down. I'd wanted a good night's sleep first and I'd needed to do laundry, but the kids were too excited. We took off that same afternoon, kids bouncing in the back, Miguel driving, and me in the passenger seat.

I'd forgotten how scary riding in a car could be. I couldn't see a thing! Just two cars ahead could be an emergency, a smashing on the brakes, and we wouldn't know it. Over and over I pressed my foot on the floorboard of Miguel's Taurus.

Miguel suggested we stop at Hagerman's. The kids could play on the swings. We'd stretch our legs.

"No, we don't want to stop." Mateo spoke for Sophie too. "We want to sleep in the tent."

We climbed into the Sierra National Forest south of Yosemite Park. First pavement, then gravel, and finally a dirt road. Miguel chose the left or right forks without hesitating. Not a breath of wind, the sky a clear blue, dust following our trail.

Miguel stuck his arm out the open window. "My Dad took us camping here when I was a kid. It's beautiful."

Ponderosa pine, black oak, incense cedar, white fir, Manzanita, and no people. Lean deciduous trees bordered the gravel road. Mateo and

Sophie didn't notice the trees, but Miguel smiled at my pleasure.

We pulled into a lone campsite next to rushing water. "That's China Creek." Miguel wiped his hands on his pants after parking the Taurus. "In August it won't look like much."

"I haven't smelled air this sweet in a long time, Miguel. Thanks for bringing me here." I inhaled deeply, stood and stretched. "This is perfect."

Sophie had her shoes off, lickety-split, even before we'd opened the trunk.

"Be careful," Miguel craned his neck.

"My toes are numb!" Sophie already had her feet in the creek.

"Mine too!" Mateo yelled, still heading toward the water with laces flying.

"You sit down, Mateo. I don't want you to fall in."

By 6:00, we had rolled out the sleeping bags. Mateo had pulled out his plastic army men, and Miguel had gathered three logs in a circle for our chairs. He put sandwiches, wrapped wax paper bags, on one log and called Mateo to come eat. Sophie pulled Cokes from the ice chest, gave me one, and balanced her dad's Coke beside the sandwiches. Sophie and I opened the wrappers. We all dined on bologna on white bread.

Miguel stuck his head in the tent. "Mateo, come eat." Sounding quite fatherly, dear, I thought.

"I want to eat in here."

I acted like Mateo's complaining was nothing, but wondered how Miguel would handle it. I didn't have a clue as to what to do.

"Come out here, buddy. We don't want ants in the tent."

Mateo came out, wolfed his sandwich down, and got back in the tent. Covered by trees, no campfires allowed, temperature dropping, Sophie, Miguel and I joined Mateo. Remembering a conversation from weeks ago at Hagerman's Park, Miguel hauled out "Beauty and the Beast", my favorite fairy tale. Miguel held the flashlight and I read aloud with Mateo, head on my thigh, examining the pictures. Before turning the page, I'd pass the book over to Sophie, who sat curled up beside her dad.

Miguel whispered to me after he scooted the kids out to pee. "It'll be impossible to get Sophie out after dark." He followed them, and a minute later I heard Sophie whisper, "Dad, is Margot going to be our Mom?"

"No, Sophie. Your Mom will always be your Mom. Margot is my friend, that's all."

"I love you, Daddy."

"I love you too, sweetie."

They all climbed back in the tent. I got out and did my thing too and then, lights out, probably around 8:00. Even though we were lying on the ground, with only a thin layer of leaves for cushion, being warm in my sleeping bag, next to Miguel's family, I slept soundly.

I'll never forget the next day for the rest of my life.

The Sierra Nevada

The Monarchs

June 1981

Not thirty yards from camp, we walked smack dab into the middle of a gargantuan swarm of orange and black butterflies. Tree trunks undulated with butterfly wings opening and closing. Butterflies drooped like leaves on branches and many were bunched together, hanging down like big orange and black gourds. More butterflies arrived, crowding in with their friends. They landed in patches on the rocks, making Halloween kaleidoscopes on the white granite. The whole area pulsed like a living organism, their fluttering wings breathing in and out. Maybe they were huddled together to keep warm in the cold morning. Maybe fluttering helped them somehow.

"Just like being on acid!" I exclaimed to Miguel, who frowned me into silence, the topic inappropriate for his kids.

"Kids, stay back." He took both their hands. Sophie, contented, watched. Mateo strained for freedom. "We don't want to hurt them, Mateo. They're migrating, just stopping for a rest."

"What's migrating, Dad?" Sophie leaned into her dad's arm.

"They're traveling, Sophie." Mateo struggled but Miguel had him by the wrist.

"Why? Where are they going?"

I stood stock still, listening to father and daughter. Some kind of ache motored around in my chest, like I wanted to cry. I watched Miguel let go of Sophie's hand and stroke her hair. More butterflies kept arriving, landing on fallen wood, covering all the leaves, more clumps resting on the granite and huddling as if they were cold.

"I think they're going somewhere to get warm, or look for food." Miguel called to me. "Margot, do you know where these butterflies are going?"

"I have no clue." I turned to ask my own question. "Do you think
276

anyone else knows about this?"

We snaked carefully through the butterflies for maybe twenty yards or so. Mateo grabbed a stick, wanting to scrape the tree trunks clean, trying to step on the ones near our feet, hit them with the stick. Sophie started yelling at Mateo, calling him a mean bully. Poor Miguel. Caught between restraining his son and taking me for a nice peaceful hike. He held Mateo's wrist, shushed both of them to no avail, and followed me onto a big slab of speckled white granite. My plan to warm up the kids in the sun failed. Mateo would not be calmed.

"Let's go back to camp." I finally said to Sophie and she took my hand. The motoring in my chest moved into my throat. Her hand was so little. I held back my longing to hug her, hold her in my arms, say thank you. Miguel followed us, dragging Mateo, who turned into a happy camper again when we got back to his tent.

We ate white bread with peanut butter and jelly, and played *I Spy*.

Mateo played army with his little rubber soldiers, Sophie colored, but by late afternoon, Mateo's complaining got on our nerves. He wanted to hunt butterflies.

Dense trees, stickers, or brush surrounded our camp. No alternate options for hiking. We didn't want to subject the butterflies to Mateo's sticks, and we didn't want to spend the day with a struggling unhappy little boy. After Mateo broke Sophie's third crayon, Sophie started crying.

We took down the tent and packed the car.

"A week would have been too long, anyway." I told Miguel. "And I wouldn't have traded seeing the Monarchs for anything. We can take the kids out for a special dinner. My treat."

"Maybe Mateo didn't sleep good last night. He's usually not this bad."

"Oh, he's a great kid, Miguel. He can't help being six." I wanted to ring Mateo's neck. Only twenty-four hours and I was exhausted.

I couldn't imagine having enough patience to raise Mateo. Yet Sophie cracked my heart open. Longing had flooded me. Grateful for the silence on the way back down the mountain, I wondered what kind of mother I would make. I wondered if I'd ever get the chance.

Eureka, California
Family

June 1981

Just down the street from Tanksley's terminal, I bought a rhinestone Kenmore brooch for my Mom in the Anderson's Split Pea Restaurant. I bought Ben, my stepfather, his favorite, chocolate caramels, and found a ridiculous trucking t-shirt for Terry. I called ahead, asked Terry if I could crash at his place until I picked up a tent, thinking Patricks Point State Park a perfect respite from all the asphalt of the last five months. I didn't stop in the Willits Bar on my way home. I hadn't had a glass of wine or a beer in over seven months.

Terry had the fire going in his guest cabin and wood already stacked for me. "I like to play music out here," he explained. "Be careful of these guitars. That one isn't mine."

"I won't touch them."

"Why don't you stay in the cabin, at least till this wind dies down?"

"Thanks. That'd be great." In Humboldt County, an intermittent, cold June wind could slice through a picnic and drive people inside. People who risked outdoor June weddings either had a good windbreak or hadn't lived here long.

I arrived at my "welcome home" dinner with presents in hand. Mom laughed at her new brooch. Ben ate a caramel. She and Ben, already half-soused, wrapped me in bear hugs. Grease popped on the coals as Ben basted a turkey in their big red barbeque. Neil Diamond serenaded us from the living room. Mom and I sat on the deck and watched a storybook sunset over the ocean, me drunk on the view, something warm flooding through me, probably love.

"I threw away your letters. I didn't think you'd want them."

Bucket of cold water. So much of what I had written I hadn't rewritten in my journal. My letters to her were the notes for my book. I was sure I'd told her to save them.

"That's okay." I must have written something awful. I must have whined or made her ashamed of me. I looked down along the corner of the deck, by the door, and on the steps. Terry's pottery.

Terry's band poster in the laundry room. Terry's music on the tape deck. Probably Terry's recipe for the green beans. Maybe I'd get that tent and set up a campsite after all.

Back at Terry's cabin, I rose early, took a hot, outdoor shower, and watched the steam dissipate amongst the ferns. I drove to Patrick's Point, hiked out to Wedding Rock, sat in the fog on a wet wood bench, and listened to surf that I couldn't see. So very happy to be here. Just eighteen months ago seemed like another lifetime. Truck driving was kind of fun, and I no longer even thought about killing myself. I couldn't help being born in a family whose talents I'd never match. I knew Mom wanted most of all for me to be happy. Maybe I could give that to her.

Maybe I could shift my perspective. My mother was happy. She made people feel special. If I'd allow it, I bet she'd help me to feel special. And I met amazing people through Terry. Why not be proud of her instead of jealous? Why not feel lucky? For God's sake, why not be grateful that I even had a family?

I listened to the California sea lions bark off shore, and twenty minutes later, as the fog lifted, I counted ten of them lying together on a sea stack about a hundred yards out. An unmistakable spray of water shot straight up. A whale! In close! Me, the sea lions, and a whale. I thanked whomever —the energy of the universe— like Alcoholics Anonymous suggested. I'd go to one of those meetings tonight. Top off an already good day.

Driving into town, I had this new good feeling about being part of my family. Funny, all those years I'd judged Daniel for finding religion as a way of life, and here I was talking to my "higher power" — the universe — and finding solace like my brother had.

I found Bobby in his studio at the Blue Ox in Eureka. The tide out, a pungent smell of the mud flats just yards from Bobby's front door, I walked over spongy earth held together by the roots of grasses. Gulls perched on rotted docking piers, unconcerned. The whoosh of wind warped and popped Bobby's window pane with every strong gust as I climbed the outside staircase three floors up to his studio, a little lookout tower on top of the huge old barn. I knocked.

"It's unlocked," my brother called. My brother lay in his bed on the floor. I turned away to look out the window.

"I love this," I told my obviously hungover brother. "How come you get to live here?" His window overlooked the entire north of Humboldt Bay. I could see Arcata underneath the fast-moving cloud cover.

No paint on the thick, old growth, redwood boards, wind blowing through the cracks, the electric heater glowing red. Bobby's workbench stretched the length of one wall. Cartoon sketches, dirty cups, fast food wrappers, pencils, pens, wadded paper and art pads rendered the bench invisible. I noticed the colored pencil set I'd given him for Christmas hidden under a foam hamburger take-out tray. I stood in the center of his room and turned a circle. A computer in the corner, tied to the wall by spider webs, mattress on the floor, one chair covered with clothes, the big picture window, and the wall of clutter, his office.

"Hey, Margot. How'd you find me?" Bobby didn't have a phone.

"Mom said you were here. Viviana showed me how to get back to your stairs." Bobby managed himself out of bed, stepped into his blue jeans, and started searching for cigarettes.

Eric and Viviana owned the *Blue Ox*, named for their two huge oxen that roamed the property. A complete working Victorian woodshop in full production, the Blue Ox restored or replaced Victorian gingerbread on historical buildings, mixed stains and varnishes, fired glass, bent iron, printed and bound books, all using methods and tools from the 1800s. Just starting their enterprise, Eric and Viviana had hired Bobby as their graphic artist, to get the word out. Instead of money, they paid him with a place to live.

Many years later, the *Blue Ox* made an exact replica of the hearse that carried President Lincoln to his grave. With vintage tools, Eric and his

280

crew built the horse-driven carriage and shipped it back east for the re-creation of Lincoln's funeral procession, but that was long after Bobby was asked to leave. He'd left the heater on all night, set the electrical plug burning and almost set the old building on fire.

"What are those?" I pointed. Lined along the shelf above his counter stood tiny pedestals, larger than toothpicks, with little leather hats on top. Cowboy hats, ladies floppy brimmed hats with tiny hatbands, a baseball cap, a civil war army hat, an old leather motorcycle helmet.

"I found all these used-up leather gloves in Eric's dumpster."

The dumpster?

"I started cutting them up. See what I could make."

"You could sell these, Bobby." I wanted Bobby to live in a house with heat, if not a beautiful view.

"I'd have to charge more than anyone would pay." Bobby brushed his clothes off the chair, sat, and lit a cigarette. I recognized his irritation, the little sister telling him what to do. "I'd make about ten cents an hour off 'em." He took a long pull and exhaled. "I just give 'em to people. Makes 'em smile."

"I love this view. My God, I could live here."

"There's no bathroom. I have to go clear to the other building to take a shit." The Blue Ox office, at the opposite end of the property, was about a block away from Bobby's hundred square feet. "There's no shower at all."

I offered to pay, and we walked to the House of Omelettes. The liquor he'd drunk the night before seeped out his pores, hung around the table. He needed a shave. He needed a laundromat. I didn't offer to taxi him around for the day. Our family didn't do that.

Bobby wolfed down pancakes, scrambled eggs, sausage, toast and coffee. We walked back to my car. As I said goodbye, he pulled out the little ten-gallon cowboy hat, the kind Hoss wore on the Ponderosa, and gave it to me. "Here. Thanks for breakfast, Margot."

Underneath the hat he had glued two white wisps of cotton, maybe a Q-tip's worth, and my hat became Yosemite Sam's. I couldn't not laugh, it was so cute. I said a cheery goodbye, felt like crying, and drove away.

We made no plans to see each other again.

I hung around Eureka till the AA meeting.

Someone at the meeting said "FEAR: False Evidence Appearing Real." Another woman called out, "FEAR: Frantic Effort to Appear Recovered." What a crack up, the awful truth being so funny! A third woman piped up. "I'm FINE! I'm having a fucked up, insecure, neurotic existence."

Bobby was likely at the Vista. I could have knocked back shots and talked a blue streak about my adventures, but I drove the twenty-five miles back to Terry's, not wanting a drink, and glad I'd chosen the meeting.

The Trinity River
Hal

Late June 1981
Gray's Falls, California

Terry spied me coming out from the forest, heading to the cars. From the far end of the field, he waved me over. Straw hat on, he fussed with his water system, then turned and faced me. "Come tubing with us Saturday. We need more females." Carol, Terry's girlfriend, an HSU oceanography major, and a group of five male colleagues had planned a day of tubing down the Trinity River.

"That sounds like fun! I've always wanted to do that!" I screeched. I saw Terry wince. *Too enthusiastic. Lower your voice. Calm down.*

"John's got the tubes. We're carpooling from the parking lot of the Comfort Inn."

"Is the water tank ok? Have I used too much already?"

"Just checking the level. We're low for June."

"Okay. I can shower at Mom's."

"Thanks. Probably nothing to worry about, but I'd appreciate it."

At the Comfort Inn on Saturday, I climbed in the back seat behind the driver of a beat-up baby-blue '67 Datsun station wagon. Squeezed in with me, two scientists kept a lively conversation going with the two scientists in the front. The driver kept looking at me in the rear-view mirror while talking in fake accents and poor grammar the whole way to Gray's Falls. I kept glancing at the mirror trying to see his face. He'd catch me looking at him and I'd look away real quick.

Arriving at Gray's Falls, we got out of his car at the same time.

"What's your name?" I asked.

He mumbled out the side of his mouth, over his shoulder. "What?"

Another impossible mumble. I leaned forward and wrinkled my forehead so as to concentrate on his answer. "What?"

"Hal. H-A-L Hal."

Wow. He's pissed.

Six foot three, faded blue jeans, Birkenstocks, blue work shirt with the sleeves rolled up, salt and pepper beard, skinny as a rail. I couldn't decide about his hair color. Brown or gray? He didn't offer to carry my tube, which was almost as tall me and much bigger around.

We baby-stepped down the steep dirt road. I slipped on sparse patches of gravel, but H-A-L didn't even turn around. Quite a change from the chivalrous truck drivers of the last five months.

We launched our huge truck tire tubes, and only a few minutes downstream, my brother called out, "What kind of bird is that?" directing his question to the nearest scientist. With necks craned, mouths open, we watched three torpedo-like birds in low flight, traveling upstream.

"Common Merganser," Hal's Australian accent answered after awarding the birds their five seconds of fame.

To prepare for the first set of rapids, he took my hand.

We bounced off rocks, twirled, and held on to each other, hollering with fun in the ice-cold water. I attempted to do a high-five with him when we reached the deep pool, but either he didn't know what it was, or the current carried him away too fast.

We paddled slowly through the calm part. Warmth from the sun, hands in the cold Trinity water, water so clean we could see the graveled bottom. I waved to a family having a picnic. Their barking black Lab followed us momentarily as we floated by.

"What's that?" I pointed to the insect that had landed on the tube next to my knee. We were traveling at a snail's pace, Hal and me side-by-side.

Hal stuck his index finger in the air and orated to the heavens. "It's a true bug. It's a hemipteran."

We perched on a huge boulder to eat our lunches. Gerald, HSU professor and Carol's boss in some ocean sampling study; Terry who worked at the Marine Lab in Trinidad; Ward, graduate and home on vacation; Ed a fisheries graduate, and Hal, who held a master's in Biology. Nobody reacted to Hal's fake accents like they thought he was strange. In fact, everyone seemed to enjoy him. They deferred to him with their scientific questions, maybe because he was the biologist and not an oceanographer. The fisheries guy didn't talk much.

"Look at this, Hal." Carol held up a reddish rock.

"Let me scratch it with my knife." Hal pulled out his pocketknife, waved it around, and scratched the rock. He waved his knife again, in the same demonstrative swirl, on its way back to his pocket. "Jaspert chert!" Hal announced in unmistakable Oklahoman.

"Huh. Unusual for up here, isn't it?" Carol again.

Another vertical index finger. "That it is." Jovial Hal.

"Why's it that color?" Me, braving a science question.

"We don't do why questions." H-A-L, answered in full-blown Texan. "*Why* questions are for the philosophy department."

Is this guy serious?

July Fourth

He's a Biologist

July 4, 1981

Terry had planned a big party for the following weekend. Because my truck driving adventures would give me notoriety, I'd be able to socialize adequately with all the scientists, musicians, and painters. I decided to extend my vacation for another week, enjoy my successful self, show everyone my comeback from the mental hospital. I didn't ask if Hal would be there.

During the week before the party, I hiked one day in the Prairie Creek State Park redwoods, avoiding the populated trail to Fern Canyon and venturing the opposite direction into the Cathedral Grove. Cool and damp, gargantuan old growth with sunbeams filtering through the canopy. Feeling so small and unimportant, humbled, my loneliness felt ridiculous. My family, a good one. They housed, loved, and wanted the best for me. I walked around the trees and I suppose I bowed my head.

I spent another day lying on my favorite little patch of sand next to where Maple Creek runs into the Mad River. Too cold for swimming; I'd wade in a bit when I wanted to cool off, in water clear to the bottom. I no longer took for granted the exquisite cleanliness or the shades of color. From river rock to madrone, and up the mountain through forest green touching blue sky. What color is clean water?

On another day, I drove all the way to Devil's Elbow a gorgeous stretch on the Trinity river, appropriately named. After parking among the oak and madrone trees, a narrow makeshift path winds down a steep cliff, cutting through poison oak bushes. Before long, the path opens to a view of the river. From a football field's length above the water, I looked down on a river rounding the cliff at white water speed. No railing. No bench. Just a drop off.

Signs posted on trees back in the parking lot warned hikers about the swift current. Every year, someone drowns in the Trinity. One year, eight people drowned. The water, being so clean, deceives people into thinking it isn't that deep. People plunge in up to their chests. Often drunk, the swift current pulls them down. Every year, the newspaper explains how cold temperatures cause a person's muscles to seize. Mostly, the Trinity takes the lives of children while their drunk parents watch in horror.

I sat in an eddy, feeling the current dig away at the bank under my feet. I splashed water on my arms, and breathed in the smell of Coppertone. Without my glasses, I traced the red madrone bark through the gray alders. A mosaic. Maybe I'd even try to paint someday.

Evenings, I drove thirty minutes each way into Eureka from Trinidad to attend AA meetings. By the time I got back and crawled into my sleeping bag, I was tuckered out and slept well. My skin a rich brown color, my spirit full of trees, sand, water and home, the people at meetings, hearing my voice, offering their stories, I felt hopeful, and happy. The week flew by. The morning of the fourth, I was ready to enjoy the day.

Hal came to the party. Right on time. The keg hadn't even been tapped yet. Blue jeans, Birkenstocks, blue work shirt with the sleeves rolled up, and a little note pad and pen in his pocket. He approached me, stood there, and didn't talk.

I got right to work. "What'd you get your masters in?"

"I studied hydrozoans."

"What are those?"

"They're related to jellyfish and coral and sea anemone."

"A jellyfish and a coral?"

"They're all cnidarians."

Give me a break. I tried again. "Well, what do they look like?"

"They're maybe half a centimeter tall." Hal put his thumb and index finger a half-centimeter apart, tilted his example around and stared at his fingers while he talked. "They're plant-like."

"You studied a tiny plant? For how long?"

"Five years."

"Five years?" *You're kidding, right?* "Where are they?"
"Where are what?"

"The hydrus things."

"Some of them are two hundred fathoms down. They live on snails. I compared them to some others that live in the intertidal zone of Humboldt Bay. I would have been done sooner but the RV Catalyst sank and I didn't have any way to get more hydrozoans."

"You mean they eat snails?"

"No. They need to live on something hard, and it's all mud out there. I wanted to see how quickly they could cover the whole snail shell before Bud and Ethel moved in next door."

What the fuck is he talking about? "Bud and Ethel?" I asked.

"The other critters."

"Why?"

"I don't do why..."

"I mean, is this important to know about?" He's speechless. "I mean, why do we care how long it takes them to cover a snail shell?"

"You mean, how can humans make money off this?"

"No, but, okay." *How can I put this?* "Of what use is this information?"

"It got me my masters!" A beat of silence. "How many times have you crossed the country?"

"Let me think about that." I started counting, thinking of how many trips I'd made with each partner and how many weekends in L.A. "Is that a notebook in your pocket? Can I borrow it?"

Hal handed me his note pad. "Want a beer?"

"No thanks." And then like a frog popped out of my mouth I said, "I'm in AA."

Hal left and I made hash marks. By the time he returned with his beer I'd counted twenty-eight trips in the last five months. I explained that I'd left for vacation in the thick of the busy season. That I was heading back to Los Banos tomorrow.

"Maybe I'll get a Coke." I walked away, rummaged through the *health* drinks, and brought back a Hansen's Cola. Terrible stuff, but at least it was carbonated.

"My poor driving partners. They wanted to drive from truck stop to truck stop and I wanted to go to a Museum of Natural History, or hang out at the public swimming pool." I watched him not drink his beer. I took a swallow of my Hansen's.

"My last partner, Kathy, had never even seen the Pacific Ocean. That kills me! That close and never been to see it."

Hal didn't say anything so I tried to keep the conversation alive. "She had no idea what an undertow was. I couldn't believe it."

"It's called a riptide. There's no such thing as an undertow."

Oh good. Nice to know.

"Hal, can I borrow your knife?" asked Carol, carrying cheese or brie or something white on a cutting board. Hal did the swirl thing again and handed Carol his pocketknife with both hands.

Terry's music blared from speakers set out on his deck. *Reggae.* Carol and her science friends were laying out the potluck dishes and people lined up to get a plateful. Hal and I joined them, leaving our drinks on the bench to save our seats. Hal took servings of salad and tamales and some slimy looking dish with nuts on top. Someone brought macaroni, so I tried that and doubled-up on the cookies.

We returned to our bench. Too much mayo in the macaroni. Too white. I ate my cookies and watched Mom and Ben laughing with a couple of Terry's friends. Terry's friends loved my parents. The women, especially, held my Mom in conversation all afternoon. Mom had an unconditional kindness that drew young people to confide in her. Often, a woman my age would spend an afternoon with my mother. I don't know what they talked about, but more than one woman told me how lucky I was to have my mother and how much my mother had helped them. I'd smile and nod, but on the inside jealousy seized my heart like a muscle cramp.

Sitting by Hal, watching my parents laugh and enjoy the crowd, my jealousy barely registered. Obviously, Hal's interested in me. He's nice. Intelligent. Handsome. I didn't even mind that we weren't talking. But I couldn't figure out what I was supposed to do. It occurred to me that

289

I'd never been sober in this circumstance. I felt absolutely confounded.

"We found a dinner knife. Thanks, Hal." Carol returned Hal's knife and Hal swirled it back into his pocket.

I thinned my voice into an accusation, and, imitating his swirling hands, I asked "What's with this?"

Twelve inches from my face, deer in the headlights, his pupils as small as pinheads inside glacial blue irises, he forced out a ridiculous Texan accent. "Aikido."

Backpedaling. Small voice. "What's that?"

"A martial art." Stiff as a board.

Can he say less?

He didn't even smile. "It's hard to explain."

Dead silence. My plate empty, I left. Dumped it in the trash and joined my parents, who were now talking to Terry's music friends. Hal followed.

"Can you believe Margot criss-crossed the country twenty-eight times in five months?" Hal started in after being introduced.

"Unbelievable! What's your handle?"

"Sunny Avenue."

"What's a handle?"

"It's a call name on the CB."

"How much time did you get to sleep?"

"It's all team driving. We sleep while the truck is moving, but it's more like bouncing around in a coffin than sleeping."

Where did you go? What did you haul? What were your partners like?

Never before, that I could remember, had the conversation centered on me, but there it was, seven of us talking about truck driving. My mother emphasized her daughter's bravery. I could tell she was proud. I offered fun anecdotes and laughed in all the right places, but on the inside, I sweated the whole twenty minutes. I finally extricated myself and stole away inside Terry's six hundred square foot house. I sat on the left end of the couch, where the springs still worked.

Fear. *Frantic Effort To Appear Recovered. I'm faking it.* I'm supposed to help someone else to get out of this ... panic attack. Get outside myself. But Jesus, I can't even bear to look at anyone right now. I saw all the potluck dishes piled on Terry's kitchen counter, walked across the room and turned on the water.

Terry bought his five acres for a dime. He'd spent several years hauling nine rusted cars off the property. He talked about fifteen dumpster loads of garbage, of having to wear a surgical mask and gloves. Ben thought he should burn the house down and start over. The people living there before had simply brought a great big log in the house and just kept pushing it into the fireplace until they finally pushed a hole clear through the stonework.

Now, the two rooms had shiny, sanded heart-redwood floors, white walls covered with Terry's big colorful abstract paintings, and a wood stove. An old, tapestry rug covered the wood floor in front of the couch, and an upright piano sat under his biggest painting.

One pan for washing, another for rinsing, I scraped waste into his mulch bucket and began. In walked Hal.

"Need some help?"

"Okay." He didn't even have a beer in his hand. I started washing vigorously. "Use that towel." I nodded toward the towel on the oven door.

"How about I wash and you dry, since I don't know where to put things."

"Deal." I hated to get my hands wet.

We didn't talk. I dried, and since I didn't know where Terry's things went either, or what was Terry's and what wasn't, I lined everything up on his kitchen table, just a few feet from the sink.

More dishes came in. Being quiet with Hal, watching his lean back, arms in the suds, I recovered from my emotional bender of just moments ago. This guy was really kind. I had no need to *get him*, to have him as my partner, and hadn't carried on like the most desirable female he'd be lucky to win for the night. That sensation of being safe, the soothing warmth of his body, his awkward nerdiness, even with all his accents there was nothing phony about him.

After the dishes, I got ready to leave, said my goodbyes and thank-yous, hugged my Mom, and told Hal I so much enjoyed talking with him.

Hal pulled out his note pad. "Want to write me?"

"Okay. Will you write me back?"

We traded addresses. I gave him the Oklahoma City address and said I had no idea when I'd be through to get his letter, but that I would write from wherever I landed.

Not wanting to reveal Terry's cabin, I headed for my Rambler. Figured I'd get to a meeting, come back to sleep, and leave early in the morning.

I'd spent a thousand dollars on my two-week vacation. Twenty per cent of what I'd saved in the last year, gone in three weeks! But my Rambler had new tires, an oil change, and a tune up. I ate out, bought clothes, boots, and gifts. I'd spent money on myself every day. None of it went to the VD or worse, to a cocaine addict. I felt pretty good.

Back on the Road
Dear Hal

July 15, 1981

Dear Hal,

I'm in Peoria, Illinois, surviving the humidity, hanging out at the public swimming pool. How do people live in this heat? This morning I delivered a load of cantaloupe and am waiting to see where they send me next. I had to wait around in Los Banos for five days before I got this load. All the trucks were stacked up out west waiting for their loads before I got one.

This tractor is horrible! It's been in a major accident and it's filthy. I broke down eight times. Three times the trailer's refrigeration quit and I had to rush to a Thermo-king to have it jump started. My air conditioner broke twice. First the fans wouldn't blow and then it wouldn't cool down. Get this: A wheel came off my right front tandem axle and almost hit a Volkswagen. I pulled the hand valve (that's the automatic cruise control) right out of the floor. The heater cord busted outside Winnemucca, Nevada, causing the engine to overheat drastically and, literally, just as I pulled into the 76, my engine quit. But I made my delivery on time even after all that.

The Queen of England couldn't persuade me to get in the sleeper. Rats wouldn't even sleep in that mattress. I'm sleeping on the doghouse.

I'm frustrated that at the party I blabbed on and on about truck driving and never got to hear about bird watching in San Blas or all the cool stuff you did in New Zealand.

My parents went to San Blas several times when I was a kid. We would have to watch hours of Dad's home movies about it. Mom standing there stock still in orange shorts and a pink and orange sleeveless blouse, waving. Mom at the restaurant table smoking a cigarette. Mom waving from their motel deck. Mom by the pool. But, I remember the lush green jungles, iguanas and cockatoos, this little boat tour going up a river — which seems more interesting and "worth it" than sleeping next to a refrigeration unit in some parking lot next to a warehouse totally surrounded by cement and litter and pollution and poor taste ... (For something I chose to be doing I'm sure sounding negative on it.)

I think I saw a big male pheasant in Los Banos. I mean, I know it was Los Banos, but I don't know if it was a male pheasant. It reminded me of a mallard. A ring around his neck, a brilliant green head, and a long, long brown spotted tail. He was a really big bird.

The sunset over the salt flats was the best. Totally pink, and the salt flats reflected back this eerie kind of blue-pink.

Just got my load. I'm headed for McMinnville, Oregon, with a load of chemicals from Ottawa, Ill. It's a good deal because I don't have to deadhead very far, but I won't be going through Oklahoma City to see if you wrote me.

They told me I'll be picking up my second-seat driver in Council Bluffs, Iowa. So much for getting to drive alone.

What were those several major changes you went through last year? Tell me more.

I look forward to hearing from you.
Take care, Margot

Paul Partner #10
Council Bluffs, Iowa

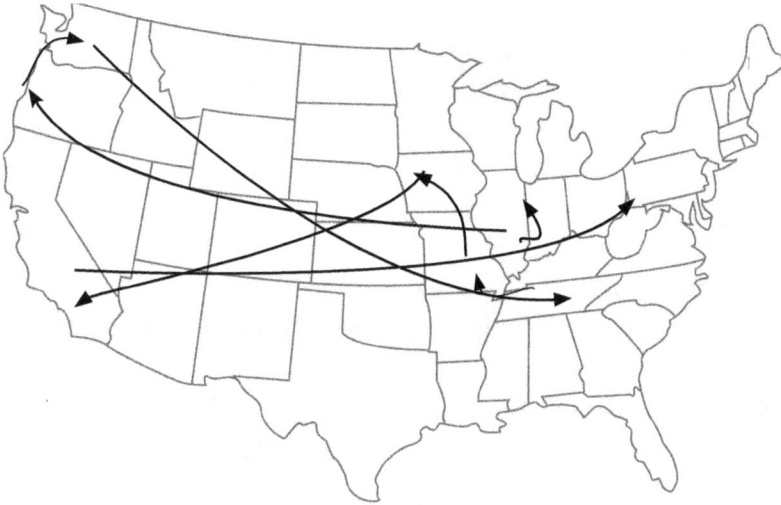

July 18, 1981

I could have killed the mechanic at Council Bluffs. Had that mechanic actually failed to tighten the bolts on purpose? How in the hell could he forget to tighten the bolts? To see my tire bouncing down the road in my rear-view mirror, that Volkswagen swerving. Thank God the tire fell flat in the median.

Indianapolis put on another tire. No, they won't go out and retrieve the blown one. Nobody cared about the danger to the Volkswagen. They scowled, like I was a whining bitch. I just shook my head, couldn't believe it.

Dispatch told me to pick up my second-seat driver in Council Bluffs. Paul. I'd have to talk to someone in that fucking terminal again.

No way would I mail Hal's letter in Council Bluffs. My letter would likely mold, maybe fall to the floor, get kicked under the counter, not to be found until after I died. I found the office at the chemical plant in Ottawa, Ill., saw a stack of outgoing mail on the counter, and stuck Hal's letter in with theirs.

Paul. Not a talker. That's not true. He told me he's twenty-five.

He's a big kid. Short curly red hair and freckles on a large square head. Tucked in collared shirt. Work pants. All neat and clean. Ship shape. All gray, like he works for Mission Linen Supply, or Chevron and it's his uniform except nothing's stitched on the front pocket.

I had stored my sleeping bag on the jump seat, not wanting to put it in the sleeper in case cockroaches lived in that mattress.

"You can sleep in the sleeper." I told him, forcing myself to put my sleeping bag in first-seat's compartment, a filthy slot at the head of the mattress. "I want the doghouse."

"Okay."

"Want to drive?"

Paul drove the speed limit, never took his eyes off the road. Privacy trumped curiosity. I figured if we didn't talk we'd might work together longer than two weeks. No wonder Tom or Donald never talked. Silence served as the boundary because our living condition had none. I didn't need to know all about Paul.

Seven hours later, outside of Cheyenne, I spoke. "I need a few hours of shut-eye before I start driving. You can get back in there if you want," I pointed, "but I need the doghouse."

"I'll wait in the coffee shop."

Trucks pulled in and out of the truck stop, waking me with their acceleration from second to third, air brakes whistling on and off. A refrigerated truck parked right next to me, and I couldn't blot out the incessant noise.

At 1 a.m., I found Paul sitting in a booth with a Coke.

"Did you eat?"

"A hamburger." He didn't look at me.

"I can't sleep. Let's go."

I drove through the sunrise, my favorite shift.

I liked that shift, even though it was the most difficult time to stay awake. I'd seen gruesome pictures of trucking accidents in pretty much every terminal lounge, but one in particular bothered me. Trucks often parked along the shoulder of the freeway during those hours, leaving their engines running and lights on while the driver got a few hours sleep. The photograph depicted a cabover tractor completely smashed in, the engine all the way back in the sleeper. The accompanying article explained how that cabover ran head on into a parked truck. Underneath, someone had written in black marker, 'Don't you do this'. I didn't trust my partners to drive the graveyard shift.

I'd roll the window down, stick my elbow out. I'd sing, and watch the stars fade to the barest twinkles as the sky turned navy blue to gray-blue to all-the-way-blue.

Paul stayed in the jump seat. Every time I looked, his eyes were closed. With the traffic being negligible, I drove with my left tires in the fast lane to avoid the potholes, hoping he'd get some rest and wouldn't tweak his back.

Paul insisted he'd slept, and started driving at Rock Springs, Wyoming. I rolled my sleeping bag out on the mattress and got in without touching anything else. I worried about cockroaches and didn't sleep.

Outside of Twin Falls, me driving again, the clutch linkage broke. Dispatch instructed us to have it fixed in Boise. A hundred miles with no clutch. I could hear when I needed to shift and no longer needed to watch the tachometer. But a full stop without a clutch would be a dead stop. I'd have to get towed. At the exit ramp's incline, I shifted all the way into low, and inched through the stop sign. I made it through two more stop signs before I reached the repair shop.

After driving down *Cabbage*, we followed the Columbia River west toward McMinnville. Paul took pictures of the river as we whizzed along.

"Want to stop? Get the camera focused?"

"No."

I wanted to impress Hal with some science fact in my next letter, like about plants. Maybe I'd find something to ask him about, like those big huge pine cones we saw up in Washington when I was riding with Tom. Tired of truck stops, sleeping in rest stops, hanging out at public swimming pools, I took an exit, parked, and let the engine cool before shutting down.

Ainsworth State Park. I'd take the day off. Have a full day of exploration.

"Want to go for a walk? Stretch your legs?"

"I'll stay here." Paul didn't even glance my way.

"You sure?"

No answer.

"Paul, you've got to get out of the truck. Do you have to pee or anything?"

His face flushed bright red under all the freckles. No answer again.

I shut the door, left him in the jump seat, and not thirty yards ahead, just out of the truck's view, a huge cascading waterfall split the forest.

I walked back to the truck. "Paul, you've got to see this. A huge waterfall!"

"I'll stay here."

Is he just going to sit there? Am I going to leave him for a whole day?

I hiked up a trail, across a stone bridge, but decided to turn around. I'd take Paul to a truck stop and come back.

He hadn't moved.

I started the engine and got out to thump the tires. Air whistled out of the right rear brake pot. A rusty bracket dangled gracefully by the one screw that was not engulfed in rust. The brake pot was only attached to the truck by its air hose. I didn't trust myself to try the penny and dime trick.

"We have an air leak." I told Paul as I shut the truck down again. "I'm going to walk up to the visitor center and call dispatch. Want to come? I don't know how far it is."

"No."

"What's going on with you?"

"I've never left home before. I don't want to leave the truck. I'll be fine here."

Cliff on one side, freeway below on the other, I took another long gander at the waterfall, continued up the road, admired a slice of meadow just visible through the trees, and listened to the birds. Wet color. The charcoal cliff side looked like shellacked teak wood. Water rivulets trickled through neon lime-green moss.

And flowers. All along the road. Red, orange, blue, yellow, white, purple. Big, little, pointed, round, tall, short. Everywhere. The air smelled like it had just rained. Fresh. Cool. More waterfalls. I walked in the shade the whole way.

A mile up the road I called dispatch at the visitor center.

"Can you move?"

"So far, yes."

"Nothing we can do. Drive to McMinnville and after you deliver, get back to Pendleton to have it repaired. If you don't make it we'll call a tow truck."

I walked back.

"This is the first time I've been around a woman." Paul offered after I climbed into the driver's seat.

"How come?"

No answer.

"Where are you from?"

"Jonesboro, Arkansas."

"What'd you do there?"

"I'm a licensed Baptist minister."

"Really! Where'd you get your degree?"

"Our church is small. We just get local people to preach. It's all volunteer."

I had questions, but I kept my mouth shut. If he started to preach, I didn't think I could take it.

"I hope we can get through Jonesboro on our return trip. I miss home. I like to drive."

With the brake pot dangling, we took off, all tires thumped and Paul driving.

The Pacific Northwest
Dear Hal

July 22, 1981
Dear Hal,

> *I'm in Oklahoma City. Just read your letter.*
>
> *"Harmonizing with the Energy of the Universe." Aikido sounds just like AA! That's cool that you want to train in Aikido for the rest of your life, and with your whole heart (and that you told me).*
>
> *I enjoyed getting your letter a lot. I didn't get to see the eclipse. The sky was all cloudy over Nebraska.*
>
> *Paul, my new partner, is 25, a licensed Baptist minister, never been around a woman, won't talk or leave the truck.*
>
> *Guess what? The brake pot was about to fall off and the clutch linkage broke. Sheesh. Dispatch told me to keep driving. They'd have me towed if I didn't make it.*
>
> *On the way back from calling dispatch, I picked one flower of every kind and ended up with a bouquet the size of Paul's head (it's really big). I stuck it in the air conditioning vent with a wet paper towel around the stems. Don't worry, I didn't pick any flower that was a loner. If you had been with me, you could have named every flower and told me all about each one. That would have been cool. Why are they all so different? In color, shape, size? What's with that? Someone ought to write*

a master's thesis: To determine the causality of flowers in relationship to the proximity of different flowers and overall survival rates.

I'm so happy you initiated this exchange of addresses. I had wanted to see you the week before the party, and I also thought about asking you to go for a walk after the party, but got shy. Now, I can still get to know you plus we'll be in contact for when I get home.

Let me see, Pendleton is a cowboy town. I watched the sun set by the Umatilla River. Finally, we drove east to Cashmere, Washington, through the Cowlitz County and Mt. Ranier National Park. You wouldn't believe the scenery. Or, maybe you've been there. So green. A clear rushing head water. (The rivers east of the Rockies look awful. I'd never get in one.) I swear I never appreciated Humboldt County's beauty till I left.

Tubing that day. I'll never forget it. I had so much fun. There was an instant when we were holding hands and I looked right at you and you let me see you and I felt you seeing me also — your eyes are so blue — but I think it might be because of that moment that I'm writing to you now.

Cashmere: Manicured lawns, perfect flowers, planned gardens, freshly painted houses, warm sunshine and clean air. Big apple industry. Lots of tourists. Christian bumper stickers. Jesus in every window. The downtown is only about two blocks long, one clothing store, a five and dime, but tons of restaurants for the tourists and every restaurant posted religious concerts and church services.

The Wenatchee River runs about a block away from downtown Cashmere. Kids had a rope attached to a bridge with a plank in the water. They were standing on the plank "waterskiing" the river's downstream flow. I thought the water was too cold, but they didn't seem to care. Loved listening to them scream, like being on a roller coaster in a theme park, but for free. I laid back in the dry, bug free heat, remembered

301

reading Mark Twain in high school, listened to the kids, and thought of you.

I want to know more about you. Where'd you grow up? Brothers and sisters? Hopes and dreams? What's your worst fear? I love talking about that stuff like that. I'd like to hear more about what it was like growing up with your Dad being an alcoholic. How long ago did he get sober? What was your Mom like?

We finally loaded apples headed for Memphis. I wrote at least ten pages in my journal about all the hassle. I can tell you what happened when I get home... but Route 97, gorgeous. And Route 14! My trailer is 12'3" high and I inched along under a wooden tunnel that was only 12'6" high. Crossing the Columbia River to hook up with I-84, the Hood River Bridge was almost as skinny as the Ferndale Bridge across the Eel. Frightening.

I'll drop Paul in Jonesboro, his home, and go on to Memphis by myself. Knowing this, Paul is pushing hard. He loves to drive, and he's a good driver. I'll have extra time to explore Memphis.

Oh, and Mom sent me a picture of you and I at the party. I taped it to my dashboard. Getting your letter sure made happy to go through Oklahoma City.

I've practically written a whole book to you. I'm kind of embarrassed.

Take Care, Margot

Memphis

Delbert

July 25, 1981

We made good time through the back roads of Missouri and Arkansas because Paul knew the way. The landscape barely rolled, with farmland marked by fences, one-block-long towns, and no rest stops. At midnight, I dropped Paul off in Jonesboro and drove the last seventy miles south into Memphis. Near Overton Square, I found a vacant parking lot for the truck. I'd have a full extra day to explore Memphis.

The next morning, I walked a couple of blocks around several corners and down into a basement restaurant for breakfast. Two men and a woman sat at one table. No food, just a large piece of paper in front of them.

"Are you open?"

"Sure," one of the men responded. Come join us. We're about to order breakfast."

Bob owned the cafe, Wendy was his lady friend, and the third, Woody, did most of the talking. He'd sketched plans for the restaurant's expansion, a small structural addition.

"This is a nice place. Where is everyone?" I sat in the chair next to Woody.

"Too early. This is an after-hours joint. Come back after midnight and check us out," Wendy winked at me.

Seven wood tables and chairs, wiped clean, sat in the shadows on a wood floor. Windows let in warm wet air. Lit by the morning sun, cigarette smoke curled above us and spread out over the tables. Iron bars on the windows split the light into thin streaks across the floor. The roof would block the sunlight within the hour. Our table, in the corner, was so dark we used a lamp.

Bob called to the woman mopping the floor behind the bar. "Maggie, we're ready to order." I could smell beer spilled from the night before.

Across from me, the woman inhaled deeply, and blew a smoke ring. I watched the ring expand and travel to the neighboring table. She left red lipstick on the filter, and ashed her cigarette with long red fingernails. Her black dress, punctuated with sequins, barely covered her thighs.

Maggie took my order. Scrambled eggs and bacon. Orange juice. To hell with grits and cornbread.

Woody leaned over the complicated drawing laid out under the lamp and was enthusiastically explaining all the details.

"Knock this wall out." He pointed. "You'll get at least five more tables outside."

The owner studied the drawing. "That's a support wall."

"We can put a beam in here." Woody drew his finger along the makeshift blueprint.

"I don't know." The owner looked up when the food arrived, "Thanks, Maggie."

Maggie had plates stacked up each arm. One dinner plate and one side plate of bacon for each of us. She had a basket of corn bread too, and deftly set all the dishes on the table without missing a beat. Ample bust and big arms, Maggie wore a faded cotton dress covered by a bib apron. I noticed her shoes, white, with thick soles. I could see thick brown shins, but no knees. A handkerchief covered her hair and I admit, I thought of Aunt Jemima.

While we were eating, Maggie mopped the floor behind the bar.

The owner and his lady friend ate quickly and left. Wendy gave me a knowing smile and I got the impression, since they left so quickly, that I had come along at just the right time to entertain Woody.

"I'm not an architect," Woody corrected my assumption before I asked. "These are just my ideas for Bob and Wendy. This is a great place. I'd like to see them succeed. They've had the place less than a year."

304

I sat back and wiped bacon grease off my chin. "Do you want to be an architect?"

"No. I manage the monkeys at the zoo. Memphis Zoo is ranked in the top twenty of all the zoos." Woody's enthusiasm for the zoo equaled his excitement about the restaurant plans.   "Are you a tourist?"

"Sort of. I'm a truck driver. I've got a load of apples to deliver in the morning."

"Really? Are you by yourself?"

"I am. I got here last night and thought I'd go exploring today."

"Take my bicycle for the day," Woody exclaimed, eyes wide. "You can explore Overton Park, Overton Square, and the zoo."

"Really? You'd loan me your bike?"

"Sure. And there's a concert in the zoo tonight. I can get you a ticket. I'm supposed to bring one of the monkeys out and let the crowd get a closer look."

We walked the few blocks to Woody's house, where he hauled out a rusted girl's bike from the weeds in his back yard.

The bike had both a flat tire and an air pump. No lock. He showed me how to pump the tire, in case it went flat again, and after a big thank you, I took-off to explore Overton Park, amazed at his trusting hospitality.

Suddenly, everyone had black skin.

After we nodded to each other, a heavyset man slowed his bike to ride along beside me. His hair was clipped short. He wore thin cotton pants gathered up in fancy Velcro straps. He looked crisp, a professional type. "I'm Delbert. You're not from around here."

"What gives me away?" I smiled.

"Your belt. I could tell right off." He had a big grin and lovely white teeth.

The bike path was wide and paved, through cut grass. I'd worn my favorite pants. Lightweight second-hand baggy, green corduroys. I'd tied the brightly patterned Mexican strap, a gift from my Dad, around my waist. Sleeveless T-shirt and flip-flops but of course, I was sweating.

Delbert, exercising in Overton Park on his bicycle, rode along beside me. "That's some bike!" He grinned and pedaled ahead, to make room for two black women walking in our path.

"Yours looks pretty good." We toured the park, sticking to the shade of very old trees, hundreds of different kinds. "How come so many different trees?" I asked.

"This park was started in 1901. It used to be an arboretum. They wanted to get trees from everywhere, get them all identified and labeled."

Hal would like to see this.

"You're lucky to see all these trees. Because of us, we stopped the Feds from putting a freeway through here. It took ten years of arguing, but now this park is on the national register for historic landmarks and they can't touch it."

We biked around a sloping curve. "Do you know you're on the black side of the park?"

"I figured as much. Is it really carved up and segregated?"

"Yep. White folk walled off Hein Park for themselves, and two years ago, the justices made it legal, only Thurgood dissented."

"Thurgood?"

"Sorry. Thurgood Marshall."

"Wow. I thought we made segregation illegal ten years ago." "So, why are you here?"

I told him.

"A truck driver? Delivering apples?"

"That's right. What do you do?"

"I'm a probation officer. I work with juveniles. Counseling mostly."

The wide paved path meandered. Delbert rang his bell to let two people know we were passing.

We fell back beside each other. "Oh, that would be hard for me. But you get to do good. Help kids turn their lives around."

"It's not like TV, Margot. I don't get too see many happy endings."

"What *is* it like?"

"Probation work is about poverty. And violence. The kids, most of them, live in foster homes. If the parents *are* around, a lot of times they're zoned out on heroin. Police come in with horror stories about my clients. The kids re-offend, end up back in the system."

"That's depressing."

"I do get connected to some of the kids. I like that part. But, I'm
306

getting burnt out. Some guys I work with have been there thirty years. I don't see how they do it."

"What would you do if you left?"

"I don't know. Maybe be a truck driver?" He smiled. "Does the job pay good?"

I shook my head. "Not even."

"Let me show you around Memphis. It's a beautiful town."

We rode all around Overton Park. Delbert learned I used to be a teacher and that I hoped to write a book. I learned about his recent divorce, his commitment to getting back in shape.

"You okay? You look pretty hot." Delbert could see the sweat pouring down my neck.

"I'm not used to this kind of heat." I stopped my bike. "Is there someplace nearby that's air-conditioned?"

We pedaled over to the Brooks Museum of Art, and I died with gratitude for the cool air. The oldest museum in Tennessee. Room after room of paintings and statues. Classrooms. A huge historical collection.

Finally, we rode back to my truck so Delbert could take a look. He praised me sufficiently and said goodbye. I cycled off to shop in Overton Square, but I was too hot. I knew if I'd tried anything on, it would have stuck to me. And I worried about leaving Woody's bike unlocked. All I really wanted was to get out of the humidity and cool off. Around 4:30, I pedaled back to the truck to check the inside temperature of the trailer.

On the back door, in fat black marker, someone had written:

A Nigger Fucker Drives this Truck.

I jumped back, like the words might have got on me. I looked around. Across the street, leaning against the garage opening of a mechanics repair shop, a pot-bellied white man leered at me. He was chewing tobacco, and when I saw him he sneered back at me and then spit a whole wad of brown goo onto the sidewalk at his feet. Then he folded his arms across the black grease on his faded red T-shirt, and I saw all his white skin through the big hole under his armpit. I stood paralyzed, staring, and he just kept sneering, putting another wad of tobacco in his mouth.

A huge Confederate Flag draped above the entrance to one of the bays.

Engines and car parts spilled out from his doublewide doors. Grease stains covered the sidewalk across the entrance to the garage. Attached to the garage, a dirty window showed a room filled with cardboard. His posture yelled at me. "Whaddayagonna do about it?"

Heart in my throat, afraid to turn my back on him, I walked up to the cab and got a rag. My knees were shaking. I walked back to the trailer doors and wiped off the black filth. My arm had no strength. So hot all day and now my shoulders were shivering. I loaded Woody's bike into the trailer, not a simple maneuver. I didn't check the inside temperature. I didn't look at the mechanic, didn't think about a plan if he approached me. My heart beat hard but I didn't put my hand on it. I took bigger breaths, but my head got fuzzed out, like hyperventilating. I tried short breaths but my heart started to race. Finally, I got back in the cab and locked the door. I never looked back to see if he was still looking. I didn't wait for the engine to warm up. I pulled out and turned left on the first wide street with a stoplight.

Memphis
Woody

July 1981

Kroger's. Perfect. Except, I pulled half-way into the gas station next door by accident. Fuck! Shit! Twenty minutes to back out and into Kroger's lot.

I sat in the parking lot and put my hand on my chest to calm my heart, warm it up. I needed food, saw black people *and* white people shopping together in Kroger's, and decided to buy groceries.

Unfortunately, I tried to walk in the exit door just as someone was walking out. The automatic door smashed my big toe. I limped back to the truck. My toe throbbed and started to swell, and I started crying, first just sniffles, but then I let loose and sobbed.

To be fair, automatic in and out doors are not standardized across America. You can't just walk on the right side and expect to go in. If you're in Memphis, you have to walk on the left side if you want to enter.

I collected myself, went back in Krogers, and bought three large Butterfingers. Back in the truck, I ate one, rested in the air conditioning, and tried to read a little. Around 6:00, I got Woody's bike out of the trailer and rode it back to his house. He invited me in.

Remembering Maggie at the restaurant that morning, her waitress/ janitor status, I had no idea what Woody would think about what had happened to me. I said nothing about the mechanic. "Thanks for the bike, Woody. What a great day!"

Woody's house reminded me of Bobby, a topsy-turvy array of furniture, books, papers, magazines, photographs, wood, appliances, windows, and stuff. Woody said he was re-modeling but hadn't worked on it recently. Extremely run down, the old three-story Victorian had plenty of character. I wondered if Woody would be the person to restore it.

Woody handed me a map of the zoo. "The Zoo started back in 1906 when the city wouldn't let this guy keep a pet bear in his back yard." He finger-walked me through to his monkeys. "We get millions of visitors." Woody concentrated on his map. "Best zoo in the country."

"You love what you do, don't you.?"

"I do. Here's a ticket for the concert. It's bluegrass tonight. Concerts every night till school starts. It'll be packed. Get there early."

"Thanks, Woody. You've been so kind. You remind me of my brother."

"Aw. I'm going to be with my lady friend, I hope, so I probably won't see you."

"Okay."

Woody seemed as scattered as his house. He jumped from the zoo to his house remodel and back to his lady friend, "Uh, I've had this friend for a long time now."

Woody paced, like he had more to say. I waited.

"I met her at the zoo."

"What's she like?"

"She's rich. Real high status, if you know what I mean."

"I see."

"Uh, well, do you think you could call her for me? I mean, if a man answers you could ask to speak to Elaine?"

"She's married."

"It's not what it looks like. She went away with her husband this weekend to either work it out or give it up. I just have to know."

I dialed the number he gave me. She answered and I handed him the phone. He smiled a thank you. I waved goodbye and left.

I didn't go to the concert. Didn't want to be in a crowd. Didn't want to hear bluegrass music. Didn't want to walk back to my truck in the dark.

Little Rock to Cape Girardeau to Red Oak
940 miles deadheading

July 1981

Kroger's warehouse refused my apples. Maybe they hadn't sold as many as they predicted. Or maybe Tanksley goofed. Whatever the reason, dispatch sent me 140 miles west. Little Rock, Arkansas, wanted apples.

I watched the lone "white-boy" lumper contract with the driver of the truck in front of mine to unload his truck. The dock crew waved me around that man's truck. I watched the dock crew wave trucks around that poor man's truck until I collected my paperwork. He would be the very last to unload. The white kid would get one truck's worth of work.

I shouldn't have split the unloading with my lumper. I think he only tolerated me *because* I was a woman. Had I been a white man, I probably would have stayed in the truck.

Around me, all the jive-ass jibberish didn't scare me like that white mechanic in Memphis, but I didn't think I'd try to unload again. I'd had enough.

Cape Girardeau, Missouri, called me in for a full service, which included a thorough cleaning, and a night in the *Ramada Inn*. I left Paul in Jonesboro, drove back to Memphis, then north on I-55, and arrived at the main dispatch center five hours later. Odd, the Cape had no drivers' lounge, only a bathroom and a telephone, two locked doors and no windows. Not even a chair. No candy machine.

I'd pictured the dispatch center as something akin to Wall Street on television, phones ringing, twenty dispatchers calling out directions, smashing phones down, cigarettes smoking in full ashtrays, arms flailing to reach the next phone call.

I picked up the telephone. "Can I come up to see the dispatch center?"

"No, sorry. Not allowed."

After a good night's sleep, I ate the only breakfast available, an old can of Tab and a Snickers Bar from the motel's machine.

I got a new mattress. A new fender, new air conditioning, and new lights. The cruise control worked. They replaced my brake pots. Even the storage compartments had been cleaned.

My truck ready, dispatch sent me to Red Oak, Iowa, to pick up a load of batteries headed for Los Angeles. They would fly Paul to Council Bluffs, and I'd pick him up in that god-forsaken terminal.

Dear Hal
Poor Paul

August 11, 1981
  Dear Hal,

  I'm in Columbus, Ohio. Let me see, here's where I've been since I last wrote you. Memphis, Little Rock, Cape Girardeau, Red Oak, Iowa; down that miserable I-80 for the millionth time into Los Angeles, back up to Bakersfield, a Barstow delay, and now I have just finished delivering these plums to Kroger's here in Columbus, the evening before they're due, which is lucky.

  How many miles is that?

  Got your letter in Oklahoma City, I like how you say 'mountains and valleys instead of ups and downs. It sounds more positive. I'm sorry you're frustrated and I hope you get a job soon. Unemployment can be really depressing. I admire you for sticking to your field. Don't move away!

  I was in a valley ... a pit, a hole, an abyss under the bottom of the ocean, from age 23 to 27. (I'm 29 now.) It was quite a valley but since then, by comparison, I've been on Mount Everest for the last two years. I understand what you said about appreciating joy after experiencing pain. This guy quoted Ernest Hemingway in an AA meeting. "This world breaks everyone and afterwards, some of us are stronger in the broken places."

You have difficulty describing yourself? Because you don't look at yourself? How lucky for you! Me, I have to purposely concentrate on others in order to quit focusing on myself. It's like I'm watching myself on a stage. Like I'm pretending all the time.

You went to Seattle with five other people! Five friends in the same car! I've never done anything like that. I wonder what training in Aikido must be like.

I layed over in Los Banos and spent time with my friend Miguel and his two kids. We raced frogs at the reservoir (my favorite). What would you tell me about frogs? Miguel's kids are a kick, and the frogs jump all over the place. I never thought anything could be fun in dry hot dusty flat central California, but I was wrong.

Poor Paul, my partner. He stayed in the truck at the terminal. Since he was right there and available, they took him off my truck and put him on this other guy's truck because the other guy needed to have a second seat to help him bring his logbook hours down within the legal limit.

So I go on alone to deliver my batteries in L.A. They send me to Bakersfield to wait two days for my load (grapes, plums, and bell peppers for Columbus) and then I'm told to pick up Paul in Barstow when I come through.

Paul's waited five days for me in the Barstow terminal. Apparently Paul's new partner was high on whites. Over Tehachapi Pass (Hwy 58) a Volkswagen bus was following their truck with the high beams on and Paul's partner went into a rage about the lights shining in his mirror. According to Paul, the guy jack-knifed the trailer in the middle of the road, took his tire thumper back to the Volkswagen and bashed out its headlights. He was starting to strike the bus's windshield when the bus finally pulled onto the shoulder of the road, barely made it around Paul's truck, and sped off.

When they got to the Barstow terminal, Paul immediately took his belongings off the truck and explained what happened to the manager. The partner got fired, but before he took off hitchhiking, he swore he'd kill Paul the first chance he got.

I can't imagine jack-knifing the trailer in the middle of a highway. But I don't think Paul would make it up, I mean, I've never heard so many words come out of Paul's mouth all at once. We pushed to West Memphis, Arkansas, where he quit. Just threw his stuff off the truck, said goodbye, and turned his back.

I wish you could have seen the butterflies on our grill this trip. Five of them. Mounted perfectly. Big ones and small ones and very colorful ones. My favorite had a half-inch border of iridescent blue along the bottom of his gray wings. I'd guess his wingspan to be about five inches. Absolutely elegant. Dispatch has agreed to put me in West Virginia before August 22nd, so I can attend a Jarvis re-union. I'm excited to see who all my relatives are. After that, I plan to come home for good in September. Hopefully I'll get a driving job for the Co-op.

Love your letters. Margot

Driving Solo

or ... Ted, partner #11, pg 317

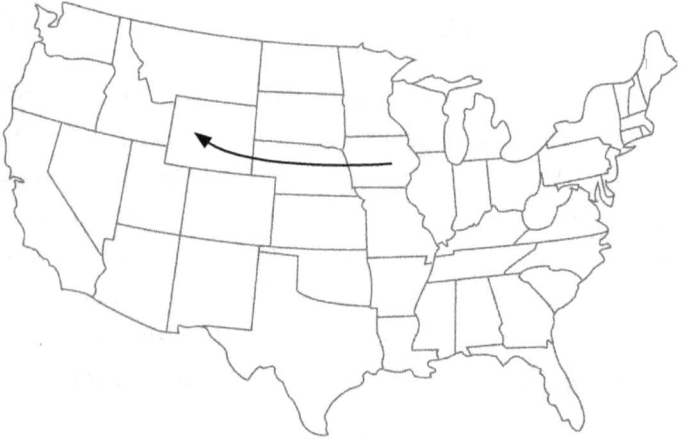

August 12, 1981

Alone. Desperately not wanting a new partner, but still required to make my deliveries on time. I did isometrics to keep alert. Squeezed my knees together and released them. Contracted my arm muscles and counted to ten before I relaxed. Often, I kept my left foot perpendicular to — and about two inches above — the floor. When I'd hit a bump, my foot would tap and I'd entertain myself listening for a rhythm. A whole note. Four-four time. Rest. Eighth notes. I thought about getting home, daydreamed for hours about fixing up my house, mowing the lawn, and seeing Hal.

Three sets of logbooks, constantly driving, but sleeping in a still truck (for five lousy hours after vibrating for the first half hour). We had to pay our own fine if we got caught with an illegal logbook. To prevent that, two illegal logs are jockeyed right along in the present tense. They run opposite of each other. At meal breaks, I'd switch logbooks and catch-up the exchanged log book as if I'd been off duty for the last five hours.

Then I'd stuff the first illegal book back in my sleeper compartment. After a delivery, on a layover, I'd catch up my legal logbook, and then whole process would start over again.

Alone, but not lonely. Want to feel comfortable being alone? Don't be alone in your small home town, that's a set-up. Drive a truck. We're all alone.

80,000 pounds of Ladies Home Journal from Columbus to Portland. I-80 again. I know every shift, every rest stop. No point in buying a radio for these last few trips. A radio would have to be turned up full volume to hear over the engine noise. Head phones weren't an option. Kathy could make the CB fun. It just made me mad.

I picked up my second-seat driver, Ted, in Indianapolis. Not in the terminal but out of the bar down the street. He sobered up and promptly got high on whites and talked about how all his friends were jerks. He asked me for money, refused to eat, and I put him off the truck in Council Bluffs, where he got fired.

Iowa, Nebraska, Wyoming, Utah, Idaho, and Oregon. Even with dark glasses, squinting against the afternoon sun exhausted my cheeks.

What if the industry paid truckers better wages? What if they hired committed team drivers? Gave them benefits. Got the partners home.

The industry would have to standardize shipping costs.

A big convoy driving to Washington D.C. Shut down the whole country in one week. But then teachers would want more money. Plumbers would demand a raise. Prices would go up. Inflation would spiral.

"Organize truckers!" I argued out loud. "Have a strike. Force the issue." When I caught myself talking out loud I tried to stop thinking, watch the scenery.

I didn't blame the trucking industry. Tanksley *wanted* us to partner with another driver. But what options did they have when partners split up?

We apologize for the delay in your delivery. Jimmy wouldn't ride with John and we couldn't find a suitable replacement.

Thank you for letting us know. We'll use Conway instead.

Maybe the whole country should just slow down.

I had the damndest time finding the U.S. Post Office in Portland. I'd written the directions wrong, had to call dispatch. Then I turned right instead of left and had to get out of that. The dock was a straight shot, but I couldn't set my truck up straight. I kept missing my line. I had such a hard time trying to update my real logbook that I gave up. Driving exhausted, not a good idea, but sleep in a still truck had to count for something.

Seeing the Country
Writing Hal

August 18, 1981

Dear Hal,
One more round trip and I'm coming home. I'm so tired. I can't even remember where I was when I last wrote to you.

I'm in Kennewick, Washington, now, having delivered Ladies Home Journal from Columbus to Portland, apples from Chelan, Washington, to Wheeling, West Virginia, and finally picked up these grape jelly jars in Pennsylvania for Welsh's in Kennewick. Thankfully, I'm laid over for a few days.

Kennewick is a trip. When I arrived I had to wait for a huge parade complete with Ronald McDonald, the A&W Root Beer Bear, a huge moving 6-pack of Ranier Beer, and a huge car-size shoe skate. Every float was plastic and had three or four queens and princesses on it. Wannabe politicians threw candy to the crowds as they drove by. Four or five high school bands and drill teams marched passed me. Twelve older men (60's) rode tiny motor scooters in the parade and called themselves "The Dirty Dozen." There was a bagpipe group. I think everyone that owned a horse rode it in the parade.

One float bothered me. A plastic religious float with a man singing through a microphone: "Oh, it ain't gonna be Buddha that comes a callin'. It ain't gonna be Buddha. And it ain't gonna be Mohammed that will save you. Oh no, it ain't gonn' be Mohammed. And it ain't gona'

319

be Hari Krishna. And we're gonna see the sun a-rising because it ain't gonna be no Mooney comin' to save you, oh no. It's only sweet Jesus and if you're a Baptist or a Methodist it's okay ... etc. etc. He wore full cowboy attire and maybe twenty small children rode on his float.

Last night, I went to the rodeo. I totally got a kick out of this clown and his dogs, which performed incredible tricks. He even had a monkey that rode around on one dog's back. Sitting in a big crowd felt foreign, that's how long it's been. I liked it!

Last week I laid over in Clarksburg, West Virginia, where my dad was raised. Dispatch kindly gave me a load to deliver near the Jarvis reunion that my Aunt had organized. I'd met my aunt and uncle before, and my three cousins, but I'd never met any of the other relatives.

Everyone was in the military! The few that weren't in the military were engineers. Shipshape in suits and slacks, leather shoes and short haircuts. In this humidity! I was so hot. I wondered if they all wore sweat pads in their armpits. I swear, nobody was sweating.

We took a group photograph. I tried to stand in the back but they pulled me to the front, the truck driver from California in short shorts and matching top. I looked practically naked next to everyone else.

I'd worried about whether I would be dressed appropriately for the party, describing to my aunt the new outfit I'd bought in Arizona for this reunion. She assured me that my cousin, was wearing a backless dress. Wait till you see the picture! Backless to my aunt meant three inches above the bra line. My cousin's dress came to the middle of her knee. I kid you not.

One guy made a point of telling me how everyone knew my Dad was real smart but that he was a totally weird kid. Growing up, my Dad explored by himself all the time. He gave me a cigar box full of the arrowheads he collected. If that's weird, I think weird's good.

320

With the truck driving, my outfit, and being from California, I stood out pretty good. I kept walking around to the other side of the house to take a breather. And boy, was I glad I wasn't drinking. I want to hear about your Dad, and what it was like growing up with him, and if he's still active in AA.

My Florida brother was at the reunion. He is a devout First Baptist Christian. Seeing him sort of flipped me back in time to being a little kid. Being unhappy. We didn't visit that much. What's your family like?

Oh, it seems like years ago now, but I got to visit the Japanese Gardens when I was in Portland. They were sculptured down to the least little weed or leaf. They made use more of shapes and shades of green than color from flowers. Even specific spider webs were purposely left untouched so that their catch of dewdrops could accentuate the sun light.

Couples held hands. Children held their parents' hands. I soaked up the cleanliness. Such formality. Peaceful. Quiet. I've got to get people back in my life. I miss you.

Have I told you about Chelan? I loaded apples there. Lake Chelan is surrounded by mountains. That evening, the sky didn't have a single cloud and the sunset reflected off the lake. Everything looked red. Even the water. Unreal.

Have you read Watership Down? Thousands of rabbits crossing the road —weeks ago — along the Columbia River. I was the "Hrududu." I'm so glad I didn't hit one. Maybe you can tell me what they were doing. Rabbits don't migrate do they?

One more round trip, and I'm coming home.
Looking forward to seeing you. Margot

Dothan, Alabama to Thomasville, Georgia
And after that, damn.

September 8, 1981

Straight out of commercial, white, religious Kennewick, Washington, I picked up a load of potatoes headed for Dothan, Alabama, and Thomasville, Georgia. Going east, the sun at my back, two log books hidden and the third ready for inspection, I drove. Slept, drove, fueled, ate. Drove. Drove.

I'd never seen the northeastern corner of Mississippi, or any of Alabama. Mostly flat and forested. Billboards advertised a pervasive Southern culture. *Jesus could save me. Make America White Again. Secede.* Confederate flags a constant visual. In one truck stop, a walk-in preacher was available.

In the most southeastern corner of Alabama, I delivered my potatoes in Dothan, and then drove east on a back road from Dothan to Thomasville. I felt transported back seventy or eighty years in time. A humid, lush green environment, house after house had a swinging chair on the front porch and maybe half the time someone was sitting in it.

No more Confederate flags. Compared with Kennewick, these houses would be called shacks. Raw gray boards, broken steps, sagging roofs. The yards looked like little overgrown fields, with a few trees or tree stumps. Plenty of rusting dead cars. I thought about *The Price Is Right* being on television inside, or maybe I'd see a man playing the banjo. Maybe because that's how television painted my picture of black people.

In Thomasville, Georgia, dispatch sent me to a single, small warehouse in the middle of the woods. Wooden dock (not painted), maybe ninety degrees with high humidity, and two jet-black men waiting to unload my truck. They started to work, and only after I inquired, they asked for a measly $15.

The boxes came off my truck, one by one. No pallet jack. No forklift. From the front of my trailer to the back end, then to the breezy shade just inside the wood double doors, they stacked boxes of potatoes for the next few hours.

Work finished, I gave one of the men an additional $15, which he immediately took inside. A moment later, a white man came out to shake hands. Kind of fat with a big head and receding hairline, he wore a short-sleeve white shirt and dark slacks. "It's not necessary to pay these folks more money."

"Oh, but I wanted to."

"Well, okay. I thank you."

I wondered if these lumpers would get the money.

I fired up the truck and pulled out. I wanted to go home.

Back to Knoxville for a load of chemicals headed for Hayward, Ca. I wondered if my last load, headed to an oil refinery, would be poisonous.

I'd filled pages and pages of illegal logs. My legal logbook would need at least a week off from driving to catch it up. I'd been driving eighteen hours a day, and sleep, even in a still truck, didn't come immediately. I'd vibrate from the day's drive, trying to wind down, and end up spinning on American culture, or the plight of truckers, or missing home.

My home.

Then, on the way up to Knoxville, I turned right at a T-section on a two-lane country road, miscalculated the corner by a mile, and rolled my right trailer tires into a ditch. In my right side-view mirror, I watched the trailer dip, stunned at the impressive visual as I stepped on the brake. I actually thought about taking a nap before doing anything about it.

I should have pulled wide, across the centerline. What was I thinking?

Traffic collected at the "T," not wanting to miss the show.

Do I pull forward now or back up? Forward, the axle would drop another foot before coming up on the perpendicular shoulder. Tractor to trailer, I estimated the angle to be 33 degrees at the kingpin. I couldn't decide how much to turn the wheel. The "V" shape I needed to navigate would be a disaster if I overshot it. I couldn't think.

Cars parked and waited. Two men came over and blabbered their opinions. They agreed that backing out of the ditch would right the trailer.

But instead of returning to the asphalt, the rear of my trailer inched further into the ditch. My 33-degree angle increased to about 40-degrees, the butt of my tractor actually stuck out across the center line.

You should have turned the steering wheel clockwise, idiot. Bottom of the wheel goes left if you want the trailer to go left, imbecile. Fuck. I did turn it clockwise! Fuck. What do I do now? Should have never become a truck driver. All these people watching. They want me to crash! I'm female. They expect me to freak out. I don't know jack-shit. Back up further and you're screwed. You've kinked the angle at the kingpin, moron. Pull forward, and you pull the rear axle down at a worse angle than it was before. Back up, you put the axle down in the ditch.

Maybe I could disconnect the trailer, realign the cab and then reconnect. Ha ha. You're funny. Do I call dispatch? Send this message down the CB trail? You're in the middle of nowhere, asshole. You can't call dispatch. Handle it. Don't fuck up.

I turned the steering counter-clockwise, as far as it would go, and inched forward. *Don't inch, just fucking drive over it. It will either tip or it won't. No one's going to get hurt.*

I drove forward and came up on the other side of the ditch, honked several times in celebration, and moved on down the road. Miracle.

My heart raced with adrenaline. I breathed deeply all the way to Knoxville. I couldn't believe I got out of that one. I vowed to get more sleep.

Chemicals loaded, I drove I-40, squinting behind dark glasses, through green Tennessee, the white highway in rolling Arkansas, the smooth road in Oklahoma, the brown Texas panhandle, the big skies of New Mexico, and the Arizona rocks. I managed the Tehatchapi pass curves and finally, drove north through central California on the forever straight I-5. CB talk chattered. I couldn't keep up with who was who. Hundreds of trucks, ahead and behind me, contracted to move produce out of the valley into cities awaiting their weekly fresh vegetables.

Hayward didn't even say thank you.

Epilogue: Between Wisdom and Home[5]

Fall 1981
Eureka, California

Home again, but home was brand new. I knew the place, intimately, but the characters had changed. I hung around AA meetings instead of the Vista. I spent time with Hal, and since my house was still rented, I spent nights with him too. For the first time in many years, I slept soundly with someone else in the bed.

We worked together as janitors cleaning Planned Parenthood. He took me to see the Monarch butterflies in Santa Cruz, explaining they were on their way to Mexico. I met his parents in San Jose. Tract home, wall sconces. "Readers' Digest" type landscapes hung on two walls in the living room. A mirror above the fireplace and an electric heater dominated the hearth. Scared the hell out of my artistic yearnings. If he hadn't been so kind, and intelligent, I'd have likely beat feet.

Once I got my house back, Hal re-roofed the shop. He helped tear out the ceiling in my living room and put in a beam. He involved himself in my production of a readers' theatre by helping me address and mail announcements. He walked with me through Old Town and HSU as I hung posters. He listened.

But for all the good news, my emotions rollercoasted something awful. Anger spiked without warning. I'd try to hide my jealousy when Hal's women friends would stop him on the street, or come by our table in The Wildflower Cafe, but it would pop out unannounced in a torrent of words. Self-pity followed guilt. A few days of calm, and the cycle would begin again. The answer came in an AA meeting. "What I wanted more than anything else was intimacy," a woman said about being newly sober, "but I'd fight you to the death if you tried to get close to me." I saw myself. I knew I needed help.

I took Hal with me to Lewis, my counselor. We put together a few rules about how to communicate: If you leave in the heat of an argument, you must state when you will return. Paraphrase back to the other person what they just said before expressing your own idea. Stuff like that. But the best part was an exercise called Mad, Sad, Glad, Scared. Every night, without interruption, we each shared and wrote down one feeling in each category. "I was scared you just wanted to get away from me." "I was mad you didn't tell me so-and-so called or this-and-such happened." "I'm sad when I'm alone." "I get mad when I have to wait for you." "I'm glad neither of us like TV." My emotions started to level out.

"Blue Highways: A Journey into America" by William Least Heat-Moon © 1982 became a famous best-selling book at the time. I struggled over my notes, trying to scratch out my story. Instead of visiting "five-calendar restaurants" while traveling through the scenic back roads of America and marveling at the beauty of our country like Least Heat-Moon, I'd complained of miserable truck driving partners, ghettos, and endless freeways. I threw my "national best-selling" book about truck driving in the bottom drawer of my dresser.

The following summer, Hal and I lived in a tent on the North Umpqua River in Oregon. I worked as a prep cook in a gourmet restaurant while he counted summer steelhead by walking all the tributaries.

In 1983, we got married. My mother was thrilled.

I started training in Aikido and going to Audubon lectures.

I quit AA.

I got a job driving the Oregon delivery route for the Arcata Co-Op. I loved my regular customers, the scenery on Highway 199, and my salary. Delivering groceries to small stores meant moving all the individual boxes to the end of the trailer, jumping down, loading a hand truck and wheeling the boxes into the back of a store. I used my back with exquisite care. My muscles toned. I could eat anything I wanted and the needle never climbed above 123 pounds. I kept that job all the way till I got pregnant and the truck's bumping made me too sick to continue.

By 1988, we had two kids.

Eureka City Schools hired me to teach in a program for gifted and talented kids. The job offered relative autonomy to decide what to offer my middle school students. The first year, we made the front page of the local newspaper. The headline read: "87% of Eureka's middle school students have looked at their Christmas presents ahead of time."

The district wouldn't allow students to ask, "Do you want to get married?" In the teacher's lounge, arguments ensued about the students' right to ask questions verses the negative consequences of students learning the answers. I wrote up the lesson plan and sold it at the Gifted and Talented conference in San Diego the following year.

I didn't need a national best-selling book about my life any more.

Back in 1965, when I was fourteen, a baobab tree popped up in one of my Dad's videos, the video he'd spliced together about his trip to Africa. That baobab tree spiraled down into my gut. In his apartment, while the four-year-long divorce drama progressed, I saw that squat, ugly tree standing out in the middle of nowhere, its branches a tangled mess pasted on the top of its trunk, and saw exactly how I felt. Thick waist. Stout. Masculine. The curly hair I worked so hard to straighten. Alone. That was me. I chose the baobab tree as my totem that night. I didn't have all these words back then. I don't I even think knew about metaphors, but the visual struck me and the memory stuck.

In 1981, I wrote The Baobab Tree, a poem for that readers' theatre Hal helped me produce. Had I spelled it correctly? I opened my 1960s Webster's dictionary. Not only had I spelled it correctly, but also, a little picture next to the definition confirmed that I had remembered the tree accurately. The definition concluded with something like: The baobab tree is revered in Africa because its roots hold water.

In 1981, the important part was being revered. Today, I know that my roots, deep in my home, hold water. And that is enough.

Bipolar Disorder

Movies that dramatize bipolar disorder, that display its worst extremes, are a disservice to the majority of people suffering from the disease. Granted, the bipolar disease affects people to the extreme, and those extremes make for great movies. The Hours (2002), and Silver Linings Playbook (2012) are excellent examples. But Infinitely Polar Bear (2014) and The Dark Horse (2014) are not. We would be better served if these movies pitted the bipolar protagonist against our fear of taking medicine, or our difficulty with finding medicine that works. A good movie about bipolar disease would leave the audience annoyed about society's stigma against mental illness.

My last chapter, Between Wisdom and Home, certainly sounds like a fairytale ending. And while I never had another psychotic episode, hindsight can easily track the evidence of my disease. My son once told the psychologist, "My Mom's the most vigorous person I've ever met." My daughter wrote a paper in high school titled, "I walk on egg shells."

When my Dad died in 1991, I broke apart. Cried, raged, and went to bed. I'd never made a connection with him. I believe he had impeccable integrity, but I resided in his blind spot. Logic and intellect counted, but self-will trumped emotion, which rated as failure. I think he saw women as objects, and didn't know how to think of a daughter. He died in July. I recovered by the time school started in September.

In 1995, Mom died. I pulled the tablecloth out from under my life and all the dishes and glassware broke. I quit my teaching job in McKinleyville Middle School at noon, waited for the substitute to arrive, went home and shut the door. I wrote poems for a solid year.

I could never understand why so many young people spent so much time with Mom, felt so connected, while I came up empty. By the time she finally passed, a stack of loving cards a foot high sat on the counter from men and women my age. One fellow visited her in last days, drove a long distance to give her the poem he had written titled, "I am your fifth child." I couldn't cope with the disparity.

Six months after Mom died, back in Lewis' office, he referred me to a psychiatrist, who started me on lithium. Astounding. I couldn't believe getting through a day was so easy. So simple.

Can all the other people on the planet think this easily?

The psychiatrist and I fiddled with different medicines and dosages for three and a half years before we hit on the right combination for me. With careful monitoring, I reported to him what I thought was a chemical imbalance and what was caused by behavioral triggers. Not drinking certainly helped. I've been taking the prescribed medicine for over twenty years.

With medicine came clarity. I developed broader perspectives, particularly about relationships. I could see how much my Mom had loved me, wanted the best for me.

Just this year, I was fortunate to have a conversation with one of the women who held my mother deep in her heart. She told me the one thing she remembers my mother saying about me was that I was a chameleon, that Mom never knew who was going to show up when Margot arrived at the door.

In social situations, people agree to obey emotional norms. But some of us, because we become flooded with emotions too extreme for particular circumstances, hide our feelings behind acceptable behavior. We don't want to appear dramatic, grandiose. We don't want to be judged. Over time, this accommodation morphs, takes on a life of its own. We build a life path with a compromised identity. We fake our behavior for so long we forget who we are.

I'm sad for people like me, who live with such a degree of chemical imbalance they develop a false self. They refuse medical help. With medicine, the ability to think, sleep, the whole deal is hard to fathom if you've spent a lifetime "holding it together". To evolve from spinning thoughts, lack of regular sleep, trying to appear normal, guilt over outbursts of rage (or effusive happiness), into a kinder, more peaceful consciousness is a gift I could never have imagined.

Bipolar illness is divided into four categories, depending on the behavior of the affected patient. My form of illness, called Bipolar 1, is defined as "At least one manic —psychotic—episode, lasting longer than seven days and so severe a person needs hospitalization. Other degrees of the disease, however, still create the painful cycling through highs and lows, and this cycling could be evened out without weight gain or loss of creativity. Unfortunately, many — if not most — of these people never discover the medicine available. Their lives look like perpetual crisis followed by chronic depression.

In 1970, the U.S. food and drug administration approved Lithium Carbonate for people with a mental illness like mine. In 1980, manic-depression first appeared as a separate illness from schizophrenia in the Diagnostic and Statistical Manual of Mental Disorders (DSM). The term bipolar gained popularity over manic-depression, but the terms are synonymous.

In 1977, I was given Thorazine, Haldol, and Melaril, in various attempts to curb what my psychiatrist thought to be schizophrenic behavior. (That psychiatrist has since been twice removed and twice re-instated into psychiatry.)

Had I been born in the 1930s, I could have received electro-shock therapy, or been given camphor to induce convulsions.

Alcoholism

In 2006, on New Year's Eve, my son a junior at U.C. Davis and my daughter a senior in high school, I got drunk for the first time in twenty-five years. For the next eight months, my life revolved around red wine. I was either drinking or thinking about drinking. In August, at two bottles a day, occasionally starting at 11:00 a.m., I was sprawled on the couch one evening when my daughter and her boyfriend walked through the living room. I'll be forever thankful for the absolute disgust she heaped on me as she stomped passed. In that moment, I saw myself clearly, looking at my own mother. I did not want my daughter to see me like that again.

I went back to AA and I've stayed. I like being with my crazy tribe and our commitment to living sober, happy lives. I'm glad I didn't progress to laying in the gutter, homeless, with a failing liver, before finding my way back to where I belong -- to where I still listen, learn, and enjoy friendship.

The thrill I've received from writing, producing, and performing my poetry has been a better high that lasted longer than any drink or drug I've ever ingested. Coming down after a performance involves pictures, celebrating, laughter, and enthusiasm. A hangover of joy that lasts for a month.

I wonder whether my mother and I could have become close had she not anesthetized her emotions with nightly black outs. I get to enjoy a growing friendship with my son and his wife. Both of them trust me, share their stories. And I'm ever so grateful my daughter is harnessing her strength and participating fully in her own life. I watch my husband with renewed curiosity as I lose my self-interest. He is ever functional. He is the rock around which I flow. I can bonk into him, hang on, or rush around to reach the deep pool. I rest and swim back. He is there. I get to fill his cracks, smooth him out. He is my constant. All is good.

Endnotes

1   Mark Vonnegut; The Eden Express, A Memoir of Insanity; (1975) First Seven Stories Press Edition; Page 129, Third paragraph.

2   Mark Vonnegut; The Eden Express, A Memoir of Insanity; (1975) First Seven Stories Press Edition; Page 113, Last paragraph.

3   Mark Vonnegut; The Eden Express, A Memoir of Insanity; (1975) First Seven   Stories Press Edition; Page 119, Last paragraph.

4   See Wikipedia.org, 1700 Cascadia earthquake. Around the year 2000, we learned   that Japan had recorded a huge tsunami on January 26, 1700 and that an   earthquake here must have caused their tsunami, which explained the enormous   change of landscape.

5   See http: tommasofiscaletti.com/stories, Between Home and Wisdom. Between   Home and Wisdom is a photographic portraits' project by Italian Tommaso   Fiscaletti who lives in Cape Town, South Africa.

Glossary of Trucking Terminology

brake pot- An air brake has a "pot," about the size of a cantaloupe, that sits near each wheel. The brake pot applies and releases air to the brakes.

com-check - A driver can request a com-check, or compensation, at a Tanksley terminal and this money will be deducted from his pay check.

dog house - The driver's seat, passenger seat, and padded area above the engine is called the dog house. The dog house is where the second seat driver sleeps when both drivers sleep in the truck at the same time.

duals - two tires on each side of one axel is a "set of duals."

geehaw - turning right, then left, then right again to wiggle out of a tight spot.

get under a slide - to regain control of the vehicle after it starts to slide on ice.

Jake brake - An engine brake to help trucks control speed while going down hill.

jumpseat - The passenger seat. The jump seat is quite rough to sit in, as it has no air-ride to cushion the shock of the road bumps.

lumper - a person who unloads a truck.

pallet jack - A piece of equipment to unload pallets off a truck by hand. A pallet jack has two forks, like a fork lift. After pumping the handle and raising the pallet off the ground, the operator can pull the pallet off the truck using the pallet jack.

service brake - a mechanical brake or emergency brake that will kick in if the air brakes fail. The mechanical brake will only release if the air brakes are operational.

tandem axels - The two axels (8 wheels) affixed to the back of the tractor and sitting under the front of the trailer.

Acknowledgements

Louise Penny nailed it in the acknowledgments she wrote for her book, *Still Life*.

> *"I went through a period in my life when I had no friends, when the phone never rang, when I thought I would die from loneliness. I know that the real blessing here isn't that I have a book published, but that I have so many people to thank."*

I am most grateful to so many people who have asked me about my memoir and encouraged me all along the way. Thank you so much, all of you, even if I haven't included your name.

Katie Elsea helped me out of my writing isolation ... and helped me enter a network of supportive writers. She countered my "paralyzing self-doubt" with encouragement on a regular basis.

Neil Tarpey, author, counselor, writing instructor, and journalist, met with me one-on-one from the beginning. His kindness, sensitivity, and expertise, coupled with his honesty and willingness have taught me so much. His edits have tightened, added depth, and clarified *Shift Happens*, as I took his suggestions back to the drawing board. I've learned so much. Thank you, Neil.

Susan Bennett, PhD writing professor and longtime friend invited me to join a writing group. She offered her tough love with the hard parts. She said, "Start at the beginning." I didn't want to start at the beginning. Months later, I knew she was right and I started over at the beginning, the hardest part for me to write. "Margot, you can't explain away the parts of your character you don't like. You have to show us the bad parts." I cut out my explaining. "Poetry does not inform prose." Right again. Thank you so much, Susan.

My writing group members, Jeff Black, Rick Benoit, Cyndy Phillips, and Erica Wright, all with over-the top writing credentials, offered their wisdom and insight. Questions took me back to my memoir again and again to strive for clarity. They went through my writing page by page, week after week, for over two years.

Thank you Cynthia Julian for reading an early draft of Shift Happens, and sending me back to revising. Thank you for your questions, comments, and compliments.

Thank you Mariah Sinclair, for imagining my cover design and offering it to me. I am ever grateful for the outrageous serendipity of how this design came about.

Thank you Paige Elizabeth Turner for your willingness to line edit my manuscript. Truly, I thought I was giving you a good read with a few errors. Thank you so much for taking all that time to read thoroughly and make all those corrections.

At my first writing conference in San Miguel de Allende, Mexico, I left David Corbett's presentation and immediately wrote the first pages of *Shift Happens* in my motel room.

I attended two Magic of Memoir conferences with Brooke Warner and Linda Joy Myers. I highly recommend these two women and their conference for anyone writing their story. They desensitized our shame. They encouraged us to tell our truth.

I would be remiss if I didn't thank Mark Dawson's Independent Publishing Classes and the Facebook Group associated with these classes. I've come to rely on the group members for answers to the many questions I've had. Thank you so much.

Chris Genger, my son, read *Shift Happens*. He wrote suggestions and comments all throughout the book. He caught mistakes that others thought were trucking terms. "Pinwheel?" he questioned when I was describing the king pin's connection to the tractor. (A pinwheel is that Hostess chocolate marshmallow cake.) A fifth wheel is the entire apparatus that connects the tractor to the trailer. I worried that Chris would be embarrassed about his mother's past, so I asked him. His answer surprised me. "That didn't bother me at all. What bothered me, is I never realized that you'd traveled around the U.S. I'd always thought of you as having lived all your life in

Eureka. I wondered why I never bothered to ask about your truck driving stories."

Michael Jenner, my Indesign Teacher from years ago, helped me through the layout process. Thanks to Michael, the maps would not have been possible.

My husband, Hal Genger, a scientist, is a man of few words. His initial comment went something like, "Maybe for those who just want to read about the truck driving, you could tell them on which page to start." A few years into the project, he finally read *Shift Happens*. This time he said, "It's good." He did the laundry, dishes, gardening, cooking, and made the money while I sat on the couch and wrote. Hal is unconditional. He's the miracle in my life.

www.ingramcontent.com/pod-product-compliance
Lightning Source LLC
Chambersburg PA
CBHW030236030426
42336CB00009B/127